1968

The Mirror of Narcissus

in the Courtly Love Lyric

The Mirror of Narcissus
in the Courtly Love Lyric

FREDERICK GOLDIN

Cornell University Press

ITHACA, NEW YORK

CORNELL UNIVERSITY PRESS

First published 1967

Library of Congress Catalog Card Number: 67–13548

PRINTED IN THE UNITED STATES OF AMERICA
BY KINGSPORT PRESS, INC.

To Emma

*s'ieu res fatz que sia benestan,
devetz n'aver lo grat e la lauzor*

Preface

THE reader may wonder about a book devoted to a close reading of the medieval lyric, which has long been regarded as a constant rearrangement of the same clichés. As Jeanroy remarked, "One is tempted to believe that all the poets loved the same lady," and it often seems equally difficult to distinguish among the poets themselves. There is no doubt that these lyrics tell the same story. The lady is always beautiful and unapproachable, the lover burns with passion but is halted by a sense of his own unworthiness; and the difficulty of their relation is aggravated by ubiquitous spies and slanderers. Since love runs this course in practically every lyric, many readers have come to regard this literature as no more than a light entertainment, in which the medieval leisure class could congratulate itself on its fine feelings. If this is true of the courtly lyric, one certainly need not waste one's time looking for any "deep meaning" in it.

Instead of quarreling with this assessment, which even the nonspecialist will recognize as an oversimplification, I merely wish to add two points to it. Precisely because the same story is told with such astonishing frequency, we may assume that it contains a revealing picture of how the best educated and most powerful secular class in the Middle Ages regarded itself and justified its existence; for in this story it must have recognized its own ideal image. If this is a reasonable assumption, then there is all the more reason to look at that story anew. Secondly, given the conventional nature of this poetry and the medieval distrust of originality, it is worth trying to discover how certain poets of genius used this rigid form to convey their own vision in some of the most beautiful lyrics of all time. Bernart de Ventadorn and Heinrich von Morungen are among the greatest lyric poets of the Middle Ages. The author of *Narcisus*, in retelling Ovid's story, dramatizes the inner life of a noble youth with such compassion that we are astonished to find in his narrative the same prescriptive diction for which literature of this sort is frequently dismissed. Ulrich von Lichtenstein was no genius, but his poetry shows how eccentric the conventional can be.

With these two considerations in mind, I have tried to present the doctrines of courtly love as a coherent ethical system and to read the courtly lyric as a coherent aesthetic structure. The result must speak for itself.

This book could not have appeared in its present form without the courtesy and help I received from many quarters. I wish to thank Professors Margaret Pelan and N. C. W. Spence for allowing me to quote from their recent edition of *Narcisus*. I am grateful to Max Niemeyer Verlag for permission to reprint texts from Carl Appel's edition of Bernart de Ventadorn, and from Carl von Kraus's edition of *Deutsche Liederdichter des 13. Jahrhunderts;* to Carl Hanser Verlag for permission to reprint texts from Carl von Kraus's edition of Heinrich von Morungen; to Northwestern University Press for permission to reprint a text and translation from William P. Shepard and Frank M. Chambers' edition of Aimeric de Peguilhan; to Professor Maurice Valency for permission to quote passages and a translation from his book, *In Praise of Love;* to Verlag Vittorio Klostermann and the editors of *Romanische Forschungen* for permission to reprint a text from Willy Ernst's edition of Guiraut de Calanso.

Preface

I am happy to acknowledge many personal debts of gratitude.

Professor W. T. H. Jackson guided and encouraged me with perfect tact from the beginning of this project through every stage of thought and composition, putting his authoritative knowledge of medieval literature at my disposal as a light to help me find my own way.

Professor Maurice Valency made many valuable and well-timed suggestions concerning the structure and style of this book.

The late Professor Kurt Lewent elucidated a number of passages in the Provençal lyrics.

Professors Lawton P. G. Peckham, David Lilien, Gail Belaief, Joan Ferrante, Robert G. Olson, Howard Schless, John C. Nelson, and Charles Blyth each read one or more versions of the text and made many important suggestions for improving it. Dione Rakita, in helping with the preparation of the manuscript, offered useful editorial criticisms.

Dr. William N. Evans gave me help and encouragement when I first began this study.

Emma Bauman helped me to formulate the basic ideas of this book by her precise and sympathetic criticism.

For the nonspecialist reader I have explained in footnotes many of the allusions to medieval works that appear in these pages. I hope that the knowledgeable reader will be tolerant of these simple notes while losing no time on them.

F. G.

New York, New York
October 1966

ix

Abbreviations

BA	St. Augustine. *De Trinitate*. Bibliothèque Augustinienne, XVI. Paris and Bruges, 1955.
DLd	*Deutsche Liederdichter des 13. Jahrhunderts*. Ed. Carl von Kraus. 2 vols. Tübingen, 1952–1958.
PG	*Patrologiae cursus completus. Series Graeca*. Ed. J. P. Migne. Paris, 1856–1866.
PL	*Patrologiae cursus completus. Series Latina*. Ed. J. P. Migne. Paris, 1845–1855.
PMLA	*Publications of the Modern Language Association of America*.
MA	*Heinrich von Morungen*. Ed. Carl von Kraus. München, 1950.
MF	*Des Minnesangs Frühling*. Ed. Carl von Kraus *et al.* 30th edition. Zürich, 1950.
MFU	Carl von Kraus. *Des Minnesangs Frühling, Untersuchungen*. Leipzig, 1939.
MU	Carl von Kraus. *Zu den Liedern Heinrichs von Morungen*. Berlin, 1916.

Contents

Contents

The Mirror of Narcissus

in the Courtly Love Lyric

Introduction

For the General Reader [1]

What we today call courtly love originated in the eleventh century as a subject of literature. It first appeared, fully endowed with its basic doctrine and imagery, in the lyrics of the Troubadours, in the south of France. These lyrics were sung before a small and close-knit audience, the most exclusive in the world at that time, the knights and ladies of the court. The poet was usually well known to them, whether he himself was a nobleman or not, and whether he or a professional singer actually performed before them. In the guise of a lover he told them of a lady to whom he had dedicated himself forever in service.

When the song began, everyone in the audience knew what to expect. There would be a testimony to one essential doctrine: the courtly man was enhanced by his love for a beautiful and virtuous lady. His love made him a better man, whether or not it was requited; the important thing was that requital had to be earned in sustained service, which demonstrated his devotion and perfected his quality. The lady was usually unattainable, far beyond the lover's reach because she was so nobly born, so accomplished, so virtuous; often also because

---

[1] The medieval specialist will lose nothing by skipping to the next section.

she was married. She was perfect, and between her and the lover stretched a vast social, legal, and moral distance.

The idea that love for a woman is ennobling was something new, having never existed before. There had certainly been love for women before, but in literature that love was destructive and humiliating. It was the love for Medea, Dido, Lesbia. And Plato had shown how love is ennobling—but not love for women. What is new in the literature of the eleventh century is that heterosexual love inspires the man to a life-long career of amelioration. All the virtues that define the courtier are perfected in the heat of love. In longing and service he becomes more skillful at arms, more graceful in song, more generous, more decorous, more humble, more noble. Seen in this way, courtly love was an ethical system, intended to perfect and justify the courtly class by depicting its ideal.

Because of the sameness of imagery and attitude among many of the poets of courtly love—because all their ladies looked alike and all their phrases were predictable—we can probably conclude that the love-experience they sang of was fictional, part of a literary tradition. The public performance of a love song suggests the same thing: this love was the hallmark of the courtly class; it was not heard as part of the poet's autobiography. At any rate, the literature of courtly love had an instant vogue. As lyric or romance, it was sung and recited all over the Continent in the twelfth and thirteenth centuries. From the Troubadours it spread to northern France, where it was carried on by the Trouvères, although nothing extraordinary was produced there. It spread east, into Germany and Austria, where it was developed into a great body of poetry, the Minnesang. It spread south into Italy, where its essential secularity was transformed; the figure of the lady became a spiritual incitement, a guiding angel who led the lover to salvation. This body of poetry, now called the *dolce stil novo*, began a development that ended in the supreme figure of Beatrice. The courtly tradition did not flourish in England until it was played out on the Continent, but then it became the impetus for some of the finest masterpieces of medieval literature: Chaucer's *Troilus and Criseyde* and his *Knight's Tale*, the Pearl Poet's *Gawain and the Green Knight*, Malory's *Morte D'Arthur*, to name the most famous.

Although the courtly tradition produced some splendid literature, it did not last long. But the doctrines of courtly love have survived for centuries, to this day in fact, with great implicit power. No one can say precisely when courtly love ceased to be confined to literature and became the substance of actual experience, although later on in this book we shall see some of the causes of this momentous change. Then, freed from its social origin in the noble class, and with certain dark features emphasized, it became the essential element of romantic love, in every aspect of that great delusive yearning, from Keats's Knight at arms to our own Great Gatsby.

Many of the images of courtly love are well known: the unattainable lady, the man held in thrall hovering near for the slightest sign that he has been seen, the solitary tears, the elegant complaint, the ecstasy when she smiles, the horror when she frowns, the glorious deeds of battle and song performed in her service. All this wonder has become so familiar that many of the questions it raises are almost never asked. Why did the lady have to be unattainable? Why did the knight become virtuous in loving and serving her? Why, in the literature of this time and this society, was sexual desire harnessed to become the energy for moral advancement? What explains the invention and appeal of courtly love?

This book tries to answer questions like these by studying an image that is crucially important, not only in the literature of courtly love, but in all medieval literature. The mirror appears in the writing of nearly every author of the Middle Ages, and it reflects all the preoccupations of that time. It was used variously to represent both God and man, and also the relation between them. It was an instrument of magical divination. It was a symbol of the Virgin, in whom the Second Person, the Imago, was made visible to the eyes of flesh. It was a symbol of all the deceitfulness of secular experience, the snare of fools like Narcissus. It stood for chastity and vanity, for the Bible and the earth, for mortal reason and divine intelligence.

One reason for the frequency of the mirror figure is that the medieval world view was essentially Platonic: the objects of actual experience were known and judged by their resemblance to an ideal Form. Now when all existence is understood as a relation between paragon and image, between one Reality and its innumerable reflections, the use of the mirror figure is inevitable. The following section will elaborate upon this point, even at the risk of being tedious, in order to prepare for what follows.

The Three Mirrors

The mirror, in the poetry we are going to study, reflects the world that Plato defined and that the Neoplatonists transmitted to the Middle Ages. As the mirror is made of matter, it has the capacity of matter to receive the image of ideal forms. From this root idea three distinct developments are possible.

We can stress the ideality of the image and ignore the materiality of the mirror. Then we praise the mirror for its clarity, and we consult it to know what we are and what we ought to be.

We can reverse this emphasis and stress the mirror's essential passivity. Then we condemn it as a snare of vain images that seduce us with a false vision of beauty and leave us with nothing, further away than ever from the ideal to which we aspired.

We can consider both matter and form together. The mirror awakens our consciousness of the ideal by translating it into sensible images. It shows us an image of eternal Beauty in the beauty of a momentary body. But that image is fleeting, it has no substance; and we must learn how to leave the mirror behind and to love a being that is invisible and immutable. The three mirrors appear frequently in texts that influenced the Middle Ages.

THE MIRROR OF THE IDEAL

The notion that the mirror reflects an ideal image explains why the Holy Scriptures are called a mirror. Sister Ritamary Bradley, in her study of mirror-titles, finds a "key text" in St. Augustine.[2] "The mirror has set its writing before you," Augustine says; "it is read to you: *Blessed are the pure in heart, for they shall see God.* The mirror is set forth in this reading; see whether you are what it has said. If you are not yet so, then groan, that you may become so. The mirror will disclose your face to you. As you will not see a flatterer in the mirror, so you will not wheedle yourself. Its brightness will show you what you are: see what you are. . . ."[3]

Elsewhere we are told that the pure soul is a mirror of God.[4] Keep this mirror clean, we are warned; for "from a soiled mirror you cannot get images; nor can the soul that is filled with worldly cares and over which the flesh spreads

[2] Sister Ritamary Bradley, "Backgrounds of the Title *Speculum* in Mediaeval Literature," *Speculum*, XXIX (1954), 100–115. She also points out the frequent use of the mirror in the titles of great compendia of knowledge or works of moral injunction throughout the Middle Ages and the Renaissance.

[3] St. Augustine, *Enarratio in Psalmum CIII* (PL, XXXII, col. 1338): Posuit tibi speculum scripturam suam; legitur tibi: *Beati mundi corde, quoniam ipsi Deum uidebunt.* Speculum in hac lectione propositum est; uide si hoc es quod dixit; si nondum es, geme ut sis. Renuntiabit tibi speculum faciem tuam; sicut speculum non senties adulatorem, sic nec te palpes. Hoc tibi ostendit nitor ille quod es; uide quod es. . . .

[4] St. Gregory of Nyssa, *De Beatitudinis*, Oratio VI; PG, XLIV, col. 1270C. Cited with many other passages by Bradley, "Backgrounds," pp. 105ff.

darkness receive the illumination of the Holy Spirit."[5] The angels are mirrors of God, mirrors without stain, reflecting his light.[6]

THE MIRROR OF MATTER

Plotinus says: "As in a mirror the semblance is in one place, the substance in another, so Matter seems to be full when it is empty, and contains nothing while seeming to contain all things. The copies and shadows of real things which pass in and out of it, come into it as into a formless shadow. They are seen in it because it has no form of its own."[7]

In its passivity and formlessness it can produce nothing but an illusion. The mirror of matter represents the delusiveness of experience in the sensible world, a world of shifting images, a world whose substratum has the "actuality of an illusion."[8] The story of Narcissus takes on the character of an exemplum:

He that has the strength, let him arise and withdraw into himself, foregoing all that is known by the eyes, turning away forever from the material beauty that once made his joy. When he perceives those shapes of grace that show in body, let him not pursue: he must know them for copies, vestiges, shadows, and hasten away towards That they tell of. For if anyone follow what

[5] St. Basil of Caesarea, *Epist.* CCX; *PG*, XXXII, col. 778AB; translated by Bradley, p. 108.

[6] Dionysius the Pseudo-Areopagite, *Celestial Hierarchy*, III, 1 and 2; *PG*, III, col. 166A.

[7] *Enneads*, III, 6, 7; translation by William Ralph Inge in *The Philosophy of Plotinus*, 2 vols. (New York and London, 1918), I, 130. Cf. Emile Bréhier, *The Philosophy of Plotinus*, trans. Joseph Thomas (Chicago, 1958), p. 179. In the following discussion of Plotinus, I shall use alternative translations, whenever they are available, in preference to MacKenna (see n. 9, below).

[8] II, 5, 5, trans. Joseph Katz, *The Philosophy of Plotinus* (New York, 1950). Cf. III, 6, 7.

is like a beautiful shape playing over water—is there not a myth telling in symbol of such a dupe, how he sank into the depths of the current and was swept away to nothingness? [9]

In the Neoplatonic world view, the figure of the mirror represents the decline of the "great chain" from God the highest to the lowest dregs of things.[10] St. Augustine cites the mirror to demonstrate that "the mother of falsity is the similitude of things which reaches the eyes." [11] The image in the mirror is a "seductive similitude," seeming to be real but really false, for it cannot be grasped, it makes no sound, it does not live.[12] "For does not your image in the mirror appear to you as though it wished to be yourself, but to be false precisely because it is not?" [13]

Within us, says Augustine, is the desire to see the whole face of truth; but often we are deluded, thinking that what we know or seek to know is all that is to be known. From our partial knowledge, "certain false colors and forms pour themselves as though into the mirror of thought. . . . Such imaginations are to be avoided with great care; they are recognized as false when they vary as if in a varying mirror of thought, whereas the face of truth remains one and immutable." [14] Again, the mirror is the natural example of instability, passivity, delusiveness.

[9] I, 6, 8, trans. Stephen MacKenna (New York, n.d.). Cf. V, 8, 2; and IV, 3, 12, concerning the souls' descent into the sensible world: they are ensnared by their own beautiful reflection into the sorrow of generation.

[10] Macrobius, *Commentarius in Somnium Scipionis*, I, xiv, 15. Cf. *Enneads*, I, 1, 18. Macrobius gave the medieval world an abridged and much simplified version of Plotinus. See Paul Henry, *Plotin et l'occident* (Louvain, 1934), pp. 147, 150ff, 190ff; also Arthur O. Lovejoy, *The Great Chain of Being* (Cambridge, Mass., 1936), p. 63.

[11] *Soliloquia*, II, vi, 10.

[12] *Ibid.*, II, vi, 11 and 12; vii, 13.

[13] *Ibid.*, II, ix, 17.

[14] *Ibid.*, II, xx, 35.

Introduction

"When we wish to ascend, we naturally use a ladder, we who are men and unable to fly. Then let use as a ladder the similitude of visible things, so that the things we cannot see by direct vision we may become able to see from this watchtower and as though in a mirror."[15]

We must love and seek to know the invisible things of God, the incorporeal essences. After a long climb, a severe regimen, we may come to know them directly and intuitively in *contemplation*. But the slow and faltering way to that knowledge is *speculation*, the inferior knowledge we work to attain through the *speculum* of the visible things of this world.[16]

The mirror unites its own material nature with a spiritual reality. The image that results is necessarily inadequate, the merest vestige of true knowledge. The beauty of bodies, the justice of men, love defined in times and places—these change, they pass away; they are poor and suffering images of Beauty, and Justice, and Love. But each image is eminently visible, and that is its value: the soul may climb upon these images, leaving each behind as it learns to contemplate the reality they reflect. By the debased but visible image of its true desire the soul is inspired to begin its ascent.

The most famous mirror is St. Paul's. Everyone knows those prophetic words:

Videmus nunc per speculum in aenigmate; tunc autem facie ad faciem.   [I Cor. 13: 12]

[15] Richard of St. Victor, *De Trinitate*, V, vi. Ubi ad alta quidem ascendere volumus, scala quidem uti solemus, nos qui homines sumus et volare non possumus. Rerum ergo visibilium similitudine pro scala utamur, ut quae in semetipsis per speciem videre non valemus, ex ejusmodi specula et velut per speculum videre mereamur. Note play on *specula-speculum*. Cf. VI, i.

[16] Richard of St. Victor, *Benjamin Major*, V, xiv; II, xvii and i–iii; *Adnotatio in Psalmum CXIII: PL*, CXCVI, cols. 96–99, 79–82, 337. N.b. the famous passage in St. Paul (Rom. i, 20).

8

Nos vero omnes revelata facie gloriam Domini speculantes, in eamdem imaginem transformamur, a claritate in claritatem, tanquam a Domini Spiritu. [II Cor. 3: 18]

(We see now by means of a mirror in an enigma; but then face to face.)

(But we all, with face unveiled contemplating as in a mirror the glory of the Lord, are transformed into the same image, from splendor into splendor, as by the Spirit of the Lord.)

St. Paul's theme is the imperfect nature of man's knowledge in this life: we may see the glory of God only in a mirror, never directly. Even in the second passage, with its great promise, the pejorative intent in the mirror metaphor is crucial.[17]

This mirror, with its antithetical meanings, will be our mirror. We shall find it in the most interesting and imaginative of the works that lie before us. It is also the most comprehensive and universal mirror: even the clearest mirror, the mirror of Scripture, is ambivalent. One final example will show this and will suggest the pervasiveness of St. Paul's theme.

St. Augustine, in the *Confessions*, speaks of the condition of the faithful in this life. Their knowledge is uncertain. They live by faith, not yet by vision. God alone can distinguish those in the light from those in the darkness, for we are all made from the same mass, some into vessels of honor, others of ignominy. For our weakness and uncertainty God made a "firmament of authority" in His divine Scripture, as our protection and guide. As the Lord clothed men in skins when by sin they became mortal, so He has spread out the firmament of His book like a skin, a tent to shelter us, a heaven to guide us.[18]

---

[17] See Norbert Hugedé, *La métaphore du miroir dans les épîtres de Saint Paul aux Corinthiens*, Thèse No. 157, Geneva (Neuchâtel, 1957). Hugedé cites many texts regarding the mirror's clarity, deceptiveness, and usefulness as an instrument of self-knowledge.

[18] *Confessions*, XIII, xiii,14—xv,17.

Introduction

We who are men must look to this firmament; but the angels read the will of God directly; they stand above that firmament, "supercelestial":

Let the supercelestial bands of your angels praise your name, let them praise you; they do not need to look up to this firmament and read there in order to know your word. They see your face, always, and there they read, without the syllables of time, what your eternal will desires. They read, they choose, they love. They read always, and what they read never passes away. For they read the very immutability of your purpose, and they read by choice, and with love.

Their manuscript is not folded nor is their book closed, for you yourself are this book to them, and you eternally are. You placed them above this firmament, which you set firmly above the infirmity of the people of this world below; you set it there so that these mortals might look up to it and recognize your mercy, which proclaims you in time, you who created time. . . . The preachers of your word pass from this life into another, but your Scripture remains spread out above the people to the end of time. Both heaven and earth will pass away, but your words shall not pass away, for the skin shall be folded up and the earth over which it was spread shall pass with all its glitter, but your word remains eternally.

Now your word appears to us in the enigma of the clouds and by means of the mirror of heaven, not as it is, for however much we are loved by your Son, it has not yet appeared what we shall be. . . . It will be ours to see him as he is, Lord, but it is not yet ours.[19]

[19] *Ibid.*, XIII, xv, 18. Text: *Œuvres de Saint Augustin*, Bibliothèque Augustinienne, deuxième série, Vol. XIV, ed. M. Skutella (Paris and Bruges, 1962). Laudent nomen tuum, laudent te supercaelestes populi angelorum tuorum, qui non opus habent suspicere firmamentum hoc et legendo cognoscere uerbum tuum. uident enim faciem tuam semper et ibi legunt sine syllabis temporum, quid uelit aeterna uoluntas tua. legunt, eligunt, et diligunt; semper legunt et numquam praeterit quod legunt. eligendo enim et diligendo legunt ipsam inconmutabilitatem consilii tui. non clauditur codex eorum nec plicatur liber eorum, quia

The firmament of Scripture was set out as an accommodation of our infirmity, that we on earth might see some sign of God, whom we shall see face to face in another life. But above that firmament there are those who do not need to search through our Scriptures, which are filled with "the syllables of time," for the angels see the will of God directly. The mirror of Scripture excites our love, as Christ incarnate made us ardent—"He looked through the nets of flesh, and caressed, and inflamed, and we run after his fragrance." [20] But it is the vague mirror of this firmament, obscured by enigmatic clouds, and in that mirror we see something of the word of God as we are enabled to see it, not as it is. The *speculum Scripturae* reflects the image of what we long for, and gazing upon it we struggle to understand what is not clear.

But beyond that mirror obscured by mortality, beyond the firmament that separates us from another heaven—a supercelestial and invisible heaven,[21] the dwelling-place of God and the elect—there is another kind of contemplation, pure, without obscurity because its object is no mere image perceived in a mirror but the very "face" of God.

The firmament, the tent of skins, the earth they cover and

---

tu ipse illis hoc es et es in aeternum, quia super hoc firmamentum ordinasti eos, quod firmasti super infirmitatem inferiorum populorum, ubi suspicerent et cognoscerent misericordiam tuam temporaliter enuntiantem te, qui fecisti tempora. . . . transeunt praedicatores uerbi tui ex hac uita in aliam uitam, scriptura uero tua usque finem saeculi super populos extenditur. sed et caelum et terra transibunt, sermones autem tui non transibunt, quoniam et pellis plicabitur et faenum, super quod extendebatur, cum claritate sua praeteriet, uerbum autem tuum manet in aeternum; quod nunc in aenigmate nubium et per speculum caeli, non sicuti est, apparet nobis, quia et nos quamuis filio tuo dilecti simus, nondum apparuit quod erimus. . . . sicuti est, domine, uidere nostrum, quod nondum est nobis.

[20] *Ibid.* Attendit per retia carnis et blanditus est et inflammauit, et currimus post odorem eius.

[21] See A. Solignac's long note in Skutella's edition (note 19, pp. 592ff), which cites these and other texts, together with an ample bibliography on the subject. Cf. XIII, xxiv, 36–37.

guide, the syllables of time, the transcribing fingers, the mirror—all these we gaze upon avidly in this life, but they shall pass away with this life, and then we shall ascend to the life of true contemplation, true knowledge, without mirrors and without images.

The intelligible heaven is distinguished from the firmament we see, whose stars guide us on earth (cf. XIII, xviii, 22–23). With the *lower* heaven St. Augustine associates the mirror of Scripture and the kind of knowledge that is possible there: it is the "speculation" of which Richard of St. Victor speaks, and it is altogether inferior to the knowledge of that other world:

ad haec tu dicis mihi, quoniam tu es deus meus et dicis uoce forti in aure interiore seruo tuo perrumpens meam surditatem et clamans: "O homo, nempe quod scriptura mea dicit, ego dico. et tamen illa temporaliter dicit, uerbo autem meo tempus non accedit, quia aequali mecum aeternitate consistit. sic ea, quae uos per spiritum meum uidetis, ego uideo, sicut ea, quae uos per spiritum meum dicitis, ego dico. atque ita cum uos temporaliter ea uideatis, non ego temporaliter uideo, quemadmodum, cum uos temporaliter ea dicatis, non ego temporaliter dico.   [XIII, xxix, 44]

(To these things you say to me, for you are my God and you speak with a strong voice to your servant in his inner ear, breaking through my deafness and calling out: "O man, it is true that what my Scripture says, I say. And yet it speaks in time, but time does not affect my Word, for it exists in equality with me, throughout eternity. Thus what you see by my Spirit, I see, just as what you speak by my Spirit, I speak. But when you see these things in time, I do not see them in time; just as when you say these things in time, I do not say them in time.")

The word of God uttered in time, the image of God perceived in time—this is the extent of what Scripture offers us. This mirror truly reflects an ideal image. But it is no more than an image, explicitly distinguished from a reality far greater and more stable. Scripture is our firmament, our tent, an accommodation of our mortality (cf. XIII, xxiv, 49). It is precisely the materiality of the mirror that enables us to see in sensible images what is in its essence invisible and inaccessible in this life. Yet it requires but the slightest shift in emphasis to see the "inferior similitudes" which Augustine condemns with great severity. Whether or not there is a pejorative intent, the ambivalence of the mirror is essential.

This mirror, which debases an ideal reality so that it may be seen by man in his mortal infirmity, is the one we shall find in the literature before us. None of the other mirrors are fully relevant—the pure mirror of self-knowledge, the mirror of all being, the catoptromantic mirror.[22]

Let us state the case, bearing in mind that we are not concerned with "sources" or "influences": as the Scriptures translate the Word of God into the "syllables of time," as the holy sacraments enact before mortal eyes the eternal will of God, as the visible world vaguely reflects in its materiality the

---

[22] The use of the mirror as an instrument of divination was widespread throughout the Middle Ages; see A. Delatte, *La catoptromancie grecque et ses dérivés* (Paris and Liège, 1932), pp. 13–39 and *passim;* also L. Thorndike, *A History of Magic and Experimental Science during the First Thirteen Centuries of Our Era* (New York, 1923), II, 158–190, 281–287, 551–582, 604–608, 778, 816f, 965; also I, 505ff, 523. A wide-ranging psychoanalytic study of the magic mirror, containing material from many countries and periods, is to be found in Géza Róheim, *Spiegelzauber* (Leipzig and Wien, 1919). A great deal of material from medieval and classical sources is offered in Carl Kiesewetter, *Faust in der Geschichte und Tradition* (Leipzig, 1893); also, on a related subject, Martin Ninck, *Die Bedeutung des Wassers im Kult und Leben der Alten* (Leipzig, 1921; republished Darmstadt, 1960); and G. F. Hartlaub, *Zauber des Spiegels* (München, 1951). All of these works contain extensive bibliographies. For an interesting study of the mirror as a representation of the knowledge that brings divine power into the hands of the virtuous mortal, see Gordon Worth O'Brien, *Renaissance Poetics and the Problem of Power* (Chicago, 1956).

invisible and immutable ideal,[23] so, as we shall see in the courtly lyric, the lady is a localization of the ideal, an image that accommodates the infirmities of secular life. Many of the courtly poets, most of them perhaps, do not go beyond this point, never questioning the moral indispensability of the figure they praise. But the most interesting poets do go on to consider everything that a mirror is, recognizing, along with its capacity to excite our love for moral perfection, its passivity, its mendacity, its dangerous innocence, its soullessness.

The mirror is the instrument of illusions, barren of every attribute except its ability to reflect what is set before it in such a way that the image seems real. It has no will to choose what it will reflect, no quality to be affected by the image it bears, no heart to pity those whom it deludes, no intelligence to aspire to the reality whose semblance it sets before our eyes.

Yet it gives to the soul its first captivating glimpse of the ideal. The soul looks into the mirror to see the promise and the task of its perfection, and the moment it turns toward its ideal it must study how to leave the mirror behind. For once enlightened, unless it passes beyond the mirror it will suffer the death that befell Narcissus.

The image is equally ambivalent. Having no independent existence, it is by its very nature inferior to what it reflects.

---

[23] Cf. Hans Leisegang, "La connaissance de Dieu au miroir de l'âme et de la nature," *Revue d'histoire et de philosophie religieuses*, XVII (1937), 161f; translated and reprinted as "Die Erkenntnis Gottes im Spiegel der Seele und der Natur," *Zeitschrift für philosophische Forschung*, IV (1949), 161-183. Rabanus Maurus, *Expositio in Epistolam ad Corinthios Primam* (PL, CXII, cols. 125-127), explains Paul's intention to signify by the mirror a partial and obscure vision, which is all that faith allows us. Similarly, in the *Allegoriae in Universam Sacram Scripturam* (PL, CXII, col. 1050), he interprets: Speculum est fides, ut in Paulo: "Videmus nunc per speculum in aenigmate," id est, per fidem; faith, as he writes elsewhere, which Paul promises shall be surpassed when we see face to face and pass "from the glory of faith to the glory of direct vision" (de gloria fidei in gloriam speciei; PL, CXII, col. 178).

Every image is a degradation. But it is therefore a vision of something higher, of an ideal reality. The idea of the image and the mirror is essential to the idea of the chain of being: all existence is a system of yearning images standing at every degree of distance from the one reality they all reflect; and the love that drives every image to perfect its resemblance to its origin is the energy that holds together all creation.[24]

In this world of images the soul alone is capable of becoming conscious of itself as an image whose ultimate reality is the One, the Divine. It alone can understand that its identity consists in resemblance, and its salvation in the enhancement of that resemblance. It knows itself as an image endowed with the ability to rise out of the mirror and become one with its Creator.

From this brief notice we can see that in the cultural climate in which the poet lived there was available to him the possibility of regarding the mirror as the most beautiful and perilous object of his secular experience, and the image as a degradation that inspires an ascent. The subject of this book requires little further introduction beyond a brief summary of its contents and a note on its method.

Outline

The first chapter consists of a detailed reading of the twelfth-century French *Narcisus*, and briefer discussions of other medieval versions of the Narcissus story. These interpretations of Narcissus define the relation between the courtly man and the lady in the "mirror lyrics." In Chapter Two some Provençal lyrics in which the mirror appears in a

---

[24] See Bréhier, p. 149; René Arnou, *Le désir de Dieu dans la philosophie de Plotin* (Paris, 1921), pp. 53–103, 197f; and Paul Aubin, "L' 'Image' dans l'œuvre de Plotin," *Recherches de science religieuse,* XLI (July–September 1953), 348–379. This idea was, of course, summarized for the Middle Ages in Boethius.

significant rôle reveal how the story of Narcissus is re-enacted in the career of the courtly lover.

Chapter Three is a study of some lyrics of the great poet Heinrich von Morungen, whose imaginative use of the mirror figure points up its essential ambivalence. Chapter Four is devoted to the development of courtly poetry in the hands of the thirteenth-century poet Ulrich von Lichtenstein. His long work, *Frauendienst*, in effect documents the turning point of the Minnesang: after Ulrich the courtly lyric declines, and its future lies with the Meistersinger, who will turn a rich tradition into a pedantic and mechanical exercise. The reasons for this decline are fully revealed in Ulrich's work, and are epitomized in his use of the mirror figure.

With Chapter Four the literary study is concluded; but I have added an epilogue, for there ought to be an attempt to say not only what the meanings of the mirror were, but also how they developed. To this end the final chapter presents an account of the *De Trinitate* of St. Augustine. Augustine's vocabulary—the terms he establishes as he seeks for an image of the Holy Trinity in the mind's effort to become conscious of itself—is in every way adequate to define the relations between the courtly man, the lady, and the love that unites them, in the secular lyric.

By this arrangement we shall see not only the changing meanings of the mirror figure and the ways in which they change, but also the mirror's capacity to reflect the preoccupations of the poet's entire work and the cultural condition of the society to which the poet belongs.

Method

One of the most admired and influential works of criticism and scholarship in our generation is Ernst Robert Curtius's *European Literature and the Latin Middle Ages*. For Curtius, European literature is a single "intelligible unit" and must be studied as such; the division of that literature into periods, into "chronological fragments," obscures its unity and causes every particular work to be read as though it had no essential antecedents and hence to be misunderstood and misrepresented. On this basis the study of European literature becomes, in Curtius's book, the study of "topics." His work accomplishes what it sets out to do; but its method is not useful for the purposes of this book.

To separate a literary figure from every specific context and then to trace it to its earliest appearance is not, after all, to study literature, however useful and even indispensable it may be as a preparation. When, for example, we trace "nautical metaphors" from Horace to Dante to Spenser,[25] we must remember that a poem is not the same as the "topic" it treats. When, beside a charming verse of Horace, who declines to set his "little sails" upon the epic sea, we place a sustained metaphor from the *Commedia*, a metaphor that sweeps from this tense moment to encompass all time since Jason and the Argonauts, we are certainly demonstrating the continuity of a literary figure, but we are also in danger of obliterating essential differences.

If Curtius's method had been followed in this book, we should look for the Ovidian mirror which competes with the poet for Corinna's love, the Pauline mirror through which we see in an enigma, the "steel glass" that shows the world its true image, the eighteenth-century mirror that reduces the vastness of the universe to a toy-like intelligibility. We should list these instances, but we should not note their different meanings— that would mean relapsing into "periods." And we could not do the job half as well as Curtius himself might have, if he had wanted to.[26]

---

[25] This appears on pp. 128–130 of Willard R. Trask's translation of Curtius's work, Bollingen Series, XXVI (New York, 1953).

[26] Unfortunately, he does not discuss the mirror figure except in two brief notes on pp. 177 and 336.

Introduction

The study of a topic is most valuable, not when it cancels the division of literary history into periods and regions, but when it makes their demarcation more clear and more meaningful.

Every now and then Curtius feels called upon to explain why in periods vastly different there should be a restatement of the same topics. At those moments, however, he does not set himself the task of examining the differences between the classical instance and the medieval, and his position regarding the "unity" of European literature will not permit him even to acknowledge that such a task might be in order. Instead, he turns to the psychology of C. G. Jung, another for whom cultural differences are unimportant beside the omnivorous and immutable "archetype." [27]

But for the study of literature what interests us is not the topic or the archetype but the cultural climate in which the topic occurs, the secular forms in which the archetype reveals itself. We who are students of literature study a thing that changes, and the study of a figure must record the differences between one age and another. We study not the archetype but the artifact, a thing that can be dated and placed in the context of a defined yet mutable "period," with its peculiar repertory of concern.

Therefore, to list the instances of the mirror figure in medieval literature is a facile task and practically of no value. What we want to know is not the number of times the figure occurs, but the number of meanings it has, and whether these changes of meaning follow any pattern, thus suggesting a literary development. We want to know, furthermore, why these various meanings are "medieval": among the several meanings of the mirror, why did the poets of the Middle Ages choose as they did? The answer to questions like this must be sought in a study of each work—and of the *whole* work—in which the figure of the mirror appears.

[27] See, for example, pp. 82 and 122f in Curtius.

18

In this study I have therefore concentrated on the text, its structure, the arrangement of all its images, the tone of its language. I have also translated all of the texts, for they are not simply illustrations of the thesis of this book but its chief source. For the same reason, I have translated literally, sometimes even with painful literalness. Since I have resolved to seek the meaning of the mirror in the whole of the text that contains the figure, and not simply in the line or strophe in which it is explicitly mentioned, I have had to restrict my discussion to a small number of lyrics, although many others are cited in the notes. As I have said, my intention is not to provide an exhaustive catalogue but to define the principal literary meanings of the figure of the mirror.

The consciousness of unlimited meaning is one of the chief pleasures of reading a literary work. I am pleasantly aware, therefore, that the poems in this book can be interpreted in many other ways than as aesthetic-ethical documents concerning the problems of identity and class. I hope for nothing more than to bring some light to a single aspect of this superb literature.

CHAPTER ONE

Narcissus

THE story of Narcissus, for the medieval period as well as for
our own, has all the attributes of an exemplum. It identifies a
peril that every human being must encounter, and shows him
how to overcome that peril in order to preserve his life.

Ovid's famous narrative (*Met.* III, 338–510) is the source of
the medieval versions of the story to be discussed in this
chapter. The tale begins with a prophecy of Tiresias, who
tells Liriope that her son will live a long time provided that he
never knows himself—*si se non noverit* (348). Sixteen years
later, Narcissus's beauty has aroused the desire of many
youths and maidens but conceals a pride so hard that none
may touch him. Hunting one day, he is seen by Echo, who
immediately loves him. Because of Juno's curse upon her,
Echo is unable to speak on her own initiative but can only
repeat the last sounds uttered by another's voice; and here, by
returning Narcissus's words, she reveals her love and asks for
his own. She is cruelly repulsed, like everyone else. She is left
with nothing but the desire that consumes her, wasting away
her body until she is reduced to a mere voice.

Another victim of Narcissus's hard-heartedness prays to
heaven to make Narcissus suffer what he has caused others to
suffer: to love and be unable to possess his beloved. This
prayer is granted by Nemesis. One day, fatigued and thirsty
from hunting, Narcissus kneels down to drink from a spring.

Then, as Ovid says, "another thirst increases within him" (415). He sees a beautiful youth in the water, whom he immediately desires. He does not know that that "youth" is his own reflection, that he himself is both lover and beloved. He begs the youth to come forward, for they are equally beautiful and nothing but the surface of the water separates them. After many passionate complaints, he suddenly realizes the truth: "*I am that youth!—Iste ego sum!*" (463). Yet he cannot stop loving what he now knows is his own reflection; he regrets that he cannot separate himself from his body. Now he already feels grief taking away his life. He loses his color, succumbs to the fire that is consuming him. Nothing remains of the beauty that Echo loved.

In his last moments she returns, and despite her anger she pities him. When he strikes his breast in grief, she returns the sound of the blows. As he dies, she repeats his last *vale*. But even after he enters the infernal regions, he gazes upon himself in the waters of the Styx. In the place where he suffered his torment on earth grows the flower that bears his name.

This is the story that the medieval poets received. No matter how they interpreted it, they were at one in suppressing all of the supernatural elements. Thus the medieval poets were constrained to show how this extraordinary story accommodates the facts of ordinary human experience. And here it is obvious what their main problems were. They had to explain, for example, why Narcissus continues to love the image even after he recognizes it as a mere reflection. Why can he not simply pick himself up and withdraw in relief? As a matter of fact, how is it possible that he could so deceived as to love a reflected image in the first place? Why could he not love any of the living youths who loved him?

For the medieval poets, and particularly for the author of the most detailed and interesting version of the story, these questions were vital. In their answers we find the key to their treatment of the story. They saw in the tale of Narcissus a representation of an indispensable human experience, the birth of self-consciousness through love.

Narcisus

The most highly developed version of the story of Narcissus is in a twelfth-century lay by an unknown Norman-French poet,[1] who makes of Ovid's tale a narrative that is truly medieval, not only in the details of manner and dress but in style and structure. In the graceful movement and formal balance of the internal monologues, for example, he hardly suffers in comparison with Chrétien. The language is at times too automatic, too obviously determined by rhetorical prescriptions; but the formality of the rhetoric results in a pleasing restraint. So too with the poem's structure: the experience of Narcisus[2] unfolds in a pattern that reveals its meaning. It is precisely when the formal elements of rhetoric and structure are united with the impression of immediate and intense emotion that medieval literature achieves its finest and most characteristic quality. Our poem has this quality. It suggests the meaning of the story of Narcissus for much of the literature of the Middle Ages.

The Old French poet "medievalizes" the Ovidian tale, which he otherwise follows quite closely. Narcisus is no longer the son of Liriope and the river-god Cephisus but a "*dameisel*," a "*vaslez*," the son of an ordinary "*dame de la cité*"

[1] *Narcisus* (*poème du XIIe siècle*), ed. M. M. Pelan and N. C. W. Spence, Publications de la Faculté des Lettres de l'Université de Strasbourg, Fasc. 147 (Paris, 1964). All of the line numbers in our text refer to this edition, which is methodologically superior to the only previous critical edition, Alfons Hilka, "Der altfranzösische Narcisuslai, eine antikisierende Dichtung des 12. Jahrhunderts," *Zeitschrift für romanische Philologie*, XLIX (1929), 633–675.

[2] I adopt the practice of Allan M. F. Gunn, and distinguish by spelling the Narcissus of the classical source from the Narcisus of the Old French versions.

(47). Echo is replaced by Dané, the daughter of the king of the city. She is a medieval beauty in her *grise pelice*, her *chemise*, and her *mantel*. It is she, not another rejected suitor, who brings the curse down upon Narcisus. The rôle of Tiresias is retained, but he becomes a nameless *"devins . . . de Tebes nés, / Qui de voir dire ert esprovés"* (41f); and, in another departure from Ovid, his prophecy—*"Gart bien qu'il ne se voie mie; / Ne vivra gaires, s'il se voit"* (52f)—is recalled a second time later in the story. Nemesis becomes Amors, the full-fledged medieval power, with his arrows and his great *"segnourie"* (160).

The following outline will give us some idea of the poet's plan:

Introduction

1–40: The power of love and the necessity for caution, knowledge and restraint. Pride and haughtiness in a beloved person are an insult to Amors, who will take vengeance. The story of Narcisus may give us an example.

41–120: The antecedent action, the seer's prophecy, the beauty of Narcisus, his indifference to love.

I. The action begins: Dané sees Narcisus and is overwhelmed by his beauty (121–404).

II. Meditation by the narrator on the power of Amors and Dané's plight (405–424).

III. The encounter and Dané's curse: she begs for his love, is scornfully rejected, prays that N. may suffer the same plight (425–630).

IV. N. falls in love with the image on the surface of the fountain; eventually he recognizes his error (631–968).

V. Dané arrives at the last moment of his life; she dies by his side (969–1010).

Parts I and IV concern the love and suffering of Dané and Narcisus respectively, each struck by the beauty of an unattainable person. Parts III and V tell of encounters between Dané and Narcisus. Dané's plea for Narcisus's love is unfulfilled; Narcisus's plea for Dané's love is unfulfillable. Part II, containing thoughts applicable equally to both, forms a transition between the experience of Dané and the first encounter.

The correspondences are much more numerous. Although the poet has, for good reasons, altered the girl's fate (which, in Ovid, is comparable to that of Narcisus), he has done many things to stress the parallelism between the experiences of Dané and Narcisus.

Dané is not, like Echo, the aural image of Narcisus, repeating his words as the image in the fountain reflected his person. This change permits the author to trace the identical course of the love-disease in each character. Love begins for each with a vision of beauty, and immediately causes pain. Driven by their suffering and terror, Dané and Narcisus seek the cause; for although they know they suffer, they do not know what that suffering is, or what name to give it.

Dané knows only that she cannot sleep that night, tossing and turning without relief. At first she thinks it is because her bed is too hard, and she wakes the poor cursing nurse to change the covers, and the mattress, and the sheets. For a while she actually feels better:

> 220 Savés por quoi? Que ele avoit
> Le jovencel entroublié;
> Mais quant ele ot un poi esté
> Et il li est menbré de lui,
> Dont recomence son anui.

(Do you know why? Because in the meantime she had forgotten the youth. But when she has lain a while and remembered him, her discomfort begins all over again.)

There is more tossing and turning for her. Why can she not lie comfortably on either side? What *rage* has she in her body? Finally:

> 237   "Or reveul a celui penser
>   Que je vi ier par ci passer.
>   K'ai ge a faire de ce vassal?
> 240   C'est la riens qui plus me fait mal
>   Quant me menbre de sa biauté."

(Now I wish to think again of the one I saw pass by here yesterday. What have I to do with that noble youth? He is what most causes my suffering, when I remember his beauty.)

Eventually she realizes that it is love which causes this suffering, and that Narcisus is the only one who can cure her.

The experience of an unaccustomed suffering, the eventual discovery of love as its cause, the ensuing determination upon a cure: the "sickness" runs an identical course in Dané and in Narcisus, in whom it finds the same essential condition of *inexperience*. The kind of love whose origin is depicted here—the consuming and irresistible power of Amors, whose vassals are all of the courtly class—presupposes the innocence of its victims. Both hero and heroine are at the beginning of things, aware for the first time of their own bodies as distinct from the terrible beauty of others. Each learns something new: that this malady arises, and can be cured, only because there is a difference between oneself and another whom one loves. This slow burgeoning of self-consciousness is the first fact of the new life that begins for both.

All this can be seen more clearly in the story of Narcisus. From the moment he sees his reflected image, he too suffers some incomprehensible pain.

At first he thinks that the reflection is a beautiful water

nymph who guards the fountain. Amors wastes no time; Narcisus, still wondering what the beautiful *chose* can possibly be, begins to love it and finds that he cannot turn his eyes away. He trains his eyes on her face, her figure, her eyes, her hands, her fingers (651–669).

670 Mout est angouseus et destrois.
     Ne set qu'il voit; l'iaue li ment:
     Il se loe, si ne l'entent.
     C'est sa biautés qu'iloques voit
     Et il meïsmes se deçoit!
675 C'est cil qui or blasmoit Amor;
     Or l'a ja mis en tel freor.
     Or li prie, souspire et pleure;
     Or li prie qu'il le seceure,
     Mais esgarés est d'une cose.
680 Ne se poeut taire et parler n'ose;
     Plaint soi, aprés fait un sospir;
     De parler ne se puet tenir:
       "Cose, fait il, que laiens voi,
       Ne sai conment nomer te doi:
685   Se dois estre ninphe apelee,
       O se tu es duesse u fee. . . ."

(He is filled with suffering and affliction. He does not know what he sees. The water lies to him: it is himself that he is praising, but he does not realize it. It is his own beauty that he sees there, and he is deceiving himself. It is he who denounced Amors just before, and now Amors has put him in such dread. Now he will pray to Amors, sigh, and weep; now he will pray to Amors for help. He is most distraught over one thing: he cannot remain silent, yet he dares not speak. He complains, then he sighs, he cannot keep himself from speaking: "Thing," he says, "that I see in there, I do not know how I ought to call you, whether you should be called a nymph, or whether you are a goddess or a fairy. . . .")

In passages like this the poet reiterates a simple but crucial feature of the story: Narcisus does not love himself, but an image that he regards as real. He does not love the image because it is his own, but because it is beautiful; it is an image of perfect beauty. His fate is sealed not because the object of his love is his own likeness, but because it is unreal and thus incapable of requiting him. So far as he knows in his certainty and blindness, he is moved by love for another person. He cannot distinguish between false separateness and true. To us, the audience, the poem tells how Narcisus wins this essential knowledge, which we have inherited from the *exemplum* of his life, and which has saved us all from a similar fate.

And so we watch him desiring this thing that he cannot name, imploring it to come to him. All of these new feelings excite an intense effort to understand. Questions are asked, possible answers are suggested; some of these possibilities are eliminated, others are tentatively accepted and lead to other questions, which in turn suggest alternatives to be examined. His torment impels his effort to understand.

690	"Vien ça! Que te trais tu ariere?
	Por qu'es orgelleuse vers moi?
	Ne sui gaires mains biaus de toi!
	Maintes fois ai esté requis;
	Or sui de male ardor espris;
695	Or sen je bien com lor estoit,
	Qu'eles se plaignoient a droit.
	Que te vais tu or reponant?
	Parole a moi, si vien avant!
	Legierement i pues passer:
700	Entre nos deus n'a nule mer,
	Mais un peu d'iaue qui m'ocit.
	Las! Entent ele que j'ai dit?
	Nenil! Espoir trop est parfont?
	Par Diu, si fait et si respont!
705	Je li voi les levres movoir,

Mais l'oïe n'en puis avoir.
L'iaue ne laist la vois venir
Et fait que ne la puis oïr.
E, las! Por quoi ne l'oi parler?
710   Que ne se vient ça fors mostrer?
U ce li vient de grant orgueil,
U el ne veut çou que je voeil,
Car, quant je ri, je li voi rire;
Quant je sospir, ele souspire;
715   Et quant je plor, ele autretel;
K'el ne fine ne ne fait el
Devant que j'autre cose face.
Je voi les larmes en la face,
Ne mes caviaus ne puis je traire
720   Que ne li voie autretel faire.
Mais por que'l fait? S'ele m'amast,
Ele iscist hors, si se moustrast.
U ensi me veut escarnir
U ne poeut pas a moi venir."

("Come here! Why do you hold back? Why are you haughty
toward me? I am hardly less beautiful than you. My love has been
sought after many times. Now I am consumed by a terrible
burning. Now I feel clearly how it was with them, that they
justly complained. What are you saying now? Speak to me, come
forward! You can easily pass over here: between us there is no sea
but a little bit of water, which is causing my death. Wretched me,
does she hear what I am saying? No, she does not; perhaps the
water is too deep. And yet, by God, she speaks and replies. I see
her lips moving; but I cannot hear what they are saying. The
water keeps her voice from reaching me and so prevents me from
hearing. Wretched me! why do I not hear her speak, why doesn't
she come show herself outside here? Either this is caused by her
great pride, or she desires what I desire; for when I smile, I see her
smile; when I sigh, she sighs, and when I weep, she does the same.
For she neither stops nor does anything else before I do. I see the
tears on her face, and I cannot pull my hair without seeing her do
the same. Why does she act this way? If she loved me, she would

come out, show herself here. Either she wants to mock me in this way, or else she is unable to come to me.")

The problem is her unattainability and indifference. The first solution to offer itself is her possible pride. This is now examined. If she *is* proud, she is so unjustly, for he is as fair and desirable as she: pride ought not to exist between equals. The thought that he has been desired in vain by others brings him back to his own unrequited desire, and in a flash he knows something he has never known before: he now understands what *they* all felt, why *they* all suffered. Forced by this inexplicable experience to become conscious of the difference between himself and what he loves, he instantly becomes aware of the difference between himself and those who loved him; and this new awareness teaches him compassion.

Now the beautiful being in the water speaks when he speaks, does everything that he does, but is inaudible. This leads to a new perplexity, but the first possible answer is eliminated: it is not pride that keeps her back, for pride would not make her imitate so perfectly his words, and weeping, and laughter. Slowly, in this deliberate scanning of possibilities, he is led to another solution: perhaps she is *unable* to come out.

Every stage in Narcisus's effort is marked by a new expression of his suffering and confusion. He is fascinated and terrified by his own reactions: sometimes he weeps, sometimes he wants to laugh; his heart warms him and then he is cold (726ff). In the rhetorical play of antitheses the poet's intention is carried forward. Every sensation leads Narcisus to the definition of his own identity:

> 730   "Quel froidure ai je? Que ce doit,
>   Desqu'il fait si grant caut ça fors,
>   Que jou ai froit dedens le cors?"

(What is this coldness that I have? How can it be that while it is hot here outside, I am cold within my body?)

29

Narcissus

The recollection of those who loved him, and his constant awareness of his own sensations, finally enable him to discover the cause of his suffering:

> 733 "Or me menbre que j'oï dire
>   Que tel torment et tel martire
> 735 Et tel vie seulent mener
>   Cil qui s'entremetent d'amer!
>   Est donc Amors qui si me maine
>   Et me fait traire mal et painne?
>   D'Amors ne doi je riens savoir."

(Now I remember, I have heard that this torment, this suffering, this life is usually experienced by those who are taken by love. Is it Amors who so rules me and makes me bear suffering and pain? I ought to know nothing about Amors.)

I have given the merest suggestion of how, in this narrative, formal and traditional rhetoric imitates the movement of impassioned thought. The long sequence of possibility and exclusion that has led to the discovery of Amors continues now in the examination of that mighty power. It leads to new sensations, and to new understanding, for not until Narcisus is completely conscious of himself can he recognize the truth about the thing he loves.

"I ought to know nothing about Amors," says Narcisus; but he does know that Amors is powerful and is tormenting him. "But where he is, or who he may be, where he dwells, where he may be seen, what people and what land are in his power —these things I cannot know by myself" (740–746).

Here he is speaking of a *thing* that he has heard about, a great power with the form and attributes of a person and therefore external and limited. This is the language of the youth who finds Dané and all of the others oppressive with their incomprehensible desires; who lives in a world of words (like "Amors") not yet defined by experience, and of objects (of which he himself is one, and Dané another) not yet called by name because they are not yet consciously distinguished. Later he will find a word for himself, and another for Dané. But the youth we are speaking of has really ceased to exist. Narcisus has already made the most important discovery of his life:

747 "C'ai jou a faire de lu querre,
De son païs et de sa terre?
Se jel demant, assés est prés:
750 Dedens moi le sent mout engrés.
Ne m'estuet pas que loig le quiere!
Or ai vëu [d]e sa maniere.
Or m'est avis que je sai bien
Dont est! Unques mais n'en soi rien!"

(But why do I have to make an inquiry concerning his region or his land? If I seek his whereabouts, he is close enough: within myself I feel him, so powerful. Nor do I have to go far to seek him! I have now seen something of his way. Now I realize that I do indeed know where he is! I never before knew a thing about him!)

He has discovered the *moi*, a body whose form and climate are distinguishable from every other, and an inner life whose events are invisible to everyone else, revealing its existence to a consciousness newly awakened by pain and desire. In a passage like this, *Amors* is transformed from an allegorical abstraction to the experience he personifies. His icy realm, his hard heart, his veins of iron, his infernal nature (755–770)—all these attributes of the allegorical figure are now rediscovered in the torment Narcisus experiences, in the suffering that reveals to him the identity of the sufferer. Here Love is not the fatuous and sentimental master of ceremonies so often found in courtly literature, but a condition of the inner life, defined and known in the sensations of experience.

Narcissus

It is the discovery of his own capacity for knowledge that amazes Narcisus:

> 771 "Or es tu ja d'Amor mout sages!
> Qui t'en a tant dit? Tes corages?
> Je ne cuit pas que ce puist estre
> Que tu en saces tant sans mestre."

(Now you are already very wise concerning Amors. Who has told you so much about him? Your heart? I do not think you could know so much without a teacher.)

He is amazed because he has learned something important by looking within himself. But then he thinks that in a way he *has* had a teacher:

> 775 "Amors est mastre qui me duist,
> Qui dedens le cors m'art et cuist.
> Il m'aprent tote sa nature
> Et si m'angousce sans mesure."

(Amors is the teacher who instructs me, who burns and scorches me within my body: he teaches me all his nature and causes me suffering without measure.)

Amors teaches by the suffering he causes. By that means Narcisus is presented with an image of his whole life, not only of his outward form in the *unbre* that soon will cease to deceive him, but of the inner life now so well known that it can be designated and defined by a word.

Everything that Narcisus thinks from the moment he first sees the image is intended to lead to the climactic moment of his disillusionment. That self-consciousness, which Amors gives him, is necessary before he can recognize himself in the image he loves. His psychic condition before he kneels at the fountain must differ in every way from the consciousness that enables him to identify the image. For if he had ever consciously perceived his own body as separate from all other bodies in the world, with a form and a name of its own; if he had ever known the figure that all those girls and boys so vainly loved, studied its beauty and cherished it as they did and thereby understood their feelings—then he would never have been deceived and would never have trained all of his love onto something truly unreal.

Thus the problem for the poet is to show how Narcisus comes to recognize the image for what it is. Narcisus cannot recognize what he does not first of all know, and what he recognizes is an image of himself. Thus he cannot be disillusioned until he knows himself so well—and not by means of any fountain or mirror—that he can address himself and say "*tu.*"

All this will be clearer if we consider the "recognition" passage in Ovid. There, too, Narcissus wonders why the boy does not come closer, for he seems willing to do everything that Narcissus does.

459   "Cum risi, arrides. Lacrimas quoque saepe notaui
      Me lacrimante tuas; nutu quoque signa remittis;
      Et, quantum motu formosi suspicor oris,
      Verba refers aures non pervenientia nostras.
      Iste ego sum; sensi nec me mea fallit imago;
464   Vror amore mei, flammas moueoque feroque."
              [*Metamorphoseon*, Liber III]

(When I have smiled, you smile back; and I have often seen your tears while I was weeping; you return my gestures by inclining your head; and, as far as I can surmise by the movement of your beautiful mouth, you return words that do not reach my ears. I am that boy. I have understood, and my image no longer deceives me; I burn for love of myself, I have lit the flames that I bear.)

Narcissus

What our poet would find missing in this passage is clear. That *iste ego sum*—where did it come from? How did the truth suddenly flash across the mind of Narcissus, who was so completely deluded in the preceding line? Both the fact of the recognition and its position in the narrative would appear gratuitous to the Old French poet.

For it is clear that when Narcissus cries out,

Iste ego sum!

J'aim moi meïsme!

he is not discovering himself, but *recognizing* himself. Something has happened between the first deluded passion and this outcry. Before he realizes that his own body has cast its image upon a reflecting surface, he has already "doubled" himself in a more significant way: into *moi* and *tu*, into knowing subject and known object. For he cannot recognize his image until he knows himself. The discovery of Amors leads to the contemplation of Amors—the reflected image is for the moment forgotten. This absorption in the meaning and sensation of love ends in the definition of the lover, in self-consciousness and self-knowledge, the condition necessary for identifying the image.

In the climax, all of the poet's deviations from Ovid reveal his constant concern to explain the recognition. For example, in Ovid the passage about Narcisus's tears disturbing the water and thus causing the image to "flee" comes after the recognition. But our poet places it before (805ff), as a further clue for Narcisus to the insubstantial and illusory nature of the image.

Narcisus tries to embrace this beautiful figure, but nothing seems to be there.

830   Lors se comence a porpenser,
           Si voit que prendre ne la pueut

Et mout est prés, si ne se muet;
Ensi li fuit, si le deçoit;
Et quide que fantosmes soit.
835   Un poi est en son se[n]s venus;
Lors connoist qu'il est deceüs
Et voit que c'est unbres qu'il ainme.

(Then he begins to reflect. He sees that he is unable to grasp it, that it is very close but does not change. Thus it flees from him and deceives him; and he thinks it is a phantom. He has begun to understand a little. Then he knows he is deceived and sees that it is an image that he loves.)

Until this moment the revenge of Amors has not, in effect, begun. Whatever suffering Narcisus has endured so far has brought with it a great reward, the birth and increase of consciousness. He loves, he knows he loves, and he knows that love teaches him. Now, because he is capable of it, he is driven by love to know its object. This is the crucial moment for Narcisus, when Amors's revenge commences. He knows he loves an image, *but he cannot stop loving it:*

838   Mout par se blasme et fol se clanme
Et neporquant ne set que faire;
Son corage n'en puet retraire.

(He much reproaches himself and calls himself mad, and yet he does not know what to do; he cannot withdraw his heart from it.)

Now Narcisus is truly lost. The consciousness that has enriched his nature immediately becomes a curse. Here the poet makes a new addition to the story as told by Ovid: the repetition of the seer's prophecy stresses the hopelessness of Narcisus's fate:

849   "Bien sai que voir dist li devins.
       Ma mors est pres; ceu est la fins,
       Car en fol liu ai mis m'entente.
       Or n'i ai je mais nule atente.
       Or sent et croi et sai de voir
       Qu'esperance n'i puis avoir
855   Et d'itant sui plus angouseus
       Et plus m'art et esprent li feus,
       Car ançois viaus, me fu depors
       Li esgarders, et grans confors;
       Et quidai veoir quanque soit
860   De l'u[n]bre qui me decevoit,
       Si me feïst auques de bien,
       Mais ore sai que nen voi rien;
       Por çou m'est li maus plus engrés;
       Or ne puis estre une ore en pés;
865   Or n'aim je nule rien vivant;
       Or ne sai je que je demant.
       Queus amors est ce dont me duel,
       Quant j'aim, si ne sa que je veul?
       Le cors, le vis que je la voi,
870   Ce puis je tot trover en moi.
       J'aim moi meïsme! C'est folie!"

("I well know that the seer spoke the truth: my death is near, it is the end, for I have put my love in a mad place. Now I have no more hope in this. Now I feel and believe and know in truth that I cannot have any hope in this, and I am all the more in anguish, and the fire burns and consumes me more; for before at least the sight was a pleasure to me, and a great comfort. I thought I saw at least a part of the reflection that was deceiving me, and thus it would have been of some good for me. But now I know that I see nothing. Therefore my affliction has increased; now I cannot have one moment of peace. Now I love no living thing. Now I do not know what I desire. What kind of love is this from which I suffer, for I love but do not know what I want? The body, the visage I see there—I can find them in myself. I love myself! It is madness!")

As Narcisus realizes that the beautiful image is his own reflection, the depth of his understanding is revealed. He knows that when he believed in the reality of the *unbre*, for all his suffering he would have gained something: *si me feïst auques de bien*. The pain of desire then was as nothing to his terror now: he has lost all hope. For even after discovering that his beloved is a mere reflection of his own beauty, he cannot refrain from loving it.

This is his crisis, and the experience of Narcisus in this moment reveals something of the origin of courtly love. Here we are anticipating the lyrics that follow, where the joy and suffering of the courtly man re-create the awe of Narcisus before an ideally beautiful figure, and the torment of his disillusionment. The moment when the courtly man realizes that the lady lacks the qualities he has cherished and is herself a reflection of the uncertainty he has sought to escape, and at the same time finds himself unable to withdraw his love, unwilling to destroy a relation from which, despite its illusory character, he has drawn real benefits—that moment defines the meaning of the "mirror lyrics" before us. Now the lover exalts the lady as the representation of his ideal nature, now he debases her as insensate, incapable of concern: this ambivalence is at the root of all the "tensions" every reader discerns as the outstanding trait of the courtly lyric. Narcisus innocently reveals the simple explanation of much that is hard to understand about courtly love: *"Jou meïsmes me fas languir"* (916: "I myself cause my suffering"). But even now he has a means of escape.

The one way out for Narcisus is to direct his love away from a lifeless object, incapable of requital, to a living woman who can love. In one of the poet's most significant additions to Ovid, Narcisus remembers Dané; and the moral awareness he then reveals is one of the rewards of the whole experience:

936   "Las! Ma mere por quoi ne set?
        Si me venist plaindre et plorer,
        Auques me peüst conforter;
        Mais dont ne m'a nus esgardé
940   Qui plaigne moi et ma biauté?
        Certes, oïl, viaus la pucele
        Que je trovai l'autr'ier si bele,
        Ki se clamoit cetive et lasse
        Et me prioit que je l'amaisse.
945   Or me puis je caitis clamer
        Por çou que ne la voil amer!
        Ahi, las, tant par fui vilains
        Et de grant felonie plains
        Et tant fui dors et de mal aire
950   K'el onques ne me pooit plaire."

("Wretched me, why does my mother know nothing about this? If she came to pity me and weep for me, she might comfort me somewhat. Has no one seen me, then, who might lament for me and my beauty? Indeed, yes! At least there is that maiden whom I found so beautiful the other day, who called herself wretched and miserable, and begged me to love her. Now I can call myself wretched for not wanting to love her. Ahi! wretched, I have been so contemptible and full of great cruelty, and I have been so hard-hearted and villainous that she could never please me.")

In her he sees his salvation:

951   "Biaus sire Dius, car venist ore!
        Espoir mestier m'aroit encore
        Plus que mere, pere ne suer!
        S'i pooie torner mon cuer
955   Et si aploier mon corage
        Que j'oubliaisce ceste rage,
        Car Amors m'a si escaufé
        C'amer m'estuet estre mon gré;
        Mais une rien cuit bien entendre
960   Que se m'amors s'eüt u prendre

Et je veïsse autru que moi,
Ne fuisce pas en tel esfroi.
Dius! S'or venoit par aventure,
La porroit estre bien seüre
965 Que ele conqueroit m'amor
Et me geteroit de langor.
Bien me devoit maus avenir
Quant onques ne le voil oïr."

("Dear Lord God, let her come now! Perhaps she would be able to save me, more than mother, father, or sister, if I could turn my heart to her, and so bend my heart that I forget this frenzy; for Amors has so inflamed me that I must love against my will. One thing I know I understand: if my love had known where to take hold and I had seen someone other than myself, I would not be in such a predicament. God! if only she would by chance come now! She could be quite sure that she would win my love, and she would cast me out of this languishing. I deserve misfortune well, for I was never willing to hear her.")

His terror of isolation shows him his moral failing regarding the *pucele*. But this in turn leads to a practical insight: the girl, in begging for his love, was herself in love. She is available as an alternative to the reflection. For Narcisus, in his peril, the crucial difference between her and the *unbre* is not that she has a different visage from his own but that she is alive, able to respond to his desire with her own. There is no question of simply recalling his love: *amer m'estuet estre mon gré*. He must love. But whether he lives or dies depends upon what he loves. His one hope is to substitute Dané for his own unretrievable image.

But that hope is fulfilled too late. In his fear and desire he faints, three times over, and loses the power to speak. He opens his eyes and sees Dané coming, all distracted. He sees her but does not say a word; for he is unable to speak (969–978).

Narcissus

979   La fontaine li mostre au doit
        Et l'onbre qui si le deçoit.

(He points out the fountain to her with his finger, and the reflection that deceives him.)

He holds out his arms to her, moves his lips, opens his eyes as much as he can, and makes a sign to her that he repents. She understands. In her torment she embraces him, kisses his eyes and face (981–990). She cannot bear the thought that her own cruel prayer has caused his death. There is no comfort for her; she must die with him (991–1002).

They die together, in the same place, at the same moment, in the same state of repentance and despair. The poet intensifies in this last scene the correspondences he has devised throughout the narrative. The whole structure of the lay reflects this: the experience of Dané occurs as a prefiguration of Narcisus's. In their death they are identical mirror images of one another. Narcisus expiring in impotent willingness takes on the character, the tragic insubstantiality of the beloved image—perhaps there is a kind of metamorphosis here, a vestige of his fate in Ovid's narrative.[3] Dané becomes to the passive Narcisus what he had been to the passive image.

The whole force of the last scene is in the despairing gesture of Narcisus as he shows Dané the fountain and the deceiving reflection, a gesture that explains to her the cause of his dying and the source of his love and hope. What he desired in the end was to find a living person with all the beauty and perfection of the image, thus to endow that image with the capacity to requite him. The last thing he learns is the necessity to love a living image.

Here again, anticipating the lyrics, we see that the experience of Narcisus is definitive. In every love relation in the

[3] Compare the following lines: 977–981 with 705f and 788f; 985 with 664; 987 with 824–826; 993f with 704–708; 998–1001 with 783–786 and 816; 974–976 with 957f; 485 with 692.

40

courtly lyric, the living lady, universally esteemed, reflects the idealized image of the man who consecrates himself to serving her. The meaning of that consecration is here, in the last hope of Narcisus: the love that he would give to Dané is the same that binds him to the image.

The discussion so far has followed the order of the narrative itself. Therefore it will be useful to assemble our observations under more comprehensive terms. Furthermore, to avoid confusing digressions I have deferred until now some important questions that must be considered. But some repetition of earlier remarks is unavoidable in what follows.

THE NECESSITY TO LOVE

Narcisus sees the *chose*; Amors acts; Narcisus loves the object without knowing what it is, and indeed without even knowing that he loves (658ff). All this happens in a flash (657). As our poet has arranged the story, Narcisus does not know what it is that he loves, and the first thing he finds out is not what it is but that he loves it. It costs him much pain to find that out, but not until he does so can he learn anything about the beautiful thing he desires. The *chose* in the fountain makes Narcisus aware first of the love that is in him, then of the knowledge that is in him. All this happens while his beloved is a "thing," whose reality and separateness Narcisus has not learned to doubt.

But why must Narcisus be able to love only his own reflection, and not any of the *dames en chambres* whom he despises and avoids (120)? And how can he love something he knows nothing about?

It is because Amors is *mestre* to Narcisus in the same way that Socrates was to the ignorant slave who did not know that he knew. Amors "teaches" Narcisus, not by pouring previously unknown facts into his mind but by making him conscious of what is already there. That consciousness is the first reward of the meditation upon love; his own heart teaches him (771f). This happens without any mediation by the beloved object. The object is still a *chose*, still unnamable, and it remains so while Narcisus turns from it to meditate upon himself and his sensations.

Thus, for Narcisus, there seems to have been a necessity to love that preceded any perceptible object to love. The object is the material cause of a new experience, but the final cause of love is the ascent to consciousness and knowledge. Only that consciousness enables Narcisus to rise above the hard-hearted estate of childhood, thereby to perfect his nature and his moral capacity. For as he achieves consciousness and knowledge of himself he becomes capable of consciousness and knowledge of others (694ff).

Here one thinks of the genesis of the legend of Narcissus in classical and pre-classical times. Narcissus was conceived as the anti-Eros, whom the God of Love had to destroy as his enemy and the greatest danger to the continuation of life.[4] In our narrative, too, as in other medieval versions, it is Amors who destroys Narcisus, for Narcisus annihilates procreative love. But Narcisus does not merely suffer and die. Here is a special irony, for precisely through the means by which he is destroyed Narcisus achieves that psychic condition which makes him no longer the anti-Eros but Love's "man." Before Narcisus dies he understands the seer's prophecy and the crucial necessity to love another.

Readers of the medieval lyric will probably have recalled the very frequent motif of the man who loves a woman he has never seen. Every courtly lyric deals, directly or indirectly, with the problem of the origin of love. In some lyrics the lady may lodge or arouse love in the heart by "arrows" of visual spirits that penetrate the lover's wondering eyes; or Amors

[4] S. Eitrem, "Narkissos," *Paulys Real-Encyclopädie der classischen Altertumswissenschaft*, XVI (Stuttgart, 1935), 1723ff.

himself may enter directly—not necessarily through the eyes, and frequently, as we have said, before the lover has seen the lady—and dictate to the already will-less man simply that he shall love, or that he shall find and love a particular lady. But every such instance represents the material cause of *consciousness*, enabling the lover to feel what is already in his heart. It is meaningless to say that the man is "given" love. Often the man has to invent a lady as a fitting recipient of his love, and then seek a real lady who will resemble the image in his mind. This is a special kind of love, and the question persists: where does it come from? how does it originate?

The figure of Amors is no help to us at all. It is true that Narcisus discovers this great power by contemplating his own condition. But the key to the meaning of Amors is the fact that he arranges Narcisus's downfall. Amors is called upon to bring justice, by one who had been truly wronged: Amors the avenger cannot be the same as Narcisus's private feelings. Amors is collective, social, distinguished from Narcisus's own love although known and understood by means of it.

We ought to ask whether love really begins with the vision of beauty in the fountain—indeed, whether, in the medieval view, love really "begins" at all. The answer is implied in everything we have seen. Self-love and self-knowledge were in Narcisus long before the encounter at the fountain. Here in this medieval narrative, love is not a temporal condition that begins in a particular moment, before which it did not exist. It is rather one of the constitutive elements of a man's existence, one whose origin and duration coincide with his very life. What "begins" is not love but the man's consciousness of his love. It is the same with Narcisus's self-knowledge: what begins is his ability to articulate that knowledge. But to say these things is to echo another voice:

Porro autem in mente non sic est: neque enim adventitia sibi est, quasi ad se ipsam quae jam erat, venerit aliunde eadem ipsa quae

non erat; aut non aliunde venerit, sed in se ipsa quae jam erat, nata
sit ea ipsa quae non erat; sicut in mente quae jam erat, oritur fides
quae non erat: aut post cognitionem sui recordando se ipsam velut
in memoria sua constitutam videt, quasi non ibi fuerit antequam
se ipsam cognosceret; cum profecto ex quo esse coepit, nunquam
sui meminisse, nunquam se intelligere, nunquam se amare destiterit,
sicut jam ostendimus. Ac per hoc quando ad se ipsam cogitatione
convertitur, fit trinitas, in qua jam et verbum possit intelligi:
formatur quippe ex ipsa cogitatione, voluntate utrumque jungente.[5]

([For the mind's knowledge of itself is not like its knowledge of
other things, which are knowable before the mind knows them.]
The mind is not adventitious to itself, as though, to the mind that
already existed, there should come from elsewhere an identical
mind that had not existed before; or, if not coming from elsewhere, as though, in the mind already existing, there should be
born an identical mind that had not existed before; just as faith,
which had not existed before, arises in the soul that has. Nor is it
true to say that, after it has gained knowledge of itself in remembering itself, it sees itself as though placed in its own memory, as
though it had not existed there before it knew itself. For from the
very moment when it began to be, the mind has never ceased to
understand itself, has never ceased to love itself, has never ceased
to remember itself, as we have already shown. And therefore
when it is turned upon itself in the act of thought, a trinity
occurs, in which one would already be able to understand what
the *word* is: for the word is formed from the very act of thought
and is joined to the memory by the will.)

Augustine, too, is concerned with the origin of self-
consciousness. Between them, Augustine and Narcisus define
the alternatives. The mind, says Augustine, always loves itself
and always knows itself—but not always consciously. When,
impelled by self-love, the mind comes to know itself consciously, its act is the utterance of a "word" that defines its
own identity and becomes an image of it. In the text we have

[5] St. Augustine, *De Trinitate*, XIV, x, 13; *PL*, col. 1047.

quoted, the *memoria* is the mind's unconscious and abiding knowledge of itself, before that knowledge is an object of conscious thought; the *verbum* is that same knowledge re-created in consciousness. That word belongs to no audible language. It is the act of consciousness. The language of nations may try to translate that word into audible terms, but in this attempt it must fail, for no language is adequate to the word. But what audible word represents all the contents of self-consciousness? It is the *moi*, the *tu*, of Narcisus.

Love and knowledge had always existed in Narcisus, and the object (as well as the subject) of both was himself. The effect of the *unbre* is to externalize that object, to make it visible. The love that Narcisus feels for the image originates in his unconscious love of himself. Narcisus has to duplicate himself, to make a sensible image of himself. Here he puts himself in the greatest peril, for an image is unreal and unlimited, while the man who sees himself in that image is a creature of flesh and blood, subject to failings and terrors and moral commitments that an image cannot accommodate. All this we shall see more clearly later. The main observation to be made now is that love can be said to begin with the vision of beauty only in the sense that it becomes conscious and is trained upon a visible reflection. But self-love is a part of the man's constitution, and in this sense love begins when the man begins.

There are two reasons for the necessity to love. Love is an innate and enduring condition, whether or not it is conscious. And love leads to self-consciousness, and thereby to the perfection of one's nature and to moral refinement.

NARCISUS'S CRISIS

The decisive moment for Narcisus occurs not while he is deceived, or while he is meditating upon Amors, but after he has recognized himself in the image (836ff), that is, when he has been undeceived. Narcisus's "*J'aim moi meïsme*" is not a discovery, but a recognition.

Narcissus

While he was discovering Love and the sensations of loving, he was granted great gifts of consciousness, and of compassion, which made him aware of his own identity and of the consequences of his life in the world. As a result, he recognizes the image of that identity in the *unbre* and thus realizes that he loves his own reflection. Now the dangerous thing for Narcisus is not that he loves himself, or that the reflection is of himself, but simply that it is a reflection. A reflection is not anything, it does not truly exist, its nature is to be "really unreal," in the words of Plotinus. This is why Narcisus is lost. To love someone who refuses to love in return is a torment; but to love something that does not exist is to be denied even the fantasy of requital.

When Narcisus first becomes conscious of himself, there is no visible reflection but another kind of self-image, a word: *tu* (771ff). But he recognizes himself in a mute and unattainable *unbre*. Thus he turns from a self-image that is internal and truly identical with himself (for there is no difference between *tu* and *moi* while he loves himself) to one that lies in another object and bears an insubstantial likeness; and it is to the latter that he gives his love. Here is another definitive moment—definitive not only for the courtly lyric but for the problem we are considering, the genesis of love. Narcisus turns from the contemplation and love of himself to the contemplation and love of his image *in another object*. It is precisely from this disposition to recognize oneself by contemplating one's image in another, that the love-relation in the courtly lyric arises.

This act of turning from oneself to another leads to a critical moment in which the mirror of the ideal is exposed as the deceiving mirror of matter, to the horrifying discovery that the beautiful image with which one longs to be united is borne in a thing without qualities; a thing that is, like matter, capable of reflecting whatever is cast before it, but, aside from this ability to reflect, defined by no other virtue whatever.

46

Narcisus's crisis begins when the lover is incapable of renouncing the image he knows to be unreal.

The false mirror of matter has captured the beautiful image of Narcisus, and he must wrest his love away, for that shadow starves him. Now there are two ways out for Narcisus, who is here to be regarded as a medieval man.

Following the way of St. Augustine, he would reform his love until it truly lighted upon himself, so that he loved not the reflection but the identity, the *tu*, the word that contains all of his consciousness. Such living self-love would impel the intelligence toward greater knowledge of the beloved, toward that *word* which would finally be revealed as an echo of the Word of God. In loving and knowing himself he would come to know that *he* was a mirror—not the lifeless glittering mirror in the fountain, but an animated mirror endowed with memory, intelligence, and will, and reflecting the God who created it. Narcisus would once again look into a mirror, the mirror of himself, and there he would see not merely his own image but all that he *could* see, in this mortal world, of the Being who created him as an image, and with whom his soul would long to be united. This way would, in every sense, save him, for so long as he kneels entranced by a reflection, he is lost. That reflection is so unstable that whenever his tears fall into the fountain and trouble the surface, he obliterates the object he loves, and thus, in a sense, he obliterates himself. So long as he requires an external image of himself to love, he is in peril.

The first escape for Narcisus—one that is not, of course, possible for him—is to love himself, not *in* an image, but *as* an image.

The other way out Narcisus understands immediately (951ff). It is to allow the image to become real. Dané becomes still another mirror, and her beauty is a reflection of Narcisus's own. "*Car assés somes d'un aé, / D'une maniere de biauté!*" (485f) she says to him—words that are reflected by Narcisus

47

as he implores the beautiful figure in the fountain: *"Ne sui gaires mains biaus de toï"* (692).[6]

The reflection in the fountain has been more than a mere likeness: it is the image of ideal beauty,[7] and nothing less can attract the love of Narcisus. Narcisus must now seek that ideal self-image in Dané, whose beauty is like his own, and who will be capable both of loving him and of being possessed.

For Narcisus the only real alternatives lie in either continuing to love the reflection now recognized as such, or turning to love the living woman. Yet he himself cannot really choose. As long as Dané is absent, he is the captive of his love for the image. *"Bien sai que voir dist li devins"* (849): his recollection of the seer's prophecy expresses his loss of will. He cannot cease to love the image. For if he turns from it, then what can he love? what can he see of himself? how can he know himself? He will not turn from this image unless another is immediately present, for without the one image or the other his life will disintegrate. And he is almost saved, but Dané comes too late, when he has suffered too much to recover. Here again is a constant element in the courtly lyric, the immobilization of the lover's will.

There were but two possibilities for the medieval man: to know himself in an image, or to know himself as an image. This may seem exceedingly strange to a twentieth-century reader, who knows a third way, expressed in any number of passages like the following:

---

[6] "For we are of the same age, and of the same kind of beauty." "I am hardly less beautiful than you" (that is, I am not at all less beautiful). It does not matter that statements like these are commonplaces in the Old French romance. Their place in the arrangement of *this* narrative gives them new meaning.

[7] See the passage on the ideal fashioning of Narcisus (62–110), where Amors exalts the already flawless work of Nature.

Mirror of Narcissus

Sie fragen, ob Ihre Verse gut sind. Sie fragen mich. Sie haben vorher andere gefragt. Sie senden sie an Zeitschriften. Sie vergleichen sie mit anderen Gedichten, und Sie beunruhigen sich, wenn gewisse Redaktionen Ihre Versuche ablehnen. Nun (da Sie mir gestattet haben, Ihnen zu raten) bitte ich Sie, das alles aufzugeben. Sie sehen nach aussen, und das vor allem dürften Sie jetzt nicht tun. Niemand kann Ihnen raten und helfen, niemand. Es gibt nur ein einziges Mittel. Gehen Sie in sich. Erforschen Sie den Grund, der Sie schreiben heisst: prüfen Sie, ob er in der tiefsten Stelle Ihres Herzens seine Wurzeln ausstreckt, gestehen Sie sich ein, ob Sie sterben müssten, wenn es Ihnen versagt würde zu schreiben. Dieses vor allem: fragen Sie sich in der stillsten Stunde Ihrer Nacht: *muss* ich schreiben? Graben Sie in sich nach einer tiefen Antwort. Und wenn diese zustimmend lauten sollte, wenn Sie mit einem starken und einfachen *"Ich muss"* dieser ernsten Frage begegnen dürfen, dann bauen Sie Ihr Leben nach dieser Notwendigkeit: Ihr Leben bis hinein in seine gleichgültigste und geringste Stunde muss ein Zeichen und Zeugniss werden diesem Drange. . . . Wenn Ihr Alltag Ihnen arm scheint, klagen Sie ihn nicht an: klagen Sie sich an, sagen Sie sich, dass Sie nicht Dichter genug sind, seine Reichtümer zu rufen: denn für den Schaffenden gibt es keine Armut und keinen armen gleichgültigen Ort.

[Rilke, "Briefe an einen jungen Dichter," 17 February 1903]

(You ask whether your poems are good. You ask me. You have previously asked others. You send them to periodicals. You compare them with other poems, and you are disturbed when certain editorial offices reject your efforts. Now (since you have allowed me to give you advice) I ask you to give all that up. You look outward, and that above all is what you must not do now. No one can advise and help you, no one. There is but one way. Go into yourself. Find out the reason that compels you to write; test whether it stretches out its roots in the deepest place in your heart; avow whether you would have to die if it were forbidden you to write. This above all: ask yourself in the stillest hour of your night: *must* I write? Dig within yourself for a deep answer. And if this answer should be affirmative, if you may meet this grave question with a strong and simple *"I must,"* then arrange your life according to this necessity; your life must become, even in its most indifferent and trifling moments, a proof and testimony of this urgency. . . . If your everyday life appears impoverished to you, do not blame that; blame yourself, say to yourself that you are not enough of a poet to evoke its richness; for to a man who creates there is no poverty and no impoverished and uninteresting place.)

We should not confuse this with the ancient injunction to "Know Thyself." For the ancients, to know oneself was to discover a whole new reality, *another* reality, the eternal ideas in which one's own nature participated and for which it ought to renounce every other value. It was to recognize oneself as an image gifted with the will to resemble the reality it reflected. But that is all quite different from what we have here. For Rilke, there is no other reference beyond "die tiefste Stelle Ihres Herzens," the only reliable source of the truth of one's nature. So the inner life becomes a garden to be cultivated incessantly, in order to see what may bloom. What is planted there is not a "seminal reason" created by a pre-existing nature, but something that never existed before and is not to be justified by its resemblance to anything. The man's task is to become conscious of the truth whose existence began with his own. The voice he hears is an echo of none other. That "*I must!*" marks the birth of consciousness: it reveals an "identity" between what he discovers about himself and what he is, not between what he is and what he resembles. The ultimate justification of his acts, the determination of their moral value, is to be sought only in the facts of his own nature.

Such a belief in the finality of character brings its own torment. It leads to a painful uncertainty about whether one has truly reached "the deepest place," to endless doubt about the motives behind one's acts and even behind one's desires. It discovers that only a part of one's nature is available to the inquiring reason, and that another part not only is influential too, but even deflects the efforts of consciousness to reach it. It is not the historical Thomas à Becket but the hero of a modern drama who suffers the dread of doing the right thing for the wrong reasons. This belief in the finality of character prohibits one from resolving these doubts by consulting a universal moral law or a pre-existing image. Rilke's letter shows the struggle of the individual consciousness to defend itself against the obliterating tyranny of a universal ideal. But this concept of personal truth, which denies the validity of the mirror, was not available to medieval man.

It is a commonplace in criticism of the medieval lyric to point out the tension that sustains as well as torments the true lover. He is torn between the ideal beauty and virtue reflected in the lady, which are visible so long as chastity keeps the mirror bright (hence her unattainability), and the physical attractiveness of the lady herself, desired as a wonderful sexual prize. But a deeper tension is revealed in this conflict. For beneath every posture of *fin amor* is the prostrate Narcissus at the moment of his crisis, liable to go one way or the other, and in peril. The lover's deepest conflict arises from his doubt as to the reality of what he loves. Then he vacillates between his faith that the lady is a mirror of the ideal, and his suspicion that she is merely the passive and glorified instrument of his own aspiration, reflecting what she does not truly possess. It is the most important conflict in the lover's life, for upon its outcome depends the intactness or the dissolution of his own identity; and it arises because the lover, like Narcissus, requires a mirror in order to know himself.

We have discovered three different mirrors in *Narcisus*. The fountain was at first the idealizing mirror, reflecting perfect beauty. Later, Narcisus is horrified by the wholly material nature of the mirror: it possesses no qualities, it contains neither the real nor the ideal but a fatal mockery of both. The third mirror is Dané, who is much like the other two, except that she is alive.

The mirror is a neutral object, without a will to deceive or a soul to emulate the ideal. And yet, in passively reflecting the forms that move before it, it exempts their images from the unceasing flux in which it is itself implicated; insensate and unaspiring, it gives the appearance of permanence and ideality. "La réalité fuit sans cesse. Le miroir est l'objet le plus réel et en même temps le plus fuyant. Le fait même (dans sa réalité) du miroir est paradoxal." [8]

The Romance of the Rose

In this episode (ll. 1425–1695), Guillaume de Lorris represents the irresistibility of love: to defy the commands of Amors is to invite his dread revenge, and no rebel against Love suffered more horribly than Narcisus. This is the clear, literal intent of the story of Narcisus in Guillaume's narrative, and as such it points a commonplace moral. Like everything else in Guillaume's work, however, the story has a deeper resonance, and the pristine experience obscured by banalities is retrieved and re-lived.

The Dreamer, continually menaced by Amors, discovers the fountain of Narcisus and is subsequently pierced by the arrows of love from Amors's bow.[9] At first, the God of Love follows him everywhere, coming closer and closer, waiting for the proper moment to let his arrows fly. In his wanderings through the Garden, which are aimless and spontaneous in contrast to Amors's single purpose, the Dreamer comes upon a fountain skillfully set by Nature within a marble rock beneath

[8] Guy Michaud, in "Discussions," *Cahiers de l'Association Internationale des Etudes Françaises*, XI (May 1959), 350.

[9] *Le Roman de la Rose par Guillaume de Lorris et Jean de Meun*, ed. Ernest Langlois, Société des Anciens Textes Français, Vol. LXXI, 5 vols. (Paris, 1914–1924). All references are to this edition.

a pine tree. It is the Fountain of Love. An inscription in small letters on the side of the rock tells that here the beautiful Narcisus died (1435–1438).

With the very next line (1439) the story of Narcisus begins, very much abridged and, as a narrative, rather uninteresting. Above all, there is no transitional passage to indicate the function of the story within the whole design of the Dreamer's adventures in the Garden. In contrast to everything that goes before it, the Narcisus story is told hastily. There is, for example, no description of Narcisus's actions while he is deceived—his entreaties to the youth to come to him, and so forth. But the narrative shows all the more starkly the danger of loving one's own image, for that image is naturally unattainable, and of refusing to love another:

1485	E cil maintenant s'esbaï,
	Car ses ombres si le traï
	Qu'il cuida veoir la figure
1488	D'un enfant bel a demesure.
	Lors se sot bien Amors vengier
	Dou grant orgueil e dou dangier
	Que Narcisus li ot mené.
1492	Bien li fu lors guerredoné.
	Qu'il musa tant a la fontaine
	Qu'il ama son ombre demaine.
	. . . . .
1497	Car, quant il vit qu'il ne porroit
	Acomplir ce qu'il desiroit,
	E qu'il estoit si pris par fort
1500	Qu'il n'en pooit avoir confort
	En nule fin ne en nul sen,
	Il perdi d'ire tot le sen,
1503	E fu morz en poi de termine.
	Ensi si ot de la meschine,
	Qu'il avoit devant escondite,
	Son guerredon e sa merite.

Narcissus

(And now he was astounded, for his reflection so deceived him that he fancied he saw the visage of an immeasurably beautiful youth. Then Amors knew well how to avenge himself for the pride and haughtiness that Narcisus had borne him. Then Narcisus received what he merited. For he gazed so long at the fountain that he loved his own reflection. . . . For when he saw that he would not be able to achieve what he desired, and that he was so irresistibly captivated that he could not have solace in any manner, he lost all his reason from chagrin, and was soon dead. Thus he received from Echo, whom he had refused before, his reward and his deserts.)

The function of this story within the whole narrative is explained by the Dreamer's reaction to it. When he recalls the fate of Narcisus, the Dreamer shrinks back and dares not look within the fountain. But then he assures himself that he really has nothing to fear, and he returns. He is frightened at first that what happened to Narcisus might also happen to him:

> 1515 . . . dedens n'osai regarder,
> Ainz començai a coarder,
> Quant de Narcisus me sovint,
> Cui malement en mesavint.

(I did not dare look within; rather, I began to tremble when I remembered Narcisus, who so painfully suffered misfortune.)

But *why* does the Dreamer escape the fate of Narcisus? He is, after all, in the same condition of youth and inexperience that caused the other's tragedy.

The answer is precisely that he knows the story of Narcisus. Therefore he has already learned many things that it cost Narcisus his life to find out. He has learned what an image is, and the conditions in which it appears; and that an image is incapable of offering *confort* to the man who loves it. Because he knows about the death of Narcisus, the Dreamer himself is not to die. In his terror when he shrinks back from the foun-

54

tain, he knows what can happen to a man entranced by the beauty of his image in a mirror, a mirror that cannot desire and must deceive. He knows why it is necessary to love another, a mirror that is alive and attainable.

That is why the Dreamer thinks he can return to the fountain without fear, and why he sees not his own image but *cent mile choses* in two crystal stones at the base of the fountain. The image is certainly there, but he by-passes it; he looks beyond it into all the other things that a mirror can reflect. That is his safeguard: he has learned to see not his own image but other things in the fountain of Narcisus.

And yet the moment has not arrived for Amors, who has been watching him carefully all this time, ready with that bow and those arrows, to do his work.

As soon as we continue Guillaume's narrative, we stumble upon another difficulty. At first the Dreamer admires the clarity of the crystal mirrors: together they reflect the whole garden, *senz decevoir* (1560); and every object in it, no matter how small, is vividly portrayed (1570).

But with no explicit indication of a change of mood, the Dreamer suddenly exclaims:

> 1571 C'est li miroers perilleus,
> Ou Narcisus li orguilleus
> Mira sa face e ses iauz vairs,
> Don il jut puis morz toz envers.

(It is the perilous mirror, where the proud Narcisus gazed upon his face and his sparkling eyes, wherefore he then lay dead upon his back.)

Whoever looks into this mirror cannot help falling in love. It has caused many a valiant man to perish, for the wisest, the noblest, the most refined are trapped there. It causes *rage*, it makes the heart unstable; against it, reason and restraint are

55

ineffectual. It leaves the beholder with nothing but the irresistible desire to love (1575–1587).

Why is the Dreamer again terrified by the fate of Narcisus, when he has already overcome that fear? Why should the bright, truthful mirror he admires suddenly become the perilous mirror that destroys reason?

This change of mood, so difficult to understand, becomes even more pronounced some lines further on:

> 1608   Las! tant en ai puis sospiré!
>   Cil miroers m'a deceü.
>   Se j'eüsse avant coneü
>   Queus sa force iert e sa vertuz,
> 1612   Ne m'i fusse ja embatuz,
>   Car maintenant ou laz chaï
>   Qui maint ome a pris e traï.

(Wretched me! how much I have sighed since then because of it! This mirror deceived me. If I had known before what force and power it had, I should never have driven myself to it, for now I have fallen into the net that has captured and betrayed many a man.)

But he did know the power of the fountain: he learned of it from the legend of Narcisus engraved there; and, because he knew it, he recoiled in horror.

It is as if Guillaume were telling the same story twice. Immediately after his exclamation of terror, the Dreamer again describes his joy in the beautiful things he sees in the mirror of the fountain, just as before. Why does the Dreamer experience everything twice? Why this double alternation between the mirror that reflects without distortion and the mirror that deceives?

The Dreamer himself tells us why, and he is quite explicit:

> 1603   Adès me plot a demorer
>   A la fontaine remirer,

E as cristaus, qui me montroient
Cent mile choses qui paroient;
Mais de fort eure m'i mirai.
1608   Las! tant en ai puis sospiré!

(Then it pleased me to remain gazing into the fountain and into the crystals, which were showing me the appearance of a hundred thousand things. But in a painful moment, *I saw myself there.*[10] Misery! how much I have sighed since then because of it!)

Just then he sees the Rose. He tries to reach it, but is repulsed by the sharp thorns. This is the moment that Amors has been waiting for. Having observed the Dreamer choose a rose more pleasing than any other, the God of Love stretches the cord of his bow to his ear and shoots the first arrow, *Biauté*, through the eye of the Dreamer and into his heart (1615–1695).

Here is an outline of the episode:

1425–1518:   The Dreamer's terror of the fountain of Narcisus.

1519–1569:   The beauty of the reflections in the fountain.

1570–1587:   The Dreamer's terror of the fountain of N.

1588–1606:   The work of Cupid in making the fountain of N. a beautiful fountain of Love; the hundred thousand beautiful reflections to be seen there.

1607–1614:   The Dreamer's terror of the fountain of N. The Dreamer sees his own reflection.

[10] Such is the simplest and most obvious translation of this line, and it is surprising how many translators blink it. Godefroy, *s. mirer,* offers three definitions for the reflexive. "Prendre soin de sa personne" is, of course, impossible in this context; "réfléchir, fixer sa pensée" would fit, but then the sequence of events would lack coherence. Guillaume uses the term *se mire,* obviously meaning "se regarder, se contempler" shortly before (line 1575). This is exactly the way Jean de Meun interprets this passage; see below. In any case, the point is that the Dreamer is saved because he knows the story of Narcisus.

1615–1695: The beautiful rose-bush and the most beautiful Rose. The Dreamer is pierced by the arrows of Love.

It is the medieval Narcisus whose memory hovers above the actions of the Dreamer. The terror of self-admiration gives way to delight in the beauty of other objects—which in turn gives way to the abiding desire to gaze upon oneself. This alternation continues until the Dreamer actually sees his own reflection and thus finds himself squarely in the footsteps of Narcisus, whose death in isolation and despair the Dreamer knows so well. It is the genesis of object-love that is represented in this episode; the story of Narcisus has shown the Dreamer how to save himself. He is able to turn his love upon another person, ideally beautiful, alive, and attainable.

Courtly love begins in the Fountain of Narcisus. Here the youth's pristine self-love is made conscious, and that consciousness grows until he is terrified by his passion for a barren image; and his survival depends upon whether he is to love a lifeless reflection of himself or a living one. Enlightened by the story of Narcisus, he does not cease to love himself. *Mais de fort eure m'i mirai*—he thought he was so safe, gazing upon the beautiful things reflected in the fountain, when suddenly he was surprised by his own countenance and by the remembered death of Narcisus. But even then he has already survived, for he sees himself in those two beautiful crystals: he beholds his image in the eyes of the lady.[11] He is now ready to be the servant of the God of Love.

In the experience that Guillaume represents there is a special courtly refinement. That Rose is not yet the rose in Gertrude Stein's complaint, but its glorious ancestor. Its color is luminous, the finest that Nature herself could produce; its

[11] On the two crystals as the eyes of the lady, see C. S. Lewis, *The Allegory of Love* (Oxford, 1936), pp. 128ff; and Erich Köhler, "Narcisse, la Fontaine d'Amour et Guillaume de Lorris," *Journal des Savants*, Avril–Juin 1963, 86–103, esp. 96ff.

four pairs of leaves are set by Nature one after another, with no single leaf missing; its stem is as straight as a rush, its bud symmetrical; its fragrance fills the air all around (1655–1670). We are in the presence of the Rose of all roses, the ideal, the perfect form toward which all others aspire.

Before the Dreamer, who naïvely thinks he can take the Rose without any trouble, now lies a long and painful education, in which his quality as a courtly man is to be tested and enhanced. What he longs to possess immediately is not a candid reflection of what he is, but an idealized image of what he is to become. It is his future identity that he loves, his image endowed with those courtly virtues perfected in the figure and retinue of the Rose. His struggle to reach the Rose is a struggle toward union with his own ideal, and that union is to be an identity.

Thus the Dreamer continues the experience that began with Narcisus, who first loved what seemed to be a beautiful nymph and then recognized the image of himself. The Dreamer begins with the sight of his own reflection, which leads to the vision of the Rose.[12]

The Mirror of the Ideal and the Mirror of Matter: Jean de Meun and the *Ovide Moralisé*

Our last two examples will not occupy us for nearly so long. Jean de Meun's explicitness regarding the meaning of the mirror deprives the figure of the suggestiveness it had in Guillaume. In the *Ovide Moralisé* the story of Narcisus although narrated with considerable verve, is clearly subservient to a preformulated moral injunction; it is, in other words, "used," and we are conscious all the while that the suffering of Narcisus is not nearly so important as the "les-

[12] Cf. the description by Alan M. F. Gunn of Guillaume's narrative technique in *The Mirror of Love* (Lubbock, Texas, 1952), p. 111.

son" we are to learn from it. It would subvert the author's intention to move us to sympathy for Narcisus. Nowhere is the moralist's hard-heartedness, his essential distrust of experience, more evident.

Genius, in his sermon, compares the mirror and fountain of Narcisus to the Mirror of God and the Fountain of Paradise. He enjoins his hearers to love one another loyally, that is, to do their part in perpetuating the human race, for which God will reward them when Atropos strikes; each man passes away, but the species is eternal (19885–19898). For God is the welfare of the body and soul, the beautiful mirror of Nature, who would not know anything if she did not have this *bel miroer* (19899–19906).

Genius forbids any comparison of the Garden of Paradise with the Garden of Deduit, unless one is consciously comparing the truth to a fable. He reviews the adventures of the Dreamer in the Garden of Deduit, where nothing is *estable* (20352), where everything is *corrumpable*, for Atropos will destroy everything there: it is altogether different from the eternal and fecund Garden of Paradise (20243–20288). Nor is the fountain of Paradise to be compared to

20409	. . . la fontaine perilleuse,
	Tant amere e tant venimeuse
	Qu'el tua le bel Narcisus
20412	Quant il se mirait iqui sus.
	Il meïsmes n'a pas vergoigne
	Dou requenoistre, ainz le tesmoigne;
	E sa cruauté pas ne cele
20416	Quant perilleus mirail l'apele,
	E dit que quant il s'i mira
	Maintes feiz puis en soupira,
	Tant s'i trouva grief e pesant.
20420	Vez quel douceur en l'eve sent!
	Deus! com bone fontaine e sade
	Ou li sain devienent malade!

E come il s'i fait bon virer
20424   Pour sei dedenz l'eve mirer!

(. . . the perilous fountain, so bitter and venomous that it killed
the fair Narcisus when he saw himself in it. The Dreamer was not
ashamed to avow it and thus he witnesses it; and he does not
conceal its cruelty when he calls it the perilous mirror. And he
says that when he saw himself, then he sighed many times because
of it, so grieved and oppressed was he. See what sweetness he feels
from the water! Lord, what a fine and agreeable fountain where
the healthy become sick! And what good it did him to turn to see
himself in the water!)

Everything in this fountain comes to it from without. And
the Dreamer's assertion that it is as clear as silver is a lie.
Rather, it is so troubled and murky that whoever puts his head
there to see himself actually sees nothing (20425–20436):

20437   Tuit s'i forsennent e s'angoissent,
        Pour ce que point ne s'i quenoissent.

(They all become mad and suffer, because they do not recognize
themselves there.)

Each of those two crystals reflects only half of what is in
the garden; for they are so obscure and murky that they must
get their light from elsewhere. If the sun's rays did not shine
upon them, they would show nothing (20439–20460).
But the Fountain of Paradise brings true restoration and
health. In it glows a carbuncle of three facets that illuminates
all the garden of Paradise; nothing dims its splendor, which
makes the sun look dim. This is the carbuncle of the Holy
Trinity; and in contrast to those two deceiving crystals,
whoever looks there sees everything at once and recognizes
himself immediately (20465–20478).

Thus one fountain makes the living drunk with death, the other brings the dead to life again (20625f).[13]

The Mirror of Nature, or the Mirror of God, is described by Nature herself in her confession. When God put beauty in Nature, he made a fountain there, from which all other beauty derives (16233ff). When God created the world, he took his model from his own thought; for God sees everything all at once, whether an event takes ten years to happen, or five hundred, or a hundred thousand (17451–17465). For no matter what kind of event it is,

17466   . . . de toujourz l'a il veüe
          Par demontrance veritable
          A son miroer pardurable,
          Que nus, fors lui, ne set polir,
          Senz riens a franc vouleir tolir.
          Cil miroers c'est il meïsmes,
17472   De cui comencement preïsmes.
          En cet bel miroer poli,
          Qu'il tient e tint toujourz o li,
          Ou tout veit quanqu'il avendra
17476   E toujourz present le tendra,
          Veit il ou les ames iront
          Que leiaument le serviront
          E de ceus ausinc qui n'ont cure
17480   De leiauté ne de dreiture;
          E leur promet en ses ydees
          Des euvres qu'eus avront ouvrees
          Sauvement ou damnacion.

(. . . from all time he saw it by its true appearance in his eternal mirror, which no one but God knows how to polish; but his seeing everything in his mirror in no way abolishes free will. This mirror is God himself, from whom we received our being. In this beautiful bright mirror, which he bears and has always borne with him, he sees when everything shall happen; and he has it

[13] *Cele les vis de mort enivre, / Mais cete fait les morz revivre.*

always present and sees where the souls shall go who loyally served him, as well as those that had no concern for loyalty and righteousness; and in his ideas of the work that they shall have done, he promises them salvation or damnation.)

Thus the Mirror of God contains the ideal form of every object that shall ever come into being, and by that ideal the moral worth of its actual condition shall be judged. Much further on (18033ff), Nature discourses at length on mirrors and optics. Mirrors have marvelous powers. Some mirrors show the exact dimensions of things; others burn the things before them; still others distort or invert things, or make four eyes appear in one head; others contain false visions (to 18238). In Jean's work the mirror of the ideal is twinned with the mirror that deceives.

In general, the *Ovide Moralisé* [14] follows Ovid's tale closely, the few changes arising from the moralizing severity of the author. Thus, as Frappier points out, the "compassionate *credule*" of the classical Ovid becomes the "*foulz mescheans*" of the moralized Ovid.[15]

According to the author, the story shows the danger of losing eternal joy in exchange for the delusive joys and fading beauty of this world.

> Qui bien veult ceste fable aprendre
> Par Narcisus puet l'en entendre
> 1905 Les folz musors de sens voidiez,
> Les orgueilleus, les sorcuidiez,
> Qui des biens temporeus abusent,
> Que se mirent et qui s'amusent,

[14] *Ovide Moralisé*, ed. C. de Boer, Verhandelingen der koninklijke Akademie van Wetenschappen te Amsterdam, Afdeeling Letterkunde, Nieuwe Reeks, XV, XXI, XXX, XLIII (Amsterdam, 1915–1936). All line numbers refer to the first volume (1915), Book III.

[15] Jean Frappier, "Variations sur le thème du miroir, de Bernard de Ventadour à Maurice Scève," *Cahiers de l'Association Internationale des Etudes Françaises*, XI (May 1959), 146.

Narcissus

	Aus faulz mireoirs de cest monde,
1910	Qui les plunge et qui les affonde
	En folie et en forsenage
	Si les enivre de bevrage
	Plain d'amertume, plain d'amer,
	Nulz ne devroit tel boivre amer,
1915	Quar qui plus en boit plus avvive
	La soif dolereuse et chetive,
	Qui ne puet estre rapaïe
	Trop doit tel fontaine haïe
	Estre, qui bevans met a dolour,
1920	A forsenage et a folour,
	A duel, a perte et a martire,
	Et, qui plus s'i amuse et mire,
	Plus li plaist et mains s'aperçoit,
	Dou mireoir qui le deçoit,
1925	C'est li mireoirs perillous
	Ou se mirent li orgueillous
	Qui les mondains delis convoitent,
	Que quant plus musent, mains exploitent.
	Et plus i fichent leur pensee,
1930	Si croist la soif qui plus assee
	Ceulz qui boivent a la fontaine
	Qui de faulse douceur est plaine:
	C'est la fontaine decevable,
	Qui fet l'ombre fainte et muable
1935	Cuidier vrai bien et parmanant,
	Et plus se croit riche et manant
	Qui plus s'i mire et puet veoir
	En ce falible mireoir
1939	La faulse ombre ou il se delite. . . .

(Whoever wishes to understand this story, let him understand by Narcisus those who delight madly, senselessly, the haughty, the presumptuous, who misuse temporal goods, who see themselves and take delight in the false mirrors of this world, which plunges them into madness and folly, intoxicates them with a drink full of bitterness and gall. No one should like such a drink, for the more he drinks the more intense becomes that dolorous and wretched thirst which cannot be quenched. Rather such a fountain ought to be hated, for it brings the man who drinks from it to grief and madness and folly and anguish and ruin and destruction; and the more one takes delight and gazes at himself in it, the more he is pleased but the less he is aware of the mirror that deceives him. It is the perilous mirror, in which the proud look upon themselves, who covet earthly delights, and the more they gaze, the less they acquire. And the more they fix their thought on that mirror the more their thirst increases, which all the more destroys those who drink of the fountain full of false sweetness: it is the deceiving fountain, which makes the faint and mutable image seem real and permanent. And he thinks himself rich and powerful all the more as he gazes upon himself and is able to see in this deceiving mirror the false image in which he delights. . . .)

One regrets, with Frappier, that the one element in the story most apt for further development is missing here, "that movement of consciousness in which the recognition of the illusion doubles the despair of Narcissus" (p. 148). Yet even in this insistent moralizing the sadness of the story is there, the despair of the man who longs to know himself in a lifeless image, a "false mirror."

Both Jean de Meun and the *Ovide Moralisé* interpret the story of Narcisus in ways already familiar to us. The mirror of the ideal, which informs human experience and measures its moral value, is somehow inseparable from the mirror of matter, which reflects the formlessness and impermanence of earthly life, and thus makes a mockery of the ideal. Whatever the obvious differences between the two works, the similarity of their response to the antithetical meanings of the mirror is more significant.

Both authors, denying that the welter of experience is in itself intelligible, look above it for a source of meaning, and find that meaning in its resemblance to an eternal, pre-human ideal. For both, only so long as life is contemplated as an image can it have form and integrity. If it is conceived as a reflection of the forms in the Mirror of God, it enjoys a moral certainty otherwise impossible, for regarded in itself it is a false mirror whose beautiful images are dangerous because they seem to be real; but nothing is real about them except their destructive effect on the seduced beholder.

In turning to the Mirror of God, both authors show that they are children of their age. The *Ovide Moralisé* contrasts the instability of secular life with the immutable truths in that Mirror; Jean de Meun perceives in it a divine sanction of man's instinctual life (God gave us our sexuality in accordance with His plan for the perpetuation of the species). Both responses are characteristically medieval.

Nevertheless, in the lyrics we shall study in the following chapters, the Mirror of God has little or no place. Those lyrics were composed for an intimate courtly audience, and they were intended to reflect both the unique behavior and the inner life of the courtier in such a way that each member of the audience could recognize his own image there, much idealized. In that image he and his class were to find their moral and aesthetic purpose, their reason for being: they were created to serve as a model for the rest of society to imitate. The Mirror of God could justify the existence of the noble class both philosophically and politically: earthly society, like the sun and the orbiting planets above, was a reflection of the heavenly community of which the center was God attended by angels of varying degree. But no amount of talk about such correspondences could answer questions concerning the immediate problems of courtly life. In the Mirror of God the courtier could never find certainty about his personal worth: how could he be sure that he deserved the wealth and privilege that his high birth brought him? If his class was intended to serve as a paragon of all earthly endeavor, how could he know whether, in his deepest inclinations and personal acts, he was truly a member of that class? What he required was not only an adequate secular ideal, but an infallible secular judgment, someone to justify his identity as a courtier. No ideal image could give him this certainty, but the idealized lady could, if she wished.

It is worth dwelling a moment longer on this matter of the knight's uncertainty regarding his station and inner value. For example, what was the difference between the strength of an ordinary man and the prowess of a courtier—it had to be a moral difference, but what was it? Or what was the difference between the common gift of speech and the *bels digz*, the edifying, orderly, and graceful conversation of which only a certain class was capable? How was simple violence to be distinguished from chivalric adventure? How was one to distinguish between the man who was merely interested in the perfection of his nature, and the man who was consecrated to it?

To answer these questions in the formulation of a code was only to exchange one uncertainty for another. If, for example, the difference between mere politeness and true courtly deportment could be defined in a number of specific and unambiguous rules—then how was one to know whether he was really following those rules? And even if he was certain about himself, how could he be sure that others were equally certain about him? For to the knight public recognition was a part of his identity: we cannot think of an Arthur who was not loved, a Lancelot who was not famous, a Parzival who was not universally acclaimed. How could the knight be certain that his noble worth was recognized by everyone else?

These questions apply specifically to the conditions of courtly society in the early Middle Ages, but at their root are two other questions that are universal and timeless. How does a man know whether he is what he thinks he is? How does he know whether he is becoming what he wants to be?

The knight desired salvation—a secular salvation in the here and now, quite distinct from the promise of his religion, although in both the reward is the same: the full knowledge and perfection of one's nature.

To reach that mortal bliss the knight would have to answer these questions with certainty. Like Narcisus, he was tortured by the indefiniteness and unattainability of an idealized self-image; but he saved himself by embodying that image in the figure of a virtuous and universally esteemed lady who could give him the assurance he sought. In the courtly lyrics that we are now to examine, we shall see how the knight attains the certainty of moral refinement in a way that is most clearly understood through the experience of Narcisus and its essential crisis.

CHAPTER TWO

The Mirror in the
Provençal Lyric

THE interpretations in this and the succeeding chapters will take little account of the historical conditions in which the lyrics were composed.[1] Much will be said about the audience, for example, and its importance to the poet and the lady. The lady and the audience are to be construed not as actual persons with dates, but as presences in the lyric, implied and to a great extent invented by the poet, who should be similarly regarded: the historic poet invents the "I" who speaks.

These lyrics are unusual because they create their own setting, a "world" of their own, like Hamlet's "Denmark." Within that imaginary world some things (such as the lady

[1] Such an account is set forth in Alfred Jeanroy, *La poésie lyrique des troubadours*, 2 vols. (Paris and Toulouse, 1934). For a quick glimpse, see the Introduction to Moshé Lazar, *Amour courtois et "Fin' Amors" dans la littérature du XII* siècle, Bibliothèque Française et Romane, Series C, VIII (Paris, 1964). Lazar's study offers a reasonable and thorough account of the main themes in the Provençal courtly love lyric and a critical review of the pertinent scholarship. Also helpful are some of the writings of Father A. J. Denomy, e.g., "An Inquiry into the Origins of Courtly Love," *Medieval Studies* (Toronto), VI (1944); and "Courtly Love and Courtliness," *Speculum*, XXVIII (1953), 44–63. For an interesting interpretation of the meaning of courtly love and its special development in Italy, see Maurice Valency, *In Praise of Love* (New York, 1958).

and the audience) are represented as real; others (such as the poet's image of the lady and his dream of winning her), as illusory. The poet's longing, the lady's remoteness, the audience's concern, may never have existed outside the setting of the lyric; but within that setting they are crucial realities. In my interpretations I confine myself to the lyric's own representation of reality and illusion.

Nearly every observation in this chapter could be made repeatedly concerning the Middle High German lyric. But in order to avoid distracting alternations between one language and another, specific Middle High German lyrics in which similar motifs are present will be cited in the footnotes.

The mirror, in these lyrics, takes on many meanings, although their common source is in the experience of Narcissus: the mirror enables a man to see himself in another. But a new necessity requires the use of the mirror. The courtly man and the class to which he claims adherence are defined by an ideal that is often difficult to delineate and always impossible to fulfill. In the mirror, however, that ineffable courtly ideal is made visible down to the last detail, and is united with the knight's own image reflected there. His quality as a courtly man is thus confirmed.

The following lyric will probably strike most readers as a rather pedestrian performance, competent but not inspiring. One readily notes that it consists entirely of clichés (standard comparisons like that of the lady to the sun; prefabricated verbal units like *beutatz e jovens*; commonplace themes like the institution of the lady as the all-powerful *Dompna e Senhor*); and, as a consequence, that its vocabulary is often diffuse and turgid (is there any real difference in meaning, in this context, between *repaus* and *sojorns* and *refrandres*, or between *joi* and *doussor*, or between *pretz* and *valor?*).

Yet precisely because it is so commonplace, it can serve us

well in introducing some general observations about the Provençal lyric. And so we shall examine its contents carefully.

Guiraut de Calanso, "Los Grieus Dezirs" [2]

Los grieus dezirs que·m solon far doler
Ai oblidatz, domna ric' e valens,
Qu'enaissi m'es camjatz lo cors e·l sens
Que res no vuelh mas sol vostre voler,
5 E·ls mals d'amor que·m solon far languir   I
Pres de la mort, quant ieu amav' alhor
Mi fatz [3] semblar ab joi plazen doussor,
Si quo·l solelhs fai la neu devenir
Aiga doussa, tant es dous sos resplandres.

10 Tot atresi com re no pot valer
Fuecs ni clartatz ni estela luzens
Contra·l solelh, m'es autres jois niens
Contra·l vostre, qu'el mon non puesc vezer   II
Neguna res, lai on pus m'o cossir,
15 Que de beutat, de pretz ni de valor
Ni de bos faitz, que·s tanhan a ricor,
Que sol apres de vos puesca venir
De la gran mar tro lai on cor Menandres.

"Belhs Diamans" devetz be nom aver,
20 Qu'aissi cum es bels dias resplandens
Clartatz del mon, dompn', etz vos onramens
D'autras dompnas, don deu om retener

[2] A. Pillet and H. Carstens, *Bibliographie der Troubadours* (Halle, 1933), 234, poem 13. Text: *Die Lieder des provenzalischen Trobadors Guiraut von Calanso*, ed. Willy Ernst, *Romanische Forschungen*, XLIV (Erlangen, 1930), 305–307. The medieval specialist will find nothing new in this section.

[3] On *fatz* instead of Ernst's reading *fai*, see the review by Kurt Lewent of Ernst's edition in *Zeitschrift für franz. Sprache und Literatur*, LVII (1933), 413f. I am grateful to the late Professor Lewent for pointing out his review in private correspondence, where he has also been most helpful in clearing up other difficulties concerning this lyric.

Vostres rics faitz de vezer e d'auzir;   III
Et atressi cum en un mirador
25   Vezon li uelh manta belha color,
Pot om en vos tot autre ben chausir,
Per que·m plai mout lo lauzars e l'espandres.

E vos, dompna, avetz tant de saber
E valetz tant que ben etz conoissens
30   Que lai on plus val beutatz e jovens,
Don valon mais li do e li plazer;
E tug li pros, que·s volon far grazir,   IV
Fan lurs belhs dos lai on pus an sabor;
E breus respos es loncs jois en amor,
35   Per que dompna non deu son joi fenir,
Cum fes Elis, la comtessa de Flandres.

Mas vos avetz en mi tan de poder
Que mil tans pus me seria plazens
Mort a sufrir que fos de ren jauzens
40   Qu'a vos fos grieus, si sabia per ver   V
Que tot lo mon agues al mieu servir;
Qu'ab vostres digz belhs e de gran onor
Avetz mon cor mes en tan gran ricor
Que bos pessars m'es, on pus vos dezir,
45   Jois e repaus e sojorns e refrandres.[4]

Tezaur e gaug e dompna e senhor
Fas tot de vos e lais los mals d'alhor,   T
Qu'anc non ac pus de son bel conquerir
49   Jois ni plazers Sesars ni Alissandres.

(I have forgotten the grievous desires that used to make me suffer, noble and worthy lady, for my heart and mind have so changed that I want nothing but your will alone; you cause the pains of love, which earlier made me languish near death when I loved another, to appear to me (now) as sweetness and pleasing joy, just as the sun makes the snow become mild water, so sweet is its resplendence.

[4] *Refrandres* ("solace") is Lewent's suggestion (p. 416), which I have accepted in place of Ernst's reading of *remandres*.

Just as fire or light or a bright star are as nothing compared to the sun, so is any other joy nothing to me compared to the joy I have of you; for in all the world, when I contemplate it ever so much, I cannot see anything which, in beauty or worth or merit or good deeds that befit nobility, could even come close to you; nothing in the world, from the great sea to where the Meander flows.[5]

You should well be named "Beautiful Diamond," for just as a beautiful resplendent day is the light of the world, so, Lady, are you the honor of other ladies; wherefore one ought to remember your deeds, which are noble to see and hear about.[6] And just as in a mirror the eyes see many a beautiful color, so can one discern in you every other good; wherefore it pleases me much to praise you and spread your fame.

And you, Lady, have so much knowledge and are so worthy that you well know that where beauty and youth are worth most, there gifts and pleasures are most valuable; and all the valiant, who wish to make themselves favored, make their beautiful gifts where they have most savor; and a brief answer is a long joy in love, wherefore a lady ought not to end the joy she gives, as did Elis, the Countess of Flanders.

But you have so much power over me it would be a thousand times more pleasant to suffer death than be pleased by a thing that would be grievous to you, even if I knew for certain that I should have the whole world in my service; for with your fair words and great honor you have placed my heart in such great nobility, that

---

[5] Ernst (p. 347) explains that *lai on cor Menandres* serves to designate the East generally, so that the sense of the line is: "no one in the whole world."

[6] On the translation of this passage, which Ernst (p. 347) misconstrues, see Lewent, p. 415. In a letter to the author dated January 7, 1963, Professor Lewent confirmed his construction of the passage: ". . . *vostres faitz rics de vezer e d'auzir* is to be rendered by 'your deeds noble to see and to hear (of).' This means: whether you are a witness of her deeds or only know them from hearsay, everyone should keep them in mind. This exhortation of the poet makes the lady really a paragon indeed, and this idea easily leads over to the picture of the mirror."

it is a pleasant thought to me the more I desire you; it is joy and repose and pleasure and solace.

Treasure and Joy and Lady and Lord—I make of you all these; and I leave the pains of elsewhere, for never did Caesar or Alexander have more joy or pleasure from their fine conquests.)

In the first strophe the poet explains the loss of his own will in his complete submission to the will of the lady. When his own will was still active, when he "loved elsewhere," the pain of love brought him close to death. His whole disposition is now "changed": he no longer has desires of his own, but desires only what the lady desires, and as a consequence he is restored to health. The snow melts and becomes "sweet water," which, beneath the great illumination of the sun, causes a regeneration that is now no longer merely personal—such is the implication if the simile is taken seriously—but worldwide.

This theme of the universality of the lady's goodness occupies the second strophe. It is developed by the same image that introduced it. Just as the sun is brighter and warmer than everything else in all creation (than fire, light, and star), so no one else can come near the lady in beauty and moral virtue and fair deportment—no one else in the whole world.

Now these two strophes have progressed from the personal *lo cors e·l sens* to *lai on cor Menandres*. The qualities he admires in her are visible to everyone else, and anyone who sees them must love them. She is like the sun because she is a brilliant figure universally esteemed, the subject of world-wide praise, the source of virtue and illumination.

The poet's love is thus in the nature of an observance, and his praise is based not on any preferences peculiar to him but on an implied doctrine. The song's very conventionality becomes the source of its strength; it says that *beutatz, pretz, valor* are not personal traits that happen to please a certain man, but objective qualities that define a class. In the lady, the poet admires not mere gestures, but "fair deeds that befit nobility." The very presence of his desire unites him with all who are noble. He is no longer the victim of the "heavy" desires that had earlier nearly done him to death, of the avaricious desire to possess, for what he loves now is no simple woman conceived as an object, but a celebrated emblem that draws the love of everyone. In her universal recognition he sees his hope. In her he finds values that are unchanging and enduring, having existed long before he found them, even long before the lady herself, in whom they are now embodied to perfection.

Thus the first two strophes are a little mirror of the courtly life. Here are the crucial themes celebrated in every courtly song: the supreme beauty of the lady as a visible expression of ethical ideals; the universal esteem she enjoys as a consequence; the implicit vindication of the poet's complete submission to her will. She is the image of every courtly virtue. She *is* what he wants to become—what he can never be, but what he can recognize and aspire to. For, like the sun, the ideal is unattainable.

So, in the following strophe, she is compared to a resplendent day, the universal, beneficent light of the world. He wants to call her "Beautiful Diamond," an object that also "befits nobility" as an emblem of the wealth, purity, and refinement of the whole class, and of its function as an aesthetic paragon. As a beautiful day is the light of the world, she is the source of the honor of all noble ladies. But her deeds ought to be noted by *everyone*, by all the men and women of the society to which she and the poet belong, before whom this song is performed.

The great value of her "noble deeds" lies in their capacity for being seen, and they alone comprise her meaning. Every other kind of secret or personal life is denied to her. Her existence as a figure in the lyric consists entirely in her immediate visibility and the unanimous acceptance of her as the realization of the highest good. As an emblem of the courtly class, she is characterized by the impersonality and repose that attend perfection; for any individualizing quality would diminish her stature. This necessary repose becomes, in other lyrics, the cause of great discomfort for the poet; it keeps him from ever knowing where he stands, and cloaks the figure of the Lady in an enigma he cannot resolve: he brings her every kind of offering, which she receives with the grandeur and insensibility of a public monument. Is it really repose that he sees in her, or is it indifference? Is she perfect, or is she merely insensate? This monumental immobility of the Lady is no accident: she cannot be the light of the world and at the same time yield to personal preferences, any more than the sun itself. These painful consequences of the lady's esteem are all but omitted from the present lyric (they are suggested in lines 34ff). But her motionless and emotionless character is implied in every image: she is a beautiful diamond, a mirror.

The mirror-comparison that follows (24ff) defines the lady's "meaning" completely. The eyes see many beautiful things in a mirror, but they are physical things, tangible things able to be reflected in a material mirror (for color is an attribute of physical objects). But in the lady one sees *tot autre ben*, an altogether different kind of virtue, spiritual qualities like *onramenz, pretz, ricor*.[7] The poet continues to compare physical beauty, instantly visible to the eyes, with an ideal that is invisible in itself but that is now embodied in the lady. As the day bestows light, she bestows honor; as a mirror

---

[7] Both Raynouard, *Lexique roman* (II, 440) and Levy, *Provenzalisches Supplement-Wörterbuch* (I, 283f) give examples of the word *color* meaning "kind, quality, manner." N.b. Levy's remarks concerning the example from Gaucelm Faidit. See also *Les Chansons de Guillaume IX*, ed. A. Jeanroy (Paris, 1927), no. VI, p. 13:

> Ben vuelh que sapchon li plusor
> D'est vers si's de bona color,
> Qu'ieu ai trag de mon abrador.

Here *color* is associated with an object brought forth from a craftsman's workshop and means "quality, character." Ernst, p. 348, misconstrues this passage.

reflects the beauty of physical things, she reflects moral perfection. She reflects honor upon us, and thus enables us to recognize the honor that is perfect in her. By her gifts we are led back to her. She is a mirror, and the light by which we see whatever is reflected in that mirror.

The lady is more beautiful than every other creature in the world that she illuminates. The lady is a mirror in which everything else is seen; that is, the poet looks not at the objects themselves but at their images. For to see the objects directly one must scan discursively the whole created universe, all up and down the chain of being and across the boundaries of space, "from the great sea to where the Meander flows." But in a mirror all existence is proportionately reduced, so that a vast extent, and all the objects in it, are rendered in one image which the eye perceives at once. Only by means of a mirror can we talk of "the whole world," of "all ladies," and of "every good"; for otherwise we are confronted with a vastness that we cannot visualize and to which we cannot respond. The world is too enormous, its meanings are too manifold. The mortal eye cannot see the height and breadth of it at once directly, but only as they are concentrated in an image in a mirror, where we see what is unavailable to the eye alone. And in the mirror we see these things not discursively and in apparent confusion, but all at once, in proportion and order.[8] The mirror, then, brings the praise of the lady as the light and virtue of the whole world within the possibilities of experience.

Thus the mirror is an instrument of knowledge. It represents our capacity to imagine the world and to inform the experience that otherwise would engulf us.

Now the mirror not only reflects, but also enhances. Seen directly, each object is essentially flawed, for it is composed of matter. But its image is emancipated from this welter, and

---

[8] This was the common view of classical, medieval, and Renaissance artists and theorists on art. See G. F. Hartlaub, *Zauber des Spiegels* (München, 1951), pp. 13–15, 87–101.

what we see in the mirror is not so much an exact likeness of the object as its perfected form, its ideal. Nothing, in its actual existence, is so beautiful as its reflected image, so defined in shape, so pure in color (*ibid.*). In transmuting the object from substance to image, the mirror purifies it, fixes it, above all the transformations of flesh and matter.

Therefore, the mirror immediately calls for a judgment. It demands a comparison between a reflection and the thing reflected, between an object as it is in itself and the perfected form it strives to attain. When the known and living lady becomes that mirror of the world, experience is resolved from a wild torrent of impressions into a stable and orderly pattern. She becomes the standard by which all things are judged, the ideal light by which they are known. Every beautiful object is to be referred to her beauty, every gracious act to her grace; every moral uncertainty is illuminated by her smile, every courtly man is made visible by her look. She informs what she reflects.

We look to her to know what we ought to be, and therefore what we are. It is for *us* that she exists. She is there to be consulted, like a mirror, by every courtly person. She reflects our future condition, the goal of our striving. She makes visible for us what would otherwise be mere concepts dissociated from experience: *ricor, pretz, valor, cortesia, digz belhs, grans onors*—we know what these things are because we know *her*.[9]

She is, therefore, the arbiter of virtue. That is why all

[9] We find the same mirror in Guiraut's lament for the death of the Infant Ferdinand (see Ernst, p. 386), *Belh senher Dieus, quo pot esser sufritz* (Pillet and Carstens 243, poem 6; no. 11 in Ernst's edition, p. 331f). Note especially the fifth strophe, where Ferdinand is called "mirror of the world, in which courtliness (*pretz*) is instructed." The idea is taken up again in the tornada: Ferdinand was the *chastiaire* for the courtly class (*als valens e als pros*). Cf. Guiraut's *Una doussa res benestan* (Pillet and Carstens, 243, poem 11; Ernst, no. 3, pp. 309–311), where the same idea is implied, although in a rigid and platitudinous formula.

courtly men try to make themselves pleasing to her with gifts (not necessarily to the lady whom Guiraut addresses, but the Lady who guides the life of each man). It is for the same reason that the poet declares he would rather suffer death than rejoice in anything that would be offensive to her: because the reward of her favor marks a real and publicly recognizable moral progress; it is the favor of the ideal conferred upon the endeavors of the aspirant. By the same token, her disfavor is a moral condemnation, denying in the rejected suitor the quality of a courtly man.

Thus the lady holds in her hands the earthly salvation of every courtly man. Her power is, in every sense, awful. But her value is indispensable: she alone "places one's heart in nobility." The very fact of the man's desire is a public declaration of his worth; and he sings of his desire to the whole society. It is her presence which gives the mark of order to all experience, and dignity to the song itself. The singing of her praise and the celebration of her fame are an observance before her, an obligation to the society, and a public sign of the singer's personal worth: *per que·m plai mout lo lauzars e l'espandres.*

All of the declarations in the first strophe are now vindicated. The poet has ceased to follow the aimless attractions of his own will, which have heretofore nearly disintegrated him, and has achieved such a condition that his will reposes in its proper object, a figure celebrated everywhere as the fulfillment of the courtly ideal. The tone of the lyric befits its point of view: the entire utterance is a direct and (as we must always remember) a public address to the lady. There is absolutely no reserve in its praise, not a single breath of doubt as to the adequacy of the real lady to the ideal of her public image. Every suspicion of a flaw is carefully ruled out, even, as we have seen, to the point of denying the materiality of the mirror.

The praise is offered as the fruit of intense experience—*lai on pus m'o cossir*—as though in the full awareness of other choices and possibilities: and we have, of course, the poet's own testimony as to the near-fatal consequences of his earlier love affair. But what is offered as experience is simply rhetoric, and here there is no reality beyond the words themselves. It is not only that all the objects which the lady surpasses have neither existence nor integrity as objects, but also that the lady herself has no reality except as a mirror. Like the mirror, like every other object mentioned in the song—the lady he once loved, the other ladies in the world, the fire, the light, the star, even Elis, the Countess of Flanders—she is without vital qualities. What is the real lady like in comparison with the figure he adores? What is her true countenance, in comparison with the mirror that everyone consults? What is her behavior, in comparison with the "noble deeds" that everyone preserves in his memory? These are the questions posed by real experience, which, as La Vieille [10] and her descendants will eagerly tell us, challenges the relevance of the ideal. Can a human creature bestow salvation? Can flesh and blood be unfaltering? Such questions have no place in the public fantasy which this lyric really is.

Who, we may ask, is Guiraut de Calanso? We do not refer to his biography (of which we know but a very few details),[11] but to the *persona*, the *ieu*, who sings and to whom love once brought pain but now brings contentment and rest. The personality of the Singer is as idealized and as unflawed by individual qualities as that of the Lady. He identifies himself as representative of the courtly men (*tug li pros*) who everywhere bring offerings to the ladies of their lives—perhaps to this very lady—in the hope of moral rewards. The song is *his* offering, and it is conscientiously optimistic. The lady is per-

---

[10] A knowing old crone in Jean de Meun's continuation of *The Romance of the Rose* (first introduced toward the end of Guillaume's portion). Many of her traits are reflected in Chaucer's Wife of Bath.

[11] See Ernst, pp. 269–289, and Lewent's criticism of these pages, pp. 410ff; the only real certainty is that one of Guiraut's lyrics was composed before 1202.

fect, his reformation is complete; the courtly-love relation is the source of supreme joy, and every achievement that lacks the sanction of love seems pathetic—neither Caesar nor Alexander had such joy from his world-wide conquests.

The song is, as a matter of fact, the performance of a wandering professional who served the courtly class in many places in southern Europe;[12] and its very conventionality of diction and sentiment finally becomes a part of its meaning. It is intended to be an idealizing mirror of the courtly life, of the humble aspirant, the concerned ideal, the moral reward; and thus everything works out perfectly. It is a kind of official art, justifying a ruling class by the depiction of its ideal. In another generation it would have been done in plaster of paris, with buxom allegorical figures and explanatory scrolls.[13]

[12] See Ernst, pp. 286ff.

[13] On the mirror as judge and guide, cf. Aimeric de Peguilhan's lament for the death of Malaspina, *Era par ben que Valors se desfai*, Pillet and Carstens, 10, poem 10; text in William P. Shepard and Frank M. Chambers, *The Poems of Aimeric de Peguilhan* (Evanston, Ill., 1950), pp. 81–84. Malaspina is a mirror which the courtly man consults in order to see himself in comparison with the ideal, and in whatever particular he is lacking, *er castiatz* (he will be reproved). Cf. the mirror of Loyalty in Guiraut de Bornelh's *Jois e chans*, Pillet and Carstens, 242, poem 40; text: *Sämtliche Lieder des Trobadors Guiraut de Bornelh*, ed. Adolf Kolsen, 2 vols. (Halle a.S., 1910), I, 290–299 (no. 47).

Compare "the mirror of shame" in the Middle High German lyrics. For example, Liutolt von Savene, "Mich wundert wie den liuten sî" (*Deutsche Liederdichter des 13. Jahrhunderts*, ed. Carl von Kraus, p. 249, no. 8): shame is a mirror of virtue. Burkart von Hohenvels, "Diu süeze klâre wunder" (*ibid.*, pp. 36f, no. 5), strophe 3: shame holds up a mirror to the lady, so that she loves purity.

Similar is the *êren spiegel*, the mirror of honor. For example, *ibid.*, p. 262 (Namenlos D230–238): the lady sees in the mirror of honor how she may escape false *Minne*. The mirror of chastity performs a similar function (*ibid.*, Namenlos III 5n, 1 and 2, p. 281). The most famous panegyric mirror is in Reimar's lament for Leopold (*Des Minnesangs Frühling*, ed. Carl von Kraus et al., [Zürich, 1950] 167, 31–168, 29).

Also to be noted is Peire d'Auvergne's "Gent es, mentr'om n'a

The Double Consciousness of the Courtly Lover

The instant the courtly man sets himself the task of fulfilling the ideal reflected in the mirror, he must make of his life one endless labor, without rest and ultimately without rewards. For it is a hopeless task, and every achievement is an injunction to go further. Moreover, the exaltation of the lady is really a denial of her humanity. The whole system of courtly love is one grand fiction in which all experience becomes a moral enterprise. Now, that fiction is a falsification of experience, and of the true motives and needs of love. All this we shall see more clearly later.

To escape from the mirror's impossible moral strictures, the courtly man may seek to reduce the power of the mirror. He may gain control of its image and manipulate it until its ideal nature is obliterated. Then, instead of experience, he seeks refuge in fantasies.

Such fantasies one can find in the poetry of Arnaut de Mareuil. Again and again he shows us that he is in the earliest stages of the courtly-love relation. He bases his supplication to the lady not on a long career of service but on the promise of

---

lezer," Pillet and Carstens, 323, poem 18; text in Rudolf Zenker, *Die Lieder Peires von Auvergne* (Erlangen, 1900), pp. 121–124, no. 15: God permits him to see, as in a mirror, what is for his good, and to avoid what would harm him. Similarly, Guillaume de Saint Didier's crusade song, "El temps quan vey cazer fuelhas e flors," Pillet and Carstens 234, poem 10; text in F. J. M. Raynouard, *Choix des poésies originales des troubadours*, 6 vols. (Paris, 1816–1861), IV, 133. Jerusalem is "the mirror that was given to all in common" (9f); as *miradors* means both "mirror" and "watch-tower," many of the implications of the metaphor are concentrated here. Later, the poet hopes for the deliverance of "the precious mirror which is the light of salvation" (32), and praises Alfons X of Castile, who is honored by the mirror and whose peace is embellished by it (39ff); that is, the peace that the king has preserved in his own land is a reflection of the perfect peace that one sees in the mirror of the ideal. Cf. Friedrich Diez, *Leben und Werke der Troubadours*, 2d ed. (Leipzig, 1882), p. 268.

82

future worth, and all his joys are joys of anticipation. Experience may yet occur, but apart from the growth of his passion there has so far been no trial, no confrontation, no opportunity for reward or refusal.[14] This separation from the experience that awaits him is paralleled by his physical separation from the lady. She is far away, unavailable; the poet is explicit about this. His real object in speaking of his love, even in addressing her directly, is not to persuade the lady to requite him but to make visible to the audience the presence of his desire, and thus to demonstrate his courtliness.[15] When he begs for her favor, his words are not intended for her ears: he speaks *on qu'ieu m'estey* ("wherever I may be"), and he bows imploringly when he is alone to *lai on vos es* (" there, where you are"). *Sai pensan*, the poet says—he goes about thinking of her *here*.[16] Thus the poet is in every way explicit concerning his total separation from the lady; he still has the joy of hope, but it is joy dissociated from experience. It is, along with his love, "locked in his heart," as he says, entirely independent of any correlative event.

In such a state the poet turns to the consolation of the dream and the fantasy—an imaginary *mise-en-scène*, not yet an event but still enjoyed, less present than the real but more present than the merely possible. The fantasy replaces the thought of action.

> 25 Ves lo païs, pros dompna issernida,
> repaus mos huoills on vostre cors estai

[14] See, for example, "Us jois d'amor s'es e mon cor enclaus," Pillet and Carstens 30, poem 26. Text: in *Les poésies lyriques du troubadour Arnaut de Mareuil*, ed. R. C. Johnston (Paris, 1935), no. iv, pp. 22–24. We know little of Arnaut. He flourished in the last quarter of the twelfth century, and spent most of his poetic life in the court of Roger II of Béziers and Carcassonne.

[15] *Ibid.* Cf. lyrics 30, 16; 30, 5; 30, 15; and Johnston's introduction, pp. xxvi–xxx.

[16] "Us jois d'amor."

e car plus pres de vos no·m puosc aizir,
tenc vos el cor ades e cossir sai   IV
vostre gen cors cortes, qui·m fai languir,
30   e·l gen parlar e·l deport e·l solatz,
lo pretz e·l sen e la beutat de vos,
don pois vos vi non fui anc oblidos.

Dompna, cui pretz e jois e jovens guida,
ja no m'ametz, totz temps vos amarai,
35   c'Amors o vol, ves cui no·m puosc gandir,
e car conois qu'ie·us ai fin cor verai,   V
mostra·m de vos de tal guisa jausir,
penssan vos bais e·us manei e·us embratz:
aquest dompneis m'es doutz e cars e bos,
40   e no·l mi pot vedar negus gelos.
                                    [Johnston, No. VII]

IV. I cause my eyes to dwell upon that land where you are, most noble and distinguished lady; and because I cannot approach closer to you, I hold you in my heart always, and I think here of your gentle and courtly figure, which makes me languish, and your gentle speech and deportment and society, of your worth and intelligence and beauty, which I have never forgotten since I saw you.

v. Lady whom worth and joy and youth guide, although you do not love me, I shall always love you, for Love wishes it, whom I cannot escape. And because he knows that I bear my heart truly and courteously toward you, he shows me a way in which I may have pleasure of you; and in my thoughts I kiss you and fondle you and embrace you: to me this kind of courting is sweet and dear and good, and no jealous one can forbid it to me.)

What is remarkable is the transformation of the image in these two strophes. Under the stress of separation the poet looks upon the internalized image, that is, the image of real deeds and attributes actually observed and called forth from the memory. But the fifth strophe is something else. It is not a memory but a fantasy, the enjoyment of an event that has not taken place and perhaps never will. Here, in contrast to the earlier strophe where the acts of the image reproduce the real acts of the lady, that unattainable lady is replaced by her manipulated image.[17] The poet seizes the only joy possible in his condition of separation and inexperience, and in the conditions of the court. "No *gelos* can forbid it to me": it is a surrogate experience free of all the risks and limitations of real experience, which is for him impossible now.

This manipulation of the image becomes a recurrent feature of Arnaut's work.[18] He finds great pleasure in the dream, the true theater of the animated image. When he sleeps, it seems to him that he is with the lady, who is really far away; when he wakes, he thinks he dies of desire; therefore he would like to sleep for a year, provided the imagined pleasure (*plazenz pensatz*) would last.[19]

The same theme is more elaborate in Arnaut's non-lyric poetry. In his love-epistle *Domna, genser que no sai dir*[20] he explains that he is sending this letter in order to say all the things he cannot say when love twists his tongue in the lady's presence. Her image in his heart is a courtly messenger from the lady; Arnaut gives us a beautiful description of the internalized image, her gentle figure, her golden hair, her straight

---

[17] Cf. Valency, *In Praise of Love*, Chapter VI ("True Love"), *passim*, e.g., p. 166: "In the case of the poet, the psychic tension is discharged in the poem. The poem itself is an act of creation, an act of love, beyond which the lover, as poet, has neither any great desire nor any need to go. For the poet, then, the ultimate object of love is not so much the lady as the fantasy of the lady—and this fantasy the song sufficiently embodies."

[18] See Johnston's introduction, pp. xxiiiff.

[19] "Aissi cum cel c'am' e non es amaz," Pillet and Carstens, 30, poem 3; Johnston no. 9. Cf. the following two lyrics in Johnston, "Aissi cum cel que anc non ac cossire," Pillet and Carstens 30, poem 4; "Ses joi non es valors," Pillet and Carstens, 30, poem 21.

[20] Karl Bartsch, *Chrestomathie provençale*, 6th ed. (Marburg, 1904), 105, 10–13.

nose, her little mouth, her breast as white as the hawthorn, her slender hands; "your delightful and refined pleasantries, your gentle society, your courtly response, the fair appearance you first showed me, when it happened that we both saw each other."

Then Arnaut animates this image of a figure actually observed. At night, when all his companions are asleep and he tosses and turns with a lover's insomnia, he imagines himself kissing her eyes and mouth. Finally falling asleep in the midst of his sighs, he sees his spirit with the lady. "Thus all as I desire my spirit courts you according to its will, night and day, and embraces you and kisses you and fondles you." [21]

In the very act of singling out this theme from Arnaut's work we have exaggerated its importance, for no matter how many times Arnaut turns to the image for solace, he still experiences, and longs to re-experience, many a real encounter with the lady. His work is, in this regard, finely balanced, its tone genuinely exalted. His restraint will be even more apparent when we examine the lyrics of Ulrich von Lichtenstein, where we shall find what amounts to an aberration.

But whether held in balance or not, the substitution of an erotic fantasy for the travail of experience is a possibility inherent in the whole courtly system; that is, in any relation

[21] *Ibid.*, 106, 1-27. The consolation of the dream is a frequent theme in the courtly lyric. Johnston cites other examples from Provençal literature. Walther von der Vogelweide finds his greatest consolation in *wænen;* through the fantasy he finds himself lying by the lady and seeing himself in her eyes, and whatever he asks of her then she grants him willingly ("Ich wil nu mêr ûf ir genâde wesen frô"; text in *Die Gedichte Walthers von der Vogelweide,* 11th ed., edited by Carl von Kraus [Berlin, 1950], 184, 1-30, p. 87f). Cf. Friderich von Hûsen, "In mînem troume ich sach" (*Des Minnesangs Frühling* 48, 23-31). For a later example, Der Schenke von Limpurc, II (*Deutsche Liederdichter des 13. Jahrhunderts,* pp. 240f). In every case, the erotic fantasy is explicitly associated with the lady's unavailability. N.b.: Hereafter, *Des Minnesangs Frühling* will be designated by the abbreviation *MF; Deutsche Liederdichter . . .* by *DLd.*

that may be figured by a mirror, and whose object is to make the future immediately available. As soon as a man becomes a mirror of the lady, he can free her image from her will and thus manipulate it. He can reverse the whole course of the Narcissus story, turning from something real but disappointing to a reflection responsive to his desire.

There can be no generalization from the poetry of Arnaut. When a man declares himself a mirror of the lady, there is no limit to the number of meanings he may intend, or may unintentionally convey. It may be that the image in that mirror is the memory of a beauty really observed. It may be that the image acts in the theater of a fantasy, granting there what the lover continues to desire; the fantasy described publicly in a song inflames the imagination, specifies the lover's desire, and is thus a step toward fulfillment. But it may be that the lover's will rests in that fantasy, which now becomes a kind of solace instead of a sharpening of desire.

This reversion to the way of Narcissus in the courting of an image is an escape from the severe and dangerous conditions of courtly love. To place all our hopes in an idealized human being; to turn our life into service to another person whom we have nominated to justify us; to seek in her for the image of our future perfection—such a personal submission is full of peril, because it is based on a lie, projecting onto the lady an ideality that her flesh and blood must betray. To turn from this to a simple erotic fantasy is to substitute one fiction for another.

The most interesting lyric poets never forget that courtly love is a lie, a precious and fruitful lie that can in fact enhance our nature, a falsehood that brings true rewards. This double consciousness of the courtly lover we can observe in the following song of Aimeric de Peguilhan.[22]

---

[22] Text and translation reprinted from *The Poems of Aimeric de Peguilhan*, William P. Shepard and Frank M. Chambers, editors (Evanston, Northwestern University Press, 1950; quoted by permission). Pillet and Carstens, 10, poem 50.

Si cum l'arbres que, per sobrecargar,
frang se meteys e pert son frug e se,
ai perduda ma belha dona e me   I
4   e mon entier sen frag, per sobramar.
Pero, sitot mi suy apoderatz,
anc jorn no fi mon dan ad escien;
enans cug far tot so que fatz ab sen,
8   mas ar conosc que trop sobra·l foudatz.

E non es bo qu'om sia tan senatz
que a sazo no sega son talen;
e si no·i ha de quasqu mesclamen   II
12   non es bona sola l'una mitatz.
Quar be·s deve hom, per sobresaber,
Nescis, e·n vai maintas vetz folhejan,
per que s'eschai qu'om an en loc mesclan
16   sens ab foudatz, qui o sap retener.

Las! qu'ieu non ai me mezeis en poder,
ans vau mo mal enqueren e cerquan;
e vuelh trop mais perdre e far mon dan   III
20   ab vos, dona, qu'ab autra conquerer;
qu'ades cug far ab aquest dan mon pro
e que savis ab aquesta folhor;
pero, a ley de fi fol amador,
24   M'avetz ades, on piegz mi faigz, plus bo.

No sai nulh "oc" per qu'ieu des vostre "no,"
per que soven tornon mei ris en plor;
et ieu cum folhs ai gaug de ma dolor   IV
28   e de ma mort, quan vey vostra faisso.
Quo·l bazalesc qu'ab joy s'anet aucir,
Quant el miralh se remiret e·s vi,
Tot atressi etz vos miralhs de mi,
32   Que m'aucietz quan vos vei ni·us remir.

A vos no·n cal quan me vezetz morir;
abans o faitz de mi tot enaissi
cum de l'enfan qu'ab un maraboti   V

36   fai hom del plor laissar e departir,
       e pueys quant es tornatz en alegrier
       et hom l'estrai so que·l donet e·l tol,
       et el adoncs plora e fai maior dol
40   dos aitans plus que non fetz de premier.

       Reys Castellas, ges vostre pretz no col   ɪ
       de melhurar, c'uey val pro mais que hier.

(Like the overloaded tree which breaks and loses its fruit and itself, I have lost my fair lady and myself and have broken down my sense, by overmuch loving. However, although I am overcome, never did I wittingly do harm to myself. Rather I think that I do all that I do with sense; but now I recognize that folly overcomes it.

It is not well for a man to be so sensible that at times he cannot follow his desire; and, if there is not a mixture of the two [sense and folly], one half alone is not good, for one becomes an imbecile by too much knowledge and goes about many a time acting foolishly. Therefore it is fitting that one should mix, sometimes, sense with folly, if one can remember that precept.

Alas! I cannot control myself, but go searching and seeking my own harm, and prefer by far to suffer loss and bring about my own hurt with you, Lady, than to prevail with another; for I always think to profit by this hurt and to act wisely by this folly. But, following the example of the faithful, foolish lover, you hold me the better when you treat me worse.

I know no "yea" for which I would give your "nay," on account of which my laughs often turn into weeping; and I, like a madman, feel joy from my grief and my death when I see your face. Like the basilisk which went joyfully to its death when it was reflected in the mirror and saw itself, even so are you my mirror, for you slay me when I see you and look upon you.

You care not when you see me die. Rather, you treat me as one does the child whom one causes to cease and put aside his crying with a penny; and then, when he has turned to rejoicing and one takes back and deprives him of what one had given him, then he cries twice as hard and has twice as much sorrow as he did at first.

King of Castile, may your fame not cease to grow, which is far more renowned today than yesterday.)

The tree dies not because of age or drought, but because of an excess of life; it destroys itself by the weight of its own fruit. In the same way, the poet suffers from an excess of love. In other words, the life-giving rewards of love are too much to bear, and may cause his death. The lethal result of an excess of virtue: that paradox is the point of the first two strophes, conveyed in the parallel terms *sobrecargar, sobramar, sobresaber*.

What is the cause of this excess? *Foudatz*, inexperience, the folly that comes of a lack of knowledge, the innocence of Narcissus. It is thus unknowing that the lover, seeking a good, binds himself to what he shall too late discover is the cause of his undoing. Because he did not know this, he has loved "overmuch" and has entrusted his whole life to an illusory thing.

But dangerous as this inexperience may be, the virtue that cures it is also dangerous, if it is in excess. To know too much means to be incapable of that devotion which, for all its illusory nature, may inspire a man to become better than he is. If he is too wise to follow his desire, then he is not wise at all. He is, in fact, a *nescis*, an ignorant man who cannot see that in his wise restraint he is acting foolishly. To be so inexperienced that one cannot see the dangerous fiction of courtly love is to expose oneself to the fate of Narcissus. On the other hand, to be so knowledgeable that one sees nothing but the lie at the heart of love is to deprive oneself of its ripe and abundant rewards. So one must "mix the two."

This tension, in which the lover's consciousness challenges his faith in an illusion and is at the same time checked by his will to love, holds the song together.

The poet's extreme awareness, his helplessness before the necessity to love, and the beloved's indifference to his imminent death, define the experience at the heart of the lyric. Practically every line in the lyric reflects his manifold consciousness. He knows he is seeking his own harm, yet this knowledge does not give him power over himself, because he thinks that the harm may be his advantage, the folly his wisdom. For all his awareness of hopelessly courting his own destruction, he no longer has the power to withdraw.

It is the whole experience of Narcissus that the poet is enacting now. He is bound forever to this hopeless yearning, for he loves what he cannot cease to love without suffering a greater loss, the eradication of his own perfected and immortal image. Like the basilisk destroyed by its own devouring look, the poet destroys himself by his longing to unite with the image she bears; yet this longing to attain his own ideal is what makes his life bear fruit. *Sobresaber, sobramar.* He knows that he is foolish and wise, and that he "loves overmuch" this unreal image of his perfected nature, this mirror.

The mixture of sense and folly that he proposes in the beginning—how is it possible?

The first commitment made in folly, the first innocent desire, holds sway, and no amount of knowledge can undo it. Through the pain of unrequital the lover learns, like Narcissus, that the beloved bears his own fascinating image. Now the lover is torn between *foudatz* and *saber*; and this tension may destroy the lover, or it may perfect him. For all his complaint of the loss of will, it is ultimately by a tremendous act of will that he continues to serve what his *saber* denounces: an image. In this condition the poet preserves intact from too much knowledge the inexperience that fostered his devotion. The concluding image of the child, the unknowing, is as much a declaration of his will as a description of his suffering.

Bernart de Ventadorn, "Can Vei la Lauzeta Mover"

The "real lady" whose gestures are so beautiful, who has a name and a life-span and a fleshly form—she is actually neither an image nor a mirror, and never becomes one but in the admiring and hopeful minds of those who remember her in solitude. Before it is possible to call her a mirror, a great psychic event has taken place: the courtly ideal and all the doctrines that define it have been translated into a visible form in the immediate image of the lady. The ideal is thereby equipped with a will and an intelligence, with a capacity for concern and judgment. The ideal is no longer remote, it can know us and love us. Similarly, the knight's image of himself in the courtly ideal—the man of the future that he is trying to become now—is also replaced by the figure of the lady. The self-image is as elusive as the reflected image in the fountain, but the lady lives and can be possessed. Thus the idealization of the lady saves the lover from the thirst and despair of Narcissus, from the fate of loving what cannot live.[23]

But the fact is that the lover must suffer from the remote-

----

[23] When the man is persuaded that the lady favors him, he is at one with his own ideal and consequently immune to every grief:

> Si com la tigr' el mirador
> Que, por remirar son cors gen,
> Oblida s'ir' e son turmen,
> Aissi, quan vei lei cui azor
> Oblit mos mals e ma dolors es mendre.

(Just like the tigress that forgets its anger and torment when it sees its beautiful body in the mirror, I forget my pain, and my grief is less, when I see her whom I adore.)

Rigaut de Barbezieux, "Be volria saber d'Amor," Pillet and Carstens, 421, poem 5. Text: "Rigaut de Barbezieux," ed. J. Anglade, *Revue des langues romanes*, LX (1918–1920), 269f, strophe iv, verses 25–29.

ness of the ideal with its impossible demands, and even from his own faith in the lady as its representation. The courtly lover must always have his doubts, and the best courtly poets make a song of their doubt. Bernart's lyric is a famous example.

Can vei la lauzeta mover
de joi sas alas contra·l rai,
que s'oblid'e·s laissa chazer,
per la doussor c'al cor li vai,   I
5   ai! tan grans enveya m'en ve
de cui qu'eu veya jauzion,
meravilhas ai, car desse
lo cor de dezirer no·m fon.

Ai, las! tan cuidava saber
10   d'amor, e tan petit en sai!
Car eu d'amar no·m posc tener
celeis don ja pro non aurai.   II
Tout m'a mo cor, e tout m'a me,
e se mezeis e tot lo mon;
15   e can se·m tolc, no·m laisset re
mas dezirer e cor volon.

Anc non agui de me poder
ni no fui meus de l'or' en sai
que·m laisset en sos olhs vezer
20   en un miralh que mout me plai.   III
Miralhs, pus me mirei en te,
m'an mort li sospir de preon,
c'aissi·m perdei com perdet se
lo bels Narcisus en la fon.

25   De las domnas me dezesper;
ja mais en lor no·m fiarai;
c'aissi com las solh chaptener,
enaissi las deschaptenrai.   IV
Pois vei c'una pro no m'en te
30   vas leis que·m destrui e·m cofon,

93

totas las dopt' e las mescre,
car be sai c'atretals se son.

D'aisso·s fa be femna parer
ma domna, per qu'e·lh o retrai,
35   car no vol so c'om deu voler,
e so c'om li deveda, fai.   v
Chazutz sui en mala merce,
et ai be faih co·l fols en pon;
e no sai per que m'esdeve,
40   mas car trop puyei contra mon.

Merces es perduda, per ver,
(et eu non o saubi anc mai),
car cilh qui plus en degr'aver,
no·n a ges, et on la querrai?   VI
45   a! can mal sembla, qui la ve,
qued aquest chaitiu deziron
que ja ses leis non aura be,
laisse morir, que no l'aon!

Pus ab midons no·m pot valer
50   precs ni merces ni·l dreihz qu'eu ai,
ni a leis no ven a plazer
qu'eu l'am, ja mais no·lh o dirai.   VII
Aissi·m part de leis e·m recre;
mort m'a, e per mort li respon,
55   e vau m'en, pus ilh no·m rete,
chaitius, en issilh, no sai on.

Tristans, ges no·n auretz de me,
qu'eu m'en vau, chaitius, no sai on.   T
De chantar me gic e·m recre,
60   e de joi e d'amor m'escon.[24]

(When I see the lark move its wings with joy toward the sun, and
forget itself, and let itself fall because of the sweetness that comes

[24] Pillet and Carstens, 70, poem 43. Text: *Bernart von Ventadorn,
seine Lieder*, ed. Carl Appel (Halle a.S., Max Niemeyer Verlag, 1915;
quoted by permission), pp. 249–254.

to its heart, alas, what envy comes to me then of those whom I see rejoicing! I marvel that straightaway my heart does not melt with desire.

Alas, how much I thought I knew about love, and how little I know! For I cannot keep myself from loving her from whom I shall have no requital; she has all my heart, and me, and herself, and all the world; and when she has thus taken all from me, she leaves me with nothing but desire and a longing heart.

Never have I had power over myself nor been my own from that moment, when she let me look into her eyes, into a mirror that pleases me much, till now. Mirror, since I beheld myself in you, my deep sighs have killed me, for I have lost myself as the beautiful Narcissus lost himself in the fountain.

I am in despair of all women; never more shall I trust in them, for just as I have been accustomed to protect them, so now I shall abandon them. Since I see that not one noble lady helps me against her who destroys and confounds me, I shall fear and distrust them all, for well I know that they are all alike.

In this my lady makes herself seem a woman indeed, for which I reproach her; for she does not desire what one ought to desire; and what is forbidden her to do, she does. I am fallen in evil grace, and I have indeed acted like the madman on the bridge, and I do not know how this has happened to me, except that I climbed too high.

Mercy is lost, in truth, and I never knew it; for she who ought to have the most of it has none, and where shall I seek for it? Ah, to whoever sees her it does not seem that she would leave this longing miserable man, who shall have no good without her, to die, because she does not help him!

Since with my lady there is no avail in my prayers, nor in mercy, nor in the rights I have, and since it does not please her that I love her, I shall never say it to her. Thus I part from love and renounce it; she has given me death, and by death I shall answer her; and I go away since she does not retain me, a miserable man in exile, I know not where.

Tristan, you shall have no song from me, for I, wretched man, depart, I know not where: I shall desist from singing, and I renounce it, and hide myself from joy and love.)

The first strophe,[25] with the famous image of the lark overwhelmed by the sweetness of the light, sets the mood of the whole song. Professor Jackson gives a perceptive reading:

The first strophe is of great importance. It is not a mere conventional tribute to the joy of spring but an important image which, in various ways, dominates the poem. The lark moves upwards towards the light; the light inspires him with love, with upward striving towards the source of light. The sensation he feels is joy, exaltation, the urge to go ever higher in pursuit of the light which inspires him. So great is the joy he feels that he can drop down again, still dazzled, and never notice it in the sweetness of desire—even though he has not attained the light he sought. The image occupies four lines. The *cauda* applies it to the poet. He too is inspired to love his lady in this way, but is prevented.[26]

The lark strives to reach "the source of light," which is truly unattainable; nevertheless, he wins requital, the *pro* from which the poet is excluded. For the lark's moment of self-forgetfulness is the prize the poet sought, a moment in which the lark is united with the light by the ray of "sweetness" that touches his heart. This is not only the sweetness of desire but the very sweetness of fulfillment; and as it becomes indistinguishable from the object of its desire, the lark even forgets itself. As its upward motion stops, so does its desire, for in the split second between that flight of desire and its fall back into

[25] In the manuscripts the order of the strophes varies considerably. They all agree in the placing of the first two strophes; and because of the *tornada* there is no question as to the final strophe. In my discussion I try to demonstrate the link between the second and third strophes, and I treat the fourth, fifth, and sixth strophes as a unit.

[26] W. T. H. Jackson, *The Literature of the Middle Ages* (New York, 1960), p. 248.

consciousness and separateness, it knows nothing but the sweet passivity of its will. It does not reach the source of light, but for one motionless instant the lark is united with its ray.

But for the poet things are very different. Both the second and third strophes are explicit in relating the poet's present suffering to the past. In the past, *tan cuidava saber d'amor;* but now, *tan petit en sai!* The fascination that began when he thought he knew all about love, and looked into the lady's eyes, has lasted to the present moment—*en sai,* "till now." In the past the lady had let him look into a mirror that delights him now. Thus the poet begins with an image of the joy he had naïvely anticipated, and contrasts it with his actual despair; he then evokes the past event that caused his present sorrow.

This clear progression of the first three strophes reveals how much the poet's mood differs from that of the lark. He is in a state of intense and painful self-consciousness; his allusion to Narcissus is entirely just. He knows that he was deceived, and when, and why. He says he is lost, yet he knows he cannot stop loving, even as he knows that the object of his love is as insubstantial as the shadow. As he understands his past, so he knows his future, for it is the future of Narcissus: he is in attendance upon his own dying, in full understanding and despair. For there are two voices that speak here, the voice of the entranced lover who is doomed, and the voice of the compassionate spectator who is powerless, who sees everything but can change nothing. The victim and his audience are identical; the lover watches himself. In this posture he is in every way different from the lark, which has forgotten even that it is flying.

He remembers his own past, he remembers the exemplum of Narcissus. And so he learns the same lesson twice: the man who looks into a mirror and thinks to be united with what he loves there is doomed to die in despair. But what is it that he sees in the mirror, that binds him to it with so great a force?

It is his own image perfected, his own form enhanced by

every courtly grace and virtue. As he believed the lady was a mirror of perfection, so he believed that in casting his own image in that mirror he would be united with the ideal, the light of the world, the living form of Beauty. She was to be his hope, a mediator between himself and something imperious and impossible. For just as the lark feels the *doussor* without ever reaching the light to which it aspired, so the inexperienced lover, who thought he knew so much, has sought to be loved by that impossible ideal in its own perfect embodiment, the lady.

But at that time he did not know what Narcissus, also, did not know at first: that although the mirror will reflect everything in an image abstracted from the failures of matter, the image has no present reality, and the mirror no true life. Both find this out in the same way, by the insensate indifference of the image to the yearning of the lover. Then the poet sees how little he knew about love.

For a mirror is a material thing, passive and formless, incapable of the ecstasy and anguish it causes. Without form itself, it is the mindless bearer of innumerable forms that pass incessantly, the epitome of impermanence, of shapeless, shifting, impoverished matter.[27]

The substance of the poet's discovery is clear enough, although its material cause is uncertain: an event described in detail is not to be found in a lyric. The efficient cause, however, is stated: it is the lady's indifference, her willingness to let him die even though he has given over all his life to her. "In this," the poet might have said, "my lady shows herself a mirror indeed." The mirror has no affect, and no moral concern; it does not care, because it cannot know, that it is loved

---

[27] Cf. Walther von der Vogelweide (?), "Ein meister las troum unde spiegelglas" (text in von Kraus's edition, 122, 24–123, 40): the mirror is associated with the dream, the wind, and the passing of the seasons, as examples of instability. See Carl von Kraus, *Walther von der Vogelweide, Untersuchungen* (Berlin and Leipzig, 1935), p. 460.

and desired, or that its admirer languishes before it. The real lady—she who has a name and a dwelling and our common mortality—shares in the imperfection of the human race; but long ago, in the sight of her beauty, the poet made a mirror out of her to reflect his future perfection. Between then and now he has come to see the difference between the real lady and the passive mirror, and from this gain in consciousness he has suffered a loss that cannot be measured. No longer can she be for him the concerned ideal beckoning to the courtly man.

In this difference between the real lady and the image he bears in his heart, the lady is denigrated. However accomplished in courtliness she may be, in the essential virtue, in *merces*, she is altogether lacking, altogether inferior to the poet's image of her. She cannot lead him to perfection, she is not to be his guide and loving judge. There is nothing left that he might have resembled more and more, nothing by which he might have measured himself and at the same time have demonstrated the reality of his courtliness. He has known himself and been known to others by means of his image in the mirror, but now that mirror is broken, the image discredited. Unreflected, he is socially and morally invisible. He belongs nowhere. He is truly *en issilh*.

What terrifies him is that even as he recognizes the mirror for what it is he cannot stop loving it. Knowing himself bound to what he knows is unreal, he is in despair.

In this light, the fourth strophe ought to be read as the reverse of an extremely frequent theme: the lover often declares that for his own lady's sake he will be courteous to all noble ladies and serve them willingly. "Service" is the form of the man's devotion to the courtly ideal; in service to all ladies he enacts his courtly quality and thereby proves his worth to his own lady and to his class. Furthermore, all the beauty, honor, grace, and refinement of other ladies, all the clear virtues that make them worthy of being served, are reflected upon them by the one Lady in whom these virtues are perfect; thus in serving them he pays homage to her, as to their source.

But now the condition for such service has been wholly destroyed; and just as earlier all other ladies were so many reflections of the Lady's goodness, so now they are reflections of her cruel unconcern. If she, who is supposed to have more *merces* than anyone else, in fact has none, then it must be that no one else has it either. Thus the failure of the Lady is a social as well as a personal calamity, removing all basis for faith in the goodness of others:

> 41 Merces es perduda per ver,
> et eu non o saubi anc mai,
> car cilh qui plus en degr'aver,
> no·n a ges, et on la querrai?

It is a universal loss, for the courtliness of everyone was to be recognized by its image in her; and because she is now no longer credible as the living embodiment of the ideal, a kind of ethical magnet holding the whole society together—for everyone is drawn by love to his ideal image reflected in her—everything must now fall apart, leaving nothing but a vast moral uncertainty.

The reproach of the lady's capriciousness, in the verses of the fifth strophe, stresses once again the difference between the living lady and the public ideal. Of these two, only the lady possesses a free will, but when that will is expressed, it does not accord with *so qu'om deu voler*. Indifferent to the ideal of courtly conduct, it desires what is forbidden. Again the lady is denigrated, and the image exposed as unreal except in the poet's need.[28]

[28] The poet's discovery that he is the victim and the lover of an illusion is almost always implied in the Middle High German lyric by the term *wân*. A splendid example is in Friderich von Hûsen's "Wâ-fenâ, wie hat mich Minne gelâzen!" (*MF* 52, 37—53, 30; p. 50f): he knows he is being destroyed by the *wân*, the illusory belief, that he

In the end we hear the last words of an exile, of a man without a place. He renounces love in the only way a courtly man can, for love alone preserves his life whole. He is, in short, going to die, like Narcissus, all alone. The shattering of the mirror has destroyed his life as a courtly man in a courtly society, and the sign of his death will be his silence:

52   *. . . ja mais no·l o dirai*
59   *de chantar me gic e·m recre*

For the song is a form of courtly service: the lover's proclaiming of his consecration to the lady before the whole courtly society is an act that defines him; and so, to cease to sing is to cease to *be*. Three times in this final strophe we learn he is going to die: the lady will not reflect him; the society will not recognize him; he will no longer sing.

Concerning the *tornada*, Ernest Hoepffner remarks that it "repeats like an echo his melancholy *adieu*." [29] Not only the rimes but many of the words of the *cauda* of the preceding strophe are repeated (*vau, caitius, no sai on, e·m recre*). As the figure of Narcissus has been vividly present in the poet's memory throughout each strophe, the conclusion of the song imitates Narcissus's death and echoing farewell. This remains true no matter how many times we are reminded of the formal tradition of the *tornada*, for what we read here is not a tradition but a single lyric, which exists but once.

---

may never find a better lady in all the world, but he will hold to that *wân* and serve her loyally. The same combination of disillusionment and resolution in Heinrich von Rugge, "Got hât mir armen ze leide getân" (*MF* 101, 15–38; p. 130f). Cf. Vriderich der Kneht, Ia (*DLd*, p. 69f), and Götfrit von Nifen, XXV (*DLd*, p. 109, strophes 3 and 4). A mocking account of the lover's captivation by the *wân* is in Hartmann von Aue, "Ich var mit iuwern hulden" (*MF* 218, 5–28; p. 303f).

[29] *Les Troubadours dans leur vie et dans leurs œuvres* (Paris, 1955), p. 53. Cf. Alfred Pätzold, *Die individuellen Eigentümlichkeiten einiger hervorragender Trobadors im Minneliede* (Marburg, 1897), p. 30, where a similar observation is made.

This is an appropriate moment to consider the value of tradition to a poet who uses the mirror-image. This tradition defined for the poet and his audience the universal meaning of the figure: the mirror reflects an ideal image and implicitly demands judgment upon an actual condition. His ability to rely on a common tradition well known to his audience is a great advantage to the poet. But this is a universal inheritance to which all poets have access, the good ones as well as the bad.

Whether or not a poet goes beyond this point depends on whether he is open to all the implications of the metaphor, whether he has the talent to see them and the courage to face them. Those implications are available to everyone. The mirror removes the form of an object from the flux of matter, or it translates a spiritual concept into a visible figure; and this is what makes the image ideal. But the mirror itself is also a part of the flux, without life and almost without attributes, and therefore must deform what it reflects; and this is what makes the image deceptive. Its double aspect can cause an infinite fascination: the mirror epitomizes all the reality of which it is but one small part; it is most private and most public; it permits the beholder to see spiritual things that transcend him, but at the cost of debasing them, and material things that surround him, but at the cost of distorting them, bringing both spirit and matter together in a way that imitates the act of creation, even though nothing is created; it is, indeed, almost nothing itself, but takes on the form of almost everything; it shows a man what he ought to be and what he is; it proves the reality of things, but what it shows has no reality. All the ambiguity of the human condition is re-enacted in the poet's confrontation with this truth-teller, this liar, this flatterer, this chastiser, this lifeless and inspiring thing.

The mirror is a great test for a poet, for it has all the richness and treachery of life itself. The great poets everywhere rejoice in its richness and suffer its treachery. But the ability to see all these things comes from the poet's talent and character, and not from any traditional inheritance.

The main themes treated thus far have made one fact clear: the presence of the mirror is implied at least as often as it is stated. The man who contemplates the image of the lady in solitude sees a mirror of perfection, and he is at the same time a mirror himself, for his heart and mind contain the image that grants him its qualities. The presence of an image, in these texts, presupposes the presence of a mirror. And the essence of the courtly-love relation, the desire of the man to see himself in another, is a condition impossible without the function of a mirror.[30] Bernart de Ventadorn's lines,

[30] The implicit mirror is common in Middle High German:
> "Ir houbet ist sô wünnenrîch,
> als ez mîn himel welle sîn.
> wem solde ez anders sîn gelîch?
> ez hât ouch himeleschen schîn.
> dâ liuhtent zwêne sternen abe,
> dâ müeze ich mich noch inne ersehen,
> daz si mirs alsô nâhen habe!
> so mac ein wunder wol geschehen:
> ich junge, und tuot si daz,
> und wirt mir gernden siechen seneder sühte baz."
> [Walther, ed. von Kraus; 54, 27–36]

(Her face is so rich in joy, as though it would be my heaven. To what else could it be compared? It also has heavenly splendor. Two stars shine forth there: would that she had me so close that I could gaze upon myself therein! Then a miracle would happen: I would become young again if she did that, and I, who am sick of longing would be cured of my torment.)

In seeing his image in the lady's eyes he sees himself rejuvenated, perfected; and the implied physical union suggests a still deeper wish for a total identity with the ideal, with "des Schöpfer's Meisterwerk," as W. Wilmanns calls it (*Walther von der Vogelweide*, II, Halle/Saale, 1924, 220ff). The following lyrics express a wish and define a situation exactly in the manner of Walther's: Götfrit von Nifen, "Nu stêt diu liebe heide bar" (*DLd*, p. 90); Der Wilde Alexander, "Mich

sai qu'en lei ma mortz se mira,
can sa gran beutat remir [31]

(My death sees itself in her when I gaze upon her beauty),
do not expressly mention a mirror, nor does the lyric in which
they occur, but the presence of Narcissus is felt none the less
vividly.

Peire Bremon's lyric *Us covinens gentils cors plazentiers* [32]
—to take another example—does begin by calling the lady
"mirror and flower of ladies and of love," but it is not in
this venerable, heaped-up phrase that we find anything interesting. Rather, it is the second strophe, which makes no
mention at all of a mirror but depends upon the figure for the
fullest meaning. As the true courtiers, says the poet, know all
the attributes of a good lord and therefore recognize him
when they find him, so he has had a clear image of the lady
whom he would serve, an image so clear that for thirty
months he could see that all the other ladies were not worthy
of the image, and that the one lady whom he calls "Belh
Dezir" alone could please him. Peire Bremon here expresses a
theme familiar to every reader of the courtly lyric, that of a
man who falls in love with an image and then seeks a mirror
worthy of bearing it, a beautiful living mirror esteemed by
every noble heart. This quest for a lady he has never met, but
whose image he adores, is the clearest indication of the meaning of the mirror-figure. Nowhere else do we see so plainly
that courtly love begins with the lover's image of his own

---

wundert, sit daz ich ez las" (*DLd*, p. 22f); Rubin, "Joch kunde ich
guoten liuten wol," strophe 3 (*DLd*, p. 339); Otte von Bottenlouben,
"Kumt er der mir dâ komen sol" (*DLd*, p. 316). Cf. Heinrich von
Missen, "Waz hât diu werlt ze gebenne mê" (*DLd*, p. 155), strophe 2;
and Der Tuginhafte Schriber, "Wol dir, wîbes güete" (*DLd*, p. 413),
strophes 2 and 3.

[31] "Bel m'es can eu vei la brolha," Appel, no. 9, v. 39f; cf. no. 12, v.
16. See Frappier, p. 153.

[32] Pillet and Carstens 330, poem 21. Text: *Les Poésies du troubadour
Peire Bremon Ricas Novas*, ed. Jean Boutière (Paris and Toulouse,
1930), pp. 10–12.

perfection, an image which later takes on the form of an honored lady in whom the ideal is considered to be realized. Without that lady, without a mirror that is alive and sentient, the man is in great peril. But the lady does not necessarily come first. She could not instantly attract the devotion of the courtly man were he not already devoted to the image he has engendered.[33]

A word of caution against being too literal: One mark of the knight is his prowess. Now we do not say that the lover sees in the lady the finest example of prowess and ferocity in battle, a Brunhilde who hangs up every puny impostor on a nail in the wall, so that to conquer her is indeed to achieve the ideal. We have to go further, for when prowess is the highest value there is no such thing as "courtly love." For prowess in itself is not a chivalric ideal: any raw imbecile brought up in the woods, and never far from the skirts of an over-protective mother, can slay even the most refined knight. Prowess must be justified, for otherwise we could not tell the difference between the quality of a courtly man and the power of a brute. It is when strength is expended in the struggle for moral perfection, and in a style demanded by the consciousness of class, that it becomes a true courtly virtue. It is not the natural endowments of a male that are perfected in the lady, but the ideal which every faculty serves and by which its worth is judged—what Parzival learns from Gurnemanz, from Arthur, from Sigune, from Trevrezent. It is this supreme secular ideal that is embodied in the knight's beloved.

[33] The theme of a man falling in love with a lady before he ever sets eyes on her is also quite frequent in the Middle High German lyric. For example: Meinloh von Sevelingen, "Dô ich dich loben hôrte" (*MF* 11, 1–25); Friderich von Hûsen, "In mînem troume ich sach" (*MF* 48, 23–31); Reinmar von Hagenau, "Ich will allez gâhen," strophe 2 (*MF* 170, 8–12); Hiltbolt von Swanegöi, "Wie schoen unde guot si wære" (*DLd*, p. 165f); Der Margrave von Hohenburg, "Ich hete ie gedâht" (*DLd*, p. 176)—a very full statement of the theme; Reinmar von Brennenberc, "Ich hân got und die minneclîchen Minne" (*DLd*, p. 325), and "Ir munt der liuhtet" (*DLd*, p. 327, especially strophe 6).

The Provençal Lyric

St. Augustine, as we saw, called the self-image conceived in the ideal a *word*. The lady is the word of man made flesh. The *beginning* of courtly love is the word, and the word is with the aspiring man. It is the mirror which incarnates the word, giving it a public form and thereby enabling it to guide and judge all secular experience.

It is that incarnate word that draws our interest. In the rest of this study, therefore, we need not restrict ourselves to texts in which the mirror is explicitly mentioned. The *image* first of all requires the mirror, and gives it its meaning.

Nor, in what lies before us, is there any advantage in continuing the present method of "surveying" the literature and moving about from one poet to another. It will now be more useful to study how the mirror reflects the whole work of a single great poet.

CHAPTER THREE

Heinrich von Morungen and the Mirror of the Audience[1]

THE lyric poet could not give to the courtly ideal the full and free representation that appears in the romance. For he had to play a double rôle: he is both the author and the hero of the experience he recounts. As author he is a real man well known to his peers, who are his audience; but as hero he assumes a fictional identity, an imaginary "I" whom he endows with his own name and quality but who has no existence outside the confines of the lyric. This double identity causes him many difficulties, as we shall soon see, but it is the source of the greatest value of his song.

With a defined rôle in both fiction and actuality, he was limited in the story he could tell: the events of his relation to

[1] For this chapter I have selected a few poems in which Heinrich's major themes are most clearly present, and I shall defer until the end a study of his famous "mirror-lyric." In this way it should be possible to see how the mirror epitomizes his whole work. Very little is known of Heinrich's life. He was a knight of the north of Thuringia in the service of the Markgraf Dietrich von Meissen, whom he accompanied to the Holy Land in 1197. He probably died in the Thomaskloster at Leipzig in 1222. It is generally agreed that his literary activity begins around 1190. See, in addition to the biographical information in the *MF* notes, Helmut de Boor, *Geschichte der deutschen Literatur*, II (München, 1960), 277f, which gives further biographical references.

the lady had to be, if not strictly true, at least clearly possible. In contrast, the romance unfolds freely in the realm of the ideal. There is no mortal limitation to the hero's career—and therefore no precise mortal relevance. Every adventure is exactly suited to his moral condition at the moment; sword-bridges and antagonists appear as they are required to train and test him, without any problems of transportation and finance. All the enemies of the courtly code he vanquishes, but the enemies of flesh and blood he never meets: his very weariness is a moral rather than a physical state. The hero suffers and triumphs; the distinctive ethics of the courtly class are vividly depicted, but there is no assurance that they fit the facts of human nature. When the romance is over, how shall we know whether the face of the hero reflects the faces of our peers, whether his life is a mirror of our own? What does he know of our politics, our jealousies, our lands, our alliances? But the lyric poet who tells of his service to a noble lady—he is a man we know.

Only the lyric poet can assure his listeners that the courtly code has been tested in the personal experience of one of their own; that he has lived through the regimen of the ideal, that it has all been worth while, that it has truly ennobled him. As a witness with an actual testimony he substantiates the ideal and preserves the solidarity of the whole class.

In his awareness of this social function of the courtly poet, Heinrich von Morungen is unsurpassed by any other poet of the Middle Ages. But what distinguishes him even more is his awareness that courtly love is a fiction, a false image that can bring the appearance of order. It is his office to present his experience as a validation of the courtly code; but he is everywhere conscious of the inadequacy of the code to the reality of that experience. Thus his poetry is characterized by a deep conflict, by a disposition to support the ideal in conflict with a desire to rebuke it.

Mirror of Narcissus

The Audience

Heinrich's lyrics, like those of any other Minnesänger, reflect a relation between the poet, the lady, and the audience. This relation is extraordinarily complex—no one may ever define it completely—but it begins in a situation that is really rather simple: the poet's song is performed before an audience of his peers.

131, 25   Ich bin iemer eine und niht eine [2]
           der grôzen minne der ich nie wart frî.
           wêren nun die huoter algemeine
           toup unde blint, swenne ich ir wêre bì,   I
           sô möht ich mîn leit
30   eteswenne mit gelâze ir künden
           und mich mit rede zuo ir gefründen,
           sô wurde ir wunders vil von mir geseit.

132, 3   Mîner ougen tougenlîchez spêen,
           daz ich ze boten an si senden muoz,
5   daz neme durch got von mir für ein flêen,
           und ob si lache, daz sî mir ein gruoz.   II
           in weiz wer dâ sanc
           'ein sitich unde ein star ân alle sinne
10   wol gelernten daz si sprêchen Minne':
           wol sprechent siz und habent des niemer danc.

           Wolte si mîn denken für daz sprechen
           und mîn trûren für die klage verstân,
           sô müese ir im, der niuwen rede, gebrechen.
           wê, sol iemen daz für fuoge hân   III

[2] Throughout this chapter the line numbers are from *MF*, but the text is from *Heinrich von Morungen*, ed. Carl von Kraus (München, Carl Hanser Verlag, 1950; quoted by permission). Any differences between von Kraus's text and *MF* are discussed in the notes. This edition of von Kraus's will hereafter be cited as *MA* (that is, Morungen Ausgabe), an abbreviation von Kraus himself uses in his other works.

15   daz er sêre klage
   daz er doch von herzen niht enmeinet
   als der eine trûret unde weinet
132, 18   und er sîn leit doch niemen kan gesage.

131, 33   Sie nesol niht allen liuten lachen
   sô von herzen sam si lachet mir,
35   und ir an sên sô minneclîche enmachen.
   waz habet ieman ze schouwen daz an ir,   IV
   der ich leben sol
   unde an der ist al mîn wünne behalten?
132, 1   jâne wil ich niemer des eralten,
   swenn ich si sê, mirn sî von herzen wol.

132, 19   Sît si herzen liebe heizent minne,
   in weiz wie ich die minne heizen sol.
   minne wonet dicke in mînem sinne:
   hête ich liebe, minne enbêre ich wol.   V
   liebe diu gît mir
   hôhen muot, dar zuo freud unde wünne:
25   sône weiz ich was diu minne künne,
   wan deich eine trûren muoz von ir.

(I am always alone, and yet never alone from powerful *Minne*, from whom I have never been free. If only the spies were all deaf and blind whenever I am with her, then I would be able to make her know my pain, courteously, now and then; and by conversation I would make myself her friend. Then wonderful things would be said to her by me.

May she, for God's sake, take for a supplication the secretive searching of my eyes, the look I must send to her as a messenger; and then if she would smile, let that be a greeting to me. I do not know who it was that sang there: "A parrot or a starling without any intelligence would have learned to say '*Minne*' ": they say it well but have no thought of what they say.

If she would understand my thinking for speaking, and my [silent] grieving for a [spoken] lamentation, then anyone who merely talks would never succeed. It would be a pity if such a one should consider it courtly when he loudly laments what he nevertheless does not feel in his heart, [and pretends to be] like one who grieves and weeps alone and can tell of his pain to no one.

She ought not to smile to all the people so much from the heart as she smiles to me, and she ought not to make her regard so lovely. What business has anyone to behold all this in her, for whom I live and in whom all my joy is enclosed? I shall never want to grow so old that when I see her my heart is not rejoiced.

Since they call heart's love *Minne*, I do not know how I ought to call *Minne*. *Minne* dwells often in my heart: if I had Love, I would gladly do without *Minne*. Love gives me an exultant mood, and also joy and pleasure. But I do not know what *Minne* can do, except that because of it I must grieve alone.)

The opening strophes must cause us to wonder. The poet tells us he is always alone because of the spies who surround the lady; but he is never free of *Minne*,[3] he never stops trying to communicate with her. If only those slandering spies were deaf and blind, how he would complain of his suffering and win her favor by his eloquence! Now in this terrible predicament, he devises one hopeful little stratagem: let her read his mind and heart, let her smile cautiously in response to his searching look. By this little secret between them, he may yet befriend her and keep her reputation safe from those crabbed gossip-mongers.

This is where we must wonder. The "secret" is spelled out in a song performed before his own society, where, as he says elsewhere, *sist zallen êren ein wip wol erkant* (*MF* 122, 1: "She is a woman well known for every virtue"). He has a

---

[3] Following von Kraus's reconstruction of the first two lines in his *Zu den Liedern Heinrichs von Morungen* (Berlin, 1916), p. 27; this work to be cited hereafter as *MU* (Morungen Untersuchungen, von Kraus's abbreviation). Cf. his *Des Minnesangs Frühling, Untersuchungen* (Leipzig, 1939), p. 301f, for further arguments against the MS. A reading (this latter work to be cited as *MFU*).

stratagem to escape the censure of society, but we hear of it in a public utterance which is, as a matter of fact, addressed to that society. Why does our poet seek to entertain his audience by revealing to it the way in which he hopes to escape its strictures?

It must be that he divides his society into at least two irreconcilable groups. The dangerous and repressive spies deprive the lover and silence the poet, and are like a poisonous cloud around the lady's illuminating figure; for being hypocrites themselves, they cannot understand the knight's exalted love, and seek to starve it by concealing its object. They are the Enemy. But there are others who are sympathetic, the real audience for the poet's song; it is to them alone that he reveals everything, how he has been immobilized by spies and silenced by parrots.

When the poet says, "I do not know who it was that sang, *'ein sitich unde ein star . . . ,'* " he relies upon his intimacy with his true audience; for he has sung these lines himself, and before *them*.[4] *They* know who the singer was, but the Enemy does not. They know that he sang as no parrot ever could, for the parrot and the starling speak words that mean nothing to them, while he speaks from the heart; and the audience knows that the love which engendered the words remains in the heart even when the words cannot be spoken. When the poet speaks to this group, he speaks as one of *them*, as one no less known than the lady he praises. And it is to them that he praises her, representing her image with an immediacy, a demonstrativeness, made possible only by the court conditions in which the lyric is sung, and his own position there:

> Sêt an ir ougen / und merket ir kinne,
> set an ir kel wîz und prüefet ir munt.
> [*MF* 141, 1f]

(Behold those eyes of hers, observe her chin, gaze upon her white throat, and study her mouth.)

[4] *MF* 127, 24f. Cf. von Kraus, *MA*, p. 100.

It is his secret love about whom he speaks, but he publishes her image with a diligence that tells a great deal about the audience and the singer's relation with it. The lady remains anonymous, but the career of the poet's service is made known in detail to an audience that is deeply concerned. Unnamed the lady may be—the spies are everywhere—but she is clearly not unknown: those who are sympathetic, those to whom Heinrich really speaks, are told that they may see her radiating light wherever she goes, standing at the window, conversing with other women, by her presence robbing all men of their senses, celebrated everywhere, smiling like the sun upon everyone (*MF* 131, 33). Whether or not the Lady in courtly poetry "really existed," this much is clear: she is represented as being real not only to the poet but to his audience as well—indeed, as the source of all praiseworthy reality, as the best known, the most brilliant, the most visible figure in the entire society.

Thus the poet, the Man We Know, here reveals to those who are deeply concerned the details of his experience in the *Minne*-relation, but in such a way as to protect both the lady and himself from the depredations of the *huoter*, who try to stifle the possibilities of the chivalric life. That is why this confidence which the poet shares with his sympathetic audience has such urgency. All of them, the audience as well as the poet, have an interest in protecting the *Minne*-relation from the *huoter*, with whom they are collectively at war. For that relation ultimately represents their own aspirations, and is the enactment of the values to which they are all dedicated.

In the second strophe, after hoping that the lady will accept the look in his eyes in place of a spoken prayer, the poet introduces a reference to one of his own lyrics, as we have seen. In this way he certifies his courtliness to the audience. He identifies this prayer for what it is: the latest utterance of devotion in a love-relation that has already shown his fidelity, that has continued, as he tells us elsewhere, since the days of his childhood.

But he goes further than this. When he referred to the parrot and starling in the earlier lyric, it was to show the lady how "easy" it would be for her to say *"Minne"* and rejoice his heart. But now the same parrot and starling represent something altogether different: they say words, important words, even the most important word of all, and they say them well; but they have not the faintest idea of what they are saying.[5] Their emptiness of head and heart is the starting-point of the poet's new theme, and he goes on to speak of those posturing courtiers who parrot words but feel nothing. But in using the *sitich* and the *star* to introduce a criticism, he must be leveling that criticism at his own early prayer to the lady, in which he asked her to say the word that would end his grief. He realizes that he has inadvertently asked her to be like those whom he now rebukes; any mindless creature can say a word, but the lady is his judge, far wiser and more virtuous than he. Therefore in referring to the earlier song he does more than demonstrate the steadfastness of his service; he also makes a partial retraction, he corrects the fault he has committed and the imperfect understanding that caused it. Here is the visible sign of his ennoblement; he has become more wise and more patient. And to what kind of audience could he show this painstaking revision of his own song? Only to one that has already been long concerned in the lover's and the poet's career; for he is one of them, a courtly man, a knight.

In the third strophe the poet says, Whoever has nothing but words shall never succeed; [6] let it not be considered courtly for a man to cry out about something he does not feel, in contrast to the man who feels deeply but must be silent.[7] This *iemen* stands in great contrast to the poet, who is *iemer eine*, always alone in his grief but never free of *Minne*. Others can

---

[5] Cf. von Kraus, *MU*, p. 24; *MFU*, p. 302.

[6] On the interpretation of this line, see *MU*, p. 24, n. 2.

[7] *Sam* modifies *meinet:* he does not feel it as one who weeps alone feels it.

talk of love like parrots; but Heinrich, who may not speak, is inflamed with it. Of course, the silence imposed on him extends only to a certain limit, for here he is singing about that silence. Before the whole society, before the spies and the parrots, he must be dumb; but before this audience he must sing. He is ever alone and yet never alone.[8]

Thus Heinrich identifies himself as a rare poet of the court. The others merely put words together, pretend to love, invent agonies; but he speaks from the heart and from actual experience. They can never know the true meaning of *fuoge*, courtliness, for they chatter about a love they have never felt, for ladies such as do not really exist and can never be really known. But Heinrich declares that *he* has truly loved; and this affirmation of the reality of his experience brings, as we have seen, the greatest social value, the sense of solidarity: it reveals in the life of the knight the efficacy of the courtly ideal—true dauntlessness of service, true consecration, true love. Those others, in contrast to the spies, pledge allegiance to *Minne* in a flawless posture, with their hands over their empty hearts; but in contrast to Heinrich and the other true lovers, they have no love to consecrate. They, too, are excluded from the poet's audience.

His relation to his true audience explains the structure of the second and third strophes. In each, the first part (*Aufgesang*) contains a prayer that the lady may understand the meaning of his silence, the second part (*Abgesang*) a certification of his own courtliness. The literal intention is simple: she is to grant his prayer because he is worthy of it. But his worth is not merely declared to her; it is made visible to the audience. The full meaning of these strophes is something like this: Since I am one of you, then observe how the code that unites us is tested in experience, and for your own sake pray that that experience may end in joy.

In the following strophe Heinrich goes on to reaffirm his

[8] Cf. *MU*, p. 24, n. 3.

service: he will never grow so old that his heart does not rejoice at seeing her. In the word *eralten* he not only dedicates his service in the future but also reminds everyone of its endurance throughout the past; for it began when he was a child, and even earlier—at the moment when, as he says elsewhere, he was born for her, and for nothing else, into the world. For the same reason he insists that she should not smile at everyone so cordially as she smiles at him, or make her gaze so full of love for everyone to behold; for no one else can look upon her with the poet's devotion, nor can her glance mean to the others what it means to him, whose life is dedicated to her and whose joy depends upon her.[9]

But from this we also know that she *does* smile upon all, that the sight of her is a beautiful thing for all to see. Heinrich, like other courtly poets, must show us that his devotion to her is not caused by some peculiar concept of beauty. Her beauty is an objective fact, her grace a gift to all the world—even to the hypocritical spies, who, after all, likewise feed their eyes upon her. Heinrich often compares her to the sun, for she is the light of the whole courtly class, she makes every true knight visible; she is "Madonna Cortesia."[10] As such she is everywhere esteemed; in serving her, the poet acts out the

---

[9] Von Kraus (*MU*, p. 24) discusses the connection between the third and fourth strophes:

The poet, who has shown her how much lies behind his silence and how little behind the words and complaints of the others, now claims the favor of her *lachen* (132, 6), for himself alone. Whoever weeps but does not mean it *von herzen* (132, 16), to such a one she should not *alsô von herzen lachen, same si lachet mir, und ir an sên sô minneclîche enmachen.*

Those others, with whom he must share the greeting they do not deserve, should not be confused with his audience, with whom he shares everything. See Julius Schwietering, "Der Liederzyklus Heinrichs von Morungen," in *Mystik und höfische Dichtung im Hochmittelalter* (Darmstadt, 1960), p. 87.

[10] See the interesting discussion by Carlo Grünanger, *Heinrich von Morungen e il problema del Minnesang* (Milano, 1948), p. 72f.

virtues of his class and therefore engages the concern of his audience.[11]

Many readers will have seen a conflict between Heinrich's claim to personal uniqueness—he is *eine*, and a rare poet—and his sense of solidarity with the audience. This is an important theme in Heinrich's poetry, and will be discussed later.

The Lyric's "Two Spaces"

The relationship between the poet and his audience is the subject of an interesting study by Wolfgang Mohr, "Minnesang als Gesellschaftskunst."[12] He is particularly attentive to the "Wechselspiel von Sänger und Hörer," the poet's alternation between distance and immediacy as he presents himself to the audience. He writes a little "Geschichte der mittelalterlichen deutschen Liebeslyrik" from the standpoint of this alternation.

The very earliest lyrics dramatize an explicit experience. The poet (for example, Der von Kurenberg or the authors of the "namenlose Lieder" in *MF*) does not speak in his own name; instead, he presents concise epitomizing life-situations,

[11] One cannot say anything definite about the final strophe because of the completely senseless readings in the manuscripts. See *MU*, pp. 25ff, and Grünanger, pp. 61ff. Much can be said in favor of von K.'s reconstruction of the text, as it is given here. For this lyric has nothing to do with the difference between "l'amore-gioia" and "l'amore-*trûren*," as Grünanger holds. The distinction on which the whole lyric rests is between those who may speak and those who may not; that is, between the behavior forced on the poet by social conditions, and that urged by his true feelings. Now this is precisely the difference between *Minne* (inseparable from the concept of courtly behavior) and *liebe* (a purely personal condition). See Herbert Kolb, *Der Begriff der Minne und das Entstehen der höfischen Lyrik* (Tübingen, 1958), pp. 38–41.

[12] First printed in *Der Deutschunterricht*, VI (1954); reprinted in *Der deutsche Minnesang*, ed. Hans Fromm (Darmstadt, 1961), to which the page numbers here refer. What follows is mostly a summary and sometimes a direct translation of pp. 214–228 of the article.

only rarely framed by formal narrative: the knight and the lady speak to us out of their situation, in fixed rôles, remaining always in the scene and seeking no contact with the audience.

With Fridrich von Hûsen and his followers there is a different sort of objectivity. The poet presents a pattern of thoughts and feelings in his own name, in the form of a monologue; the lyric comes forth in the guise of a personal experience, sung as though out of an inner necessity and as a model for the noble society who hears it. That society is therefore implied as being always present, but it is never explicitly addressed, and neither is the lady herself. Every lyric is a solo performance, a reflection upon what at least appears actually to have been experienced by the poet. The first and third personal pronouns, the "I" and the "she," predominate; "we," "you," "thou" are excluded. This distance results in the objectification of inner personal experience, which is neither enacted nor responded to in the present (in contrast to the work of the earliest poets). For what appears to be purely personal to the poet is really a paragon of the love-experience of every courtly man. Those who practice this art before a noble audience appear not as professionals but as amateurs.

But the next generation begins to play with breaking the barrier between poet and audience. The art of the nobility is adopted by composing and performing *ministeriales*. The great poets now practice their art as a vocation—Heinrich von Morungen says he was *born* to sing. His whole relation to the society is different: he now appears not simply as a paragon of the courtly lover, but as an individual with specific alliances and animosities; he stands face to face with his audience. It is true that he imitates the earlier poets; Reimar scrupulously preserves the posture of Friedrich von Husen and his circle: neither the society nor the lady is addressed directly. Nevertheless, the distance from the audience is diminished: the poet comes to specific terms with his audience, takes up an attitude toward them, individualizes them into friend, enemy, helper, and so forth.

And with Heinrich all the inherited forms fall away. He can, says Mohr, cross over the limits because there is the understanding between him and the audience that what he says is a play of fantasy, not reality. In other words, there is no danger that his song will be misconstrued as autobiography. It is a kind of play, and in play the poet has much more freedom.

I cannot accept Mohr's assertion that the poet's song is taken entirely as fantasy or play, for the social value of his song is precisely that the experience it recounts comes forth as a validation of the courtly ideal by "one of us." What really protects the poet from the danger that his song will be misunderstood as literal autobiography is the situation in which the song is performed: the singer takes on the double identity we have already noted; he is "the man we know" and "The Courtly Man" at the same time, so that the lyric is heard not as a "fantasy" but as the universal form of every particular experience. But with this one reservation, Mohr's study is truly illuminating, and we shall take it up again.

The awareness of the audience is also a grave stricture. What if the poet has things to say that cast doubt on the validity of courtly love? Such a predicament challenges both the poet's tact and his integrity. He cannot deny that he doubts the truthfulness of this enormous fiction; yet as a courtier he cannot fail to believe in its moral rewards. His standing as a courtly poet prevents his complete isolation from his class, but his doubt prevents his complete identification with it.

137, 27   Obe ich dir vor allen wîben guotes gan
          sol ich des engelten, frouwe, wider dich,
          stê daz dîner güete sêliclîchen an,
   30   sô lâz iemer in den ungenâden mich.   I
          habe ich dar an missetân, / diu schulde rich,
          daz ich lieber liep zer werlte nie gewan:
          nâch der liebe sent iedoch mîn herze sich.

Heinrich von Morungen

Obe ich iemer âne hôhgemüete bin,
35 waz ist ieman in der werlte deste baz?
gênt mir mîne tage mit ungemüete hin,
die nach fröiden ringent, den gewirret daz.   II
indes wirt mîn ungewin / der valschen haz.
138, 1 die verkêrent underwîlent mir den sin.
nieman solde nîden, erne wiste waz.

Frouwe, ob du mir niht die werlt erleiden wil,
sô rât unde hilf: mir ist ze lange wê;
5 sît si jêen ez sî niht ein kinde spil,
dem ein wîp sô nâhen an sîn herze gê.   III
ich erkande mâze vil / der sorgen ê:
disiu sorge gêt mir für der mâze zil,
hiute baz und aber dan über morgen mê.

10 Ich hân ir vil grôzer dinge her verjên,
herzeclîcher minne und ganzer stêtekeit.
des half mir diu rehte herzeliebe spên.
wol mich, habe ich al der werlte wâr geseit.   IV
habe ich dar an missesên, / daz ist mir leit.
15 mir mac elliu sêlde noch von ir geschên:
in weiz niht waz schœner lîp in herzen treit.

(If it befits your nobility that I must make amends to you for
wishing you well before all other women, then let me forever
remain without grace. If in this I have done a misdeed, then
punish this sin: that I have never in this world won a dear love.
Yet my heart still longs for love.

If I am always without joy, how is anyone in the world so much
the better? If my days pass away in sadness, it will distress those
who strive for joy. And so my misfortunes will arouse the hatred
of the false ones, who everywhere turn back my desires. No one
should envy what he does not know.

Lady, if you do not wish to make the world painful to me, then
give me counsel and help: my grief has lasted too long. For they

120

say it is no child's play for a man when a woman has gone so deep into his heart. I have previously known a great measure of cares: but this care goes over the limit of measure, today more, and ever again more tomorrow.

I have affirmed very great things of her so far, heartfelt love and total constancy. True heart's love helped me to see these things. Happy am I if I have spoken truly to all the world. But if I have seen mistakenly in this, it causes me grief. I may yet receive every kind of bliss from her: I do not know what such a beautiful figure bears in her heart.)

The first strophe is addressed directly to the lady. If, according to her moral obligations as a noble lady, he deserves punishment for loving her alone, then let him remain forever without any favor. The implication in the appeal to her *güete,* the ethical aspect of her nobility, is reinforced in the adverb *sêliclîchen.* At stake now is not only the poet's happiness but the moral condition of the lady: does her *güete* really exist? For if service is the essential act of the knight, then *lôn,* requital, is the corresponding act of the lady, as it makes her quality visible.

Thus we find Heinrich in his characteristic mood, denying and affirming all at once, and trying to discern the invisible. In the *Abgesang* he resolves his uncertainty regarding the lady: if he has done wrong in loving her and not being loved in return, then let her punish this "guilt"—and even then his heart will remain steadfast. And so he demonstrates his own worth.

The second strophe begins with the same *obe*-construction as the first, but it cannot be directed to the lady. It speaks of "those who strive for joy," and of "the false ones"—in other words, of the entire courtly society in which the lyric takes place. Here again we recognize the poet's double consciousness; and now we must both review and develop somewhat further what we have seen concerning the poet and his audience.[13]

One can speak of the "two spaces" of the medieval lyric. The first is the space defined by the lyric itself, the poetic space across which the lady's image bounds into the eyes of the courtly lover; in this space the poet expresses his adulation and his complaint, his offerings to the lady's perfection and his doubt regarding the reality of that perfection. In other words, it is the space defined by the *Minne*-relation itself, the measure of separation that spurs the man to resemble the ideals embodied in her, and thus to narrow the distance between them; this space inspires him, even as it threatens to destroy him.

But apart from the "space" which the lyric defines, there is another which it occupies as an event, an act of singing before a known audience whose values and requirements the poet always remembers. The courtly singer is therefore required to look in two directions at once; and this alternation of consciousness is revealed in our present lyric by the arrangement of the strophes, the first and third being appeals addressed directly to the lady, the second and fourth "objective" meditations performed with the following essential thought: *wol mich, habe ich al der werlte wâr geseit.* This second strophe is sung entirely in the second "space" by the poet in his aspect as Minnesänger, as a courtly man in the service of a clearly defined society; while in the first strophe the poet sings in the rôle of an ideal courtly lover.

Even though this matter of the two spaces is simply a construct, it can help us to see how the medieval lyric differs from the poetry of other ages. It was, as in no other age, socially determined:

[13] For some suggestions in the discussion that follows, I am indebted to S. L. Bethell's *Shakespeare and the Popular Dramatic Tradition* (London, 1944).

The topic of the audience for the courtly romance and lyric has been much discussed, not always realistically. Certain facts are clear and can be simply restated. The more settled conditions of life in the twelfth century, particularly in southern France, produced, for the first time since the Roman Empire, a relatively leisured, wealthy, and cultivated audience for literature. This class was, of course, the aristocracy of the day, educated by chaplains or clerics but not influenced to any large degree by the stricter moral standards of the church. . . .

What is important is that there were enough people in the audience who could appreciate the artist's use of an idealized world and new standards of knightly conduct to make it possible for him to write. The same is true of the love lyric. Only a highly sophisticated audience could appreciate it and that audience must have been there. . . .

The writers of the courtly romance wished to use the idealized world they created to set before their audience a new standard of values which could act as a model for behavior. . . .

In the small groups which formed the audience for courtly poetry, writer and audience were very close. The ideas of the audience could be shaped by the artist, but he in his own turn was personally affected by their reaction and bound to follow their needs. His heroes were forced to behave in the patterns with which they were familiar and which they expected. It is clear that the widening of this audience or a lowering of its standards could have a bad effect on literature. . . .[14]

As an event, the lyric takes place in "the world," as Heinrich calls it, the special class to which the poet himself belongs. Before this world he takes on the rôle of the lover longing for the grace of a Lady unnamed and unnamable, yet well known. He becomes, in a sense, a different person from what he was before the song, and this new posture lasts as long as the lyric and would be inconceivable apart from it. Thus the

[14] W. T. H. Jackson, *The Literature of the Middle Ages*, pp. 57f. Cf. Schwietering, "Liederzyklus," pp. 72ff.

whole situation in which the song takes place is essentially theatrical; the audience is called on to make believe that one of its own is, for a while, somebody else. This "new person" exists only to enact the fictional relationship described in the lyric, and it is this relationship that marks out the "inner space," the little world of the lyric, in which the singer is usually the only visible inhabitant. But as such he is insulated from the audience that surrounds him and that knows him in another life. The instant the song begins, a theatrical space encloses him, and he is, like all actors onstage, unapproachable, uninterruptible, without a past, without a future. He is the Courtly Man, and his theater is the lyric; its dimensions coincide with the space that separates him from the Ideal Lady.

That lady, like the poet, must occupy two spaces at once. Her beauty and virtue are immediately visible and universally acknowledged; for it is through no faulty perception that the poet loves her. "She is well known for every honor," the poet says, "for fair deportment, for joy with decorum, so that her praise resounds throughout the whole nation, and her splendor fills all the world, and everyone calls her the crown of all women." [15] In serving her, the courtly man proclaims his allegiance to the ideals of his class and confirms his knighthood. Thus she has a double value for him: she is the clarifying and present form of what he wants to become, the reflection of his future life; and at the same time she is the mirror of his class. Every aspect of the courtier's life is therefore united in his service to "the good one." The personal *Minne*-relation is also a social fact: his service to her consists in the acts that define courtliness.[16]

And so the distinction between the "two spaces" requires considerable modification. For the poet never ceases to be "the

[15] Heinrich, "Sist zallen êren," *MF*, 122, 1–123, 9.
[16] Cf. Wolfgang Mohr's discussion of Walther, which gives a fine demonstration of these points: "Minnesang als Gesellschaftskunst," pp. 211–214.

man we know." At the moment he takes on a rôle, he is also the man who takes that rôle: he is both impersonator and impersonation, and with that double consciousness he pronounces every word. Service informs his life and justifies his claim to the public title of knight; that service is dramatized in the "theatrical space," but it is performed in the real space as the song is performed, for the song *is* his service. This double consciousness reflects the double nature of the lyric: it defines, on the one hand, the private aspirations of the singer, and on the other the public image of the courtly class.

For this reason, the relation between singer and audience is reversible. Not only is the singer a courtly man taking on the rôle of the ideal knight; at the same time he may be seen as the paragon who is recognized as one of us. The instant the lyric poet says *ich*, he becomes an ambiguous figure. For while the lyric is presented as a fiction, the name and figure of its hero are identical with those of the singer. This, as Mohr observes, is a hazard for the poet, for should the double-consciousness of the audience falter, his lyric will be heard as simple autobiography.[17] But the social advantages of this ambiguity are great. The courtly code requires the test and sanction of experience, for only so can the ideal be distinguished from a mere fantasy. And it is only in the lyric, where the poet is a part of the society to whom he relates the events of his service, that the sanctioning experience comes forth and the ideal is shown to accommodate the facts of courtly life. The service performed by the courtly lyric is to bring together the distinguishing ideal of the courtly class and the experience of one member of that class, in such a way that the ideal is authorized by experience, and experience is informed by the ideal. The song is a social necessity, a proof of the validity of the courtly ethic. That is why the whole society participates in the love-suit of

---

[17] Mohr, pp. 197ff.

the poet as soon as he shows *hôher muot:* all its members want the experience to end in joy, from the moment the exalted disposition of the lover attests to the validity of the chivalric code.

But what we have so far seen as a harmony between two objects of consciousness—as a neat coincidence of two spaces—is at the same time really a conflict. The poet stands before his class under the obligation to tell them what they want to hear—and to suppress what they do not want to hear. This is practically an obligation to falsify. The poet may doubt the reality of the perfections he extols in the lady. He may doubt the adequacy of the chivalric code to the real experience of courtly life. But there is one reality he cannot doubt, the reality of his grief. Yet it is precisely this grief that isolates him from his society and makes him the object of the slanderers' mockery. The courtly poet is therefore torn between the demands of his public image and the reality of his private sorrow.

He can never forget his audience, his peers, the *werlt* that appears explicitly in each strophe of the present lyric. Before them, the doubtfulness of his experience is a difficult, even a dangerous secret to bear. If he casts doubt on the lady's ideality, he destroys the basis of all service, of all the moral aspirations that justify this "world." But if he can validate this experience, he validates his class—"Happy am I, if I have spoken truly to all the world."

One final word about the poet and his audience: It makes no difference whether the song, on any particular occasion, was performed by the knight himself or by one of his *Spielleute.* The song was the knight's mark, and it was by the song that he identified himself: *"in weiz wer dâ sanc / 'ein sitich unde ein star . . .' "* [18] The *persona* who presented the song had the same ambiguous identity, the double figure of the

[18] Cf. Heinrich's "Solde ich iemer / frouwen leit," *MF* 140, 11–31.

Courtly Man and the man we know. When Heinrich referred to his earlier songs, he knew he could expect the immediate recognition of his particular audience. The performance of the song by another singer might still further multiply the consciousness of the listeners, requiring them to see in the performer the figure of the poet they knew, but it would not change the manifold relations between the poet and his audience.

Returning now to the second strophe, we find the poet asking, "What good would it do anyone in the world if I must remain without joy?" As we have seen, this question is not addressed primarily to the lady. It considers the effect of the poet's rejection upon the society in which the song takes place—the whole society, both the true lovers and the crabbed slanderers.

In the second strophe [writes Carl von Kraus] the poet treats of the dilemma into which he is brought by his vocation as a poet and by his love grief. If he should remain silent because of his grief (for the song is born only from joy), it would be a loss to all who strive for joy. But if despite his grief he sings lyrics, it will be misconstrued by the false ones, since they doubt the sincerity of this grief.   [*MA*, p. 99]

In his concern for "those who strive for joy," the poet is thinking of the social consequences of his misfortune. No one would benefit from his sorrow, but it would do great harm to all the other knights devoted to the chivalric ideal. Why would they be harmed? For one thing, because, as von Kraus says, they would suffer the loss of the poet's song. But that would only be the result of a greater damage: they would be set back by the *exemplum* of the poet's career. They would see this life of devotion ending, not in grace, but in grief and the moral obliteration of knighthood.

If the listeners suffer because they are deprived of the song, this must mean, as von Kraus makes clear, that the song they crave originates in and affirms the joy of the *Minne*-relation. Yet if that song is to be forthcoming, it must deny the fact of the singer's grief and thereby make Heinrich the victim of the false ones who pervert the meaning of his songs and indict his sincerity.

There is more to the poet's dilemma, however. We have seen that the first strophe already implies the fear that is to be made explicit in the last: *habe ich dar an missesên, daz ist mir leit.* The worst social consequence of Heinrich's *ungewin* is precisely this doubt as to the reality of the lady's grace and perfection. Now the hatred of "the false ones" will be aroused, for they are envious. They do not know what it is they begrudge him, because they themselves must be without it. They are thus explicitly distinguished from "those who strive for joy": *nieman solde nîden, erne wiste waz.* They are the ones who have never committed themselves to the regimen of courtly love; they are excluded by nature from the *Minne*-relation and are ignorant of its ethical results, and in their total ignorance they envy the *vrowenritter*, the man who has dedicated himself in service to a lady, and to all ladies. They are the un-knights, the ones who mock and disbelieve; yet their hypocrisy is betrayed in their envy. They point out the poet's distress and hold it up as evidence that the *Minne*-relation is nothing but pointless suffering and self-destruction. For this reason the lady must show grace to the poet before the world, for otherwise there is nothing to disarm *die schimpfere, die falschen. Rât unde hilf,* the poet calls to her: not for myself but for the world that follows the course of my devotion and service to you, give me counsel and help.

Thus when, in the third strophe, the poet turns back to the lady and addresses her directly, his appeal is based on the social consequences he has just defined. "For they say that it is no child's play for a man when a woman has such power over his heart": *they* are the ones who would be hurt by the continued misfortune of the poet, the ones who observe his experience as a paragon of the courtly life. This is not to say that the poet does not plead for himself—he does. But by the lyric's very form, this personal appeal is inseparable from his awareness that his own love experience is the chief way in which his society expresses itself. This personal appeal continues in the *Abgesang*, but once again it is reinforced by an objective social doctrine; this suffering goes beyond the limits of *mâze*, one of the cardinal virtues of the courtly life, and one formally designated by that term; her behavior ignores the courtly forms and threatens to eradicate them.

He will rejoice, he says at the end, if it turns out that he has spoken the truth to all the world when he told everyone of her heartfelt *Minne* and real concern. Here is the whole statement of the lady's nobility and its universal significance, of the knight's service, his offerings of song. By this service he hopes to attain, not his "wages," but her grace. It is in her *genâde* that he sees the chances for his own salvation.

The posture of the true lover is so familiar that we have come to accept it as the hallmark of medieval culture. A seal attributed to the *trouvère* Conon de Bethune (1150–c. 1220), for example, represents it perfectly. This depicts, in an oval cartouche, an armed knight on his knees before a lady. His body is shrouded in a mail hauberk. His head is completely concealed in his helmet. He wears spurs but no sword. The lady stands at arm's length, chastely robed, her regular nondescript features framed in long braids, presumably blonde, and between her outstretched palms the knight's hands are placed in the formal gesture of homage. Within the cartouche, in the space above the helmet of the kneeling knight is inscribed the single word: *Merci*.

The entire concept of *fin amor* is implicit in this image. The relation of the knight and the lady is obvious. As for the motto, if we could digest the entire corpus of love-poetry into a single word, the word would be *merci*.[19]

[19] Maurice Valency, *In Praise of Love* (New York, 1958), p. 145. Cf. Kolb, p. 42.

Heinrich von Morungen

To compare the *Minne*-relation with the feudal relation has long been a commonplace: the lover stands before his lady like the "man" before his lord, with mutual obligations of service and requital (*dienst* and *lôn*). However revealing this commonplace is, it requires great care in the application. The principle of the feudal relation is the contract; and the crucial assumption of the contract is that the value of a defined service can be, and ought to be, equaled by a defined recompense. But there are many relations in which such a principle would be blasphemous or degrading; when Milton asks, "Doth God exact day labor?" he reminds us of one. It is also out of place in the *Minne*-relation. The knight does not, cannot, serve for wages. He cannot oblige the lady to love him or to give him the least sign of favor; if he did, that would be a cynical denigration of the lady's worth, and would make something meretricious of his service.

His devotion to her is a secular counterpart of a religious service, an offering, an observance. In her ideality she is not wholly contained in either of the "two spaces"; for these are available, but she is beyond us, like a future that is deeply concerned. Now we are uncertain and incapable, but *then* . . . She has the dignifying and heartbreaking reality of a promise. That is her permanent value. The knight does not look to win her. His hope is his renunciation.

For she is defined by her unattainability, she is a victory too great to be won. His only triumph is to make an observance of his devotion. All of his acts, therefore, take on the nature of a sacrament, a formal celebration of love, without hope of reward. This celebration is the substance of his knighthood, and for the knightly poet the song is his sacrament.[20]

It can "earn" him nothing, for it cannot make him worthy now of what is perpetually in the future. But in this service he dignifies his life by formalizing its essential aspiration. His

[20] See the beautiful article by Hugo Kuhn, "Zur inneren Form des Minnesangs," in *Der deutsche Minnesang*, ed. Hans Fromm (Darmstadt, 1961), pp. 167–179.

service assumes nothing except the grace of its object. But the communal nature of a sacrament gives an additional meaning to his song: in the singing of her praise he expresses the unifying doctrine of his class.

Therefore, the knight can never constrain the lady by his service. Rather, the lady is constrained by her own nature. For it is of the essence of grace that, first of all, it cannot be earned; and secondly, insofar as it is a secular virtue, it cannot be refused to the genuine supplicant, who proves his genuineness in service without the thought of wages. The *ungenâde* of the lady can have only two causes: either there is a flaw in the knight's service, or there is no grace in her. But the song begins with an affirmation of the steadfastness of Heinrich's service. So the whole utterance comes down to the question whether the virtues that have been attributed to her, the *vil grôzer dinge*, do in fact exist.

It is just this question that the poet faces in the last strophe. He is explicit about the basis of his doubt: *des half mir diu rehte herzeliebe spên*. It was the love in his own heart that enabled him to see the virtues in hers. But now a chasm yawns at his feet. This heart's love—what was its object? It was just those virtues, the *herzeclîcher minne und ganzer stêtekeit*. The love he already bore for the lady revealed to him the virtues within her—which aroused his love to begin with. This instinctual begging of the question is full of peril. It could be that, impelled by love, he came to know its object. On the other hand, he could have "mis-seen." It could have been Virtue itself that he loved and wrongly attributed to the lady. And so he says, "*wol mich, habe ich al der werlte wâr geseit.*" If he has been correct in the things he has told his audience, then he may rejoice; for the lady in her grace will not withhold some sign of recognition; she will not abandon him to an endless search, nor fail to reflect some assurance of his standing and worth.

However, *habe ich dar an missesên, daz ist mir leit.* The courtly poet is never free of this possibility. The danger he faces is more than personal, for the moral basis of the noble class would become an empty mockery. *Minne* is the love of an idealized image whose status is uncertain, the love of a mirror in all its ambivalence:

> in weiz niht was schoener lîp in herzen treit.

The Poet's Isolation

The poet is always conscious of the audience's participation in his experience. It is because of this participation that his relation with the lady is a *Minne*-relation. The universal esteem in which she is held becomes a force for the solidarity of the class, and the universal belief in her perfection becomes a form of allegiance.

But this same experience isolates him from the audience even as it unites him with it. The social value of his song lies in its confirmation of the lady's fame through the poet's experience, but the reality of that experience casts doubt upon the basis of her fame.

This alternation between faith and doubt runs parallel to the poet's union with, and isolation from, his audience; and the conflict is intensified by his continual awareness of the courtly poet's function.

His further awareness of a difference between the real lady and her adored image was entirely unexpected, as a like experience was for Narcissus, in the moment when the poet dedicated himself to her service, but it was forced on him by the *Minne*-experience. If the appearance of the image falsifies the reality of the lady, then the moral structure of the knight's life is imperiled: he has been in the service of an illusion, and there is a pejorative reflex upon the meaning of all his acts. The pain of this recognition is intensified by its social resonance: the whole courtly class is depicted as participating in that illusion.

His grief is caused by the lady's irrelevance to the image that he and all the others esteem. Soon he will be forced to conceal that grief and assume the appearance of joy—the grieving man is anti-Eros in the fiction of courtly love. The audience's interest is strictly limited: it will sympathize with his discomfort, it will applaud his gentle stratagems, but it will despise his doubt.

His great hope and his last illusion are that the audience will join him in his anguish.

138, 17   Ich wêne nieman lebe der mînen kumber weine,
          den ich eine trage,
          ez entuo diu guote, diech mit triuwen meine,
20   vernimt si mîne klage.   I
          wê wie tuon ich sô, daz ich sô herzeclîche
          bin an si verdâht, daz ich ein künicrîche
          für ir minne niht ennemen wolde,
          obe ich teilen unde welen solde?

139, 3   Dô si mir alrêrst ein hôhgemüete sande
          in daz herze mîn,
5   des was bote ir güete, die ich wol erkande,
          und ir liehter schîn.   II
          si sach mich güetlîch ane mit ir spilnden ougen;
          lachen si began ûz rôtem munde tougen.
          sâ zehant enzunte sich mîn wunne,
10   daz mîn muot stuont hô alsam diu sunne.

138, 25   Swer mir des erban, ob ich si minne tougen,
          sêt, der sündet sich.
          swenne ich eine bin, si schînt mir vor den ougen.
          sô bedunket mich   III
          wie si gê dort her ze mir aldur die mûren.
30   ir red und ir trôst enlâzent mich niet trûren.
          swenn si wil, sô füeret si mich hinnen
          mit ir wîzen hant hô über die zinnen.

          Ich wêne, sist ein Vênus hêre, diech dâ minne:
          wan si kan sô vil.

35 si benimt mir leide, fröide und al die sinne.

swenne sô si wil,   IV
sô gêt si dort her zuo einem vensterlîne,
unde siht mich an reht als der sunnen schîne:

139, 1 swanne ich si dan gerne wolde schouwen,
ach, sô gêt si dort zuo andern frouwen.

11 Wê waz rede ich? jâ ist mîn geloube bœse
und ist wider got.
wan bit ich in des daz er mich hinnen lœse?
ich was ie ir spot.   v

15 ich tuon sam der swan, der singet swenne er stirbet.
waz ob mir mîn sanc daz lîhte noch erwirbet,
swâ man mînen kumber sagt ze mêre,
daz man mir erbunne mîner swêre?

(I imagine that no one lives who would weep for my grief, which I bear alone, unless *diu guote*, whom I love faithfully, should do so; that is, if she hears my lament. Alas, how have I come to such a state where I with all my heart am so lost in thought of her that I would not exchange a kingdom for her love, if I should [ever have the occasion to] divide and choose?

When she first sent a joyful mood into my heart, her goodness, which I clearly recognized, was the bearer of it, and her bright splendor. She looked graciously upon me with her sparkling eyes; and then she smiled secretly with her red mouth. Instantly my joy was enkindled, so that my disposition rose as high as the sun.

Whoever begrudges me this, that I love her secretly—behold, he does great wrong. Whenever I am alone, she appears to me before my eyes. Then it seems to me she goes there through the walls here to me. Her words and her solace do not let me grieve. Whenever she wishes, she then leads me away from here, with her white hand, high over the battlements.

I imagine she is a noble Venus whom I love there; for she is able to do so much. She takes from me my pain, my joy, and all my senses. Whenever she so wishes, then she comes hither to a little window there, and looks down upon me like the splendor of the sun: every time I would then most willingly gaze upon her, ach, then she goes away to other women there.

Alas, what am I saying? Indeed, this belief of mine is despicable and against God. Why do I not pray to Him that He deliver me away from here? I was always the butt of her scorn, her laughingstock. I do as the swan does, who sings when he is about to die. What if my song perhaps should still gain me this, that wherever they tell the news of my grief, they envy me my pain?)

In the first strophe the poet believes that he must bear his grief alone, unless the lady should hear his cry and pity him. In other words, insofar as there is a complaint, its subject is not his grief (whose cause we expect to discover in the course of the lyric), but his loneliness, his having to grieve in complete solitude; and his hope is not explicitly that this grief may end but that the beloved may witness it and share it—with the implication that in doing so she would indeed cure his *kumber*. Here, then, the poet voices his wish to be free from isolation, for his grief sets him apart.[21]

In the *Abgesang* it is as though he had awakened from this solitude to find he had been *verdâht*, lost in thought of her; it is not the lady herself he has been contemplating, since he is alone, but the image of her that he carries in his heart. The poet asks, How have I come to this state, for I am so deep in thought of her that I would not exchange a kingdom for her *Minne?* Solitude is thus his usual condition, and suddenly it makes him wonder: he has been alone so much in the contemplation of her image that his whole disposition has become fixed upon it.

In this new consciousness of his isolation, he looks to the

---

[21] Cf. Helmut de Boor on this lyric in *Die deutsche Lyrik,* ed. Benno von Wiese, I (Düsseldorf, 1956), 45: "Die erste Strophenhälfte zeichnet die Grundsituation der Minne: sie löst das minnende 'Ich' aus der Gemeinschaft. . . ."

past for its cause.[22] Once, the lady's goodness, which he clearly recognized, came as a messenger to bring him *hôhgemüete*, a joyful mood. That messenger was the smiling image of virtue and nobility; the joy that was potential in his heart was activated by that *bote*, the lady's image perceived as a portrait of the ideal.[23] In that moment the quality within him found the image of its fulfillment, and he knew immediately what he ought to resemble and how he might be judged. Now he remembers that his present painful isolation began in joy. She smiled graciously upon him, she laughed with her red mouth in secret, as the "messenger" flew to his heart. That kindly look, that discreet smile—they were fraught with promise. His joy was aroused by a vision of being loved by the ideal. The "message" was that he would gain salvation upon earth.

Tougen: secretly she smiled at him that time, and "whoever resents my loving her secretly—behold, such a one does wrong." The secret has persisted, a triangle between him, and her, and her image. But in the third strophe we are no longer in the past. The poet has come back to the very condition of solitude that he lamented in the beginning, isolated by the incomprehension of all the others.[24]

Once again, he is *verdaht*. "Whenever I am alone, she appears before my eyes, and I think I see how she comes through the walls here to me." As in the first strophe, he is alone with the image of the lady; as in the second, the image "comes to him" to forestall his grief and to cause his disposition to soar. With her white hand she leads him high over the battlements of the court, above the castle, above the audience.

At what point in time are we now?

---

[22] Cf. *MU*, p. 42; Schwietering, "Liederzyklus," p. 76f.

[23] Cf. H. de Boor, p. 45: "In the unity of inner ("*güete*") and outer beauty ("*liehter schîn*"), the perfect image of the ideal lady is drawn."

[24] Cf. H. de Boor, p. 45f.

The sweet irony of being all alone and yet in perfect unison with that consoling image is altogether different from the hopeless complaint that began the song. For this solitude is no anguish. It is an imaginary fulfillment of the singer's dearest hope, an inner amplification of the message she once sent him. Thus the present tense here must denote a kind of habitual present: this is the way it always was; but now, as we know from the first strophe, it is all quite different. Something has happened between this private fulfillment in the distant past and the public outcry with which the song began.

That something is revealed to us in the next strophe, but meanwhile it is clear that the second *tougen* means not "discreetly" like the first, but "in my imagination": to begrudge him this imaginary love is wrong, because no harm comes from the enjoyment of a fantasy. However, the singer's explicit recognition of the fantasy is the first step toward his disillusionment, and it brings doubt upon the meaning of his first encounter with the lady, that time when her "goodness" filled his heart with joy. She smiled at him then *tougen*— discreetly? or only in his imagination? Were her goodness and the consoling promise it brought him real or only his fantasy? Nothing is certain, for something has made him aware that his whole relationship with her was a lonely invention.[25] "Thus all his heavenly joy is nothing but the illusion of a solitary man" (*MA*, p. 104).

Ich wêne: this utterance of doubt [26] begins the song and sets the mood, and it is repeated in the fourth strophe when he sees her as the very goddess of Love, powerful, and generous, and full of grace. "I fancy she is the noble Venus whom I love there"—with the demonstrative *dâ* pointing backwards to the image that soared with him to heaven, and forwards to the cold but substantial lady who turns away from him. In

[25] Cf. Schwietering, p. 77.
[26] See above, p. 100, n. 28.

Strophe III the image, *swenn si wil*, came miraculously to lead him high over the battlements; in Strophe IV the lady, *swenne sô si will*, appears high up and alone, and her splendor shines down upon him like the sun. But from the instant that there is a question of *swanne ICH wolde*, of gazing upon her as he would wish, the mood is in every sense subjunctive; she goes away "to other women," she abandons him, unmindful of his love.[27] The third and fourth strophes were made to contrast with one another. The lady who denies his wish to gaze upon her, who turns away from him, cannot be the same as the image of the lady which passes through the walls to where he is, and keeps him from grieving by her words (the "message") and her consolation.

The harsh reality in the fourth strophe is a careful reversal of the fantasy in the third, and the difference to the poet is staggering. In solitude he was united with an image responsive to his desire; in "the world" he is deprived of the real lady, who turns away from him, lofty as the sun and as indifferent to his desire.

The willfulness and above all the indifference of the real lady force the poet toward a recognition like Narcissus's. He has spent all his passion (*diech mit triuwen meine*) on a mere image; and even worse, the real lady is no Dané full of love, yearning to reflect his will and become his mirror. The poet stands, like Narcissus, in the crucial moment of recognition. The final strophe presents a kind of resolution.

The poet says that his "belief" is despicable and offensive to God.

The belief in her goodness (Strophes I, II) is vain, like the hope that this song will move her to compassion (*MU*, p. 43).

The belief in Venus is not only offensive to God, it is untenable and worthless because it includes the belief in the compassion of

[27] Cf. *MA*, p. 105; Schwietering, p. 97.

the lady as Venus's earthly personification, and this belief proves
vain.   ["Liederzyklus," p. 98.]

In other words, it was his vain belief that the lady's idealized
public image (Venus) and the living lady herself were identical; that what he imagined in solitude must coincide with
what he found in the world; that another human being could
be exempted from the defects of our common humanity, and
that anyone could nominate another person as his savior.
Immediately afterward in this strophe, the indifferent lady
becomes the one who has deceived him, and it is not he who
has deceived himself—*ich was ie ir spot.* The blame is incor-
rectly attributed, however, for the lady has been as unin-
volved as the reflection in the fountain, and ultimately just as
passive.

Schwietering's interpretation of the last four lines is illuminating: the poet sings his death-song, like the swan, perhaps
with the result that others in his society will envy him now for
his pain, as they envied him earlier for his secret love; for they
may recognize that it is also pain, and not only joy, that
enables him to sing (p. 99). All the illusions of the first strophe
are destroyed. The poet's hope to be free of solitude through
the compassion of another will be fulfilled by those whom he
doubted at first, and not by the lady, as he desired.

The reference to God is an expression of total hopelessness.
For he does not say that he will turn to God and pray to be
freed from pain: rather he wonders why he does *not* do so. If
his only hope is to begin a new life in God, then he has no
hope at all; for he is a knight, a courtly man of secular
aspirations, and to turn from service means to cease to be a
knight. Aware of the insubstantiality of the image, he must
yet remain fixed upon it, like Narcissus; not God, but death
alone can free him. His life on earth must remain to the end in
despair.

For there is no hope from the lady—she is unaware. He will

have one ironic consolation as others witness the beauty of his song and are even envious of the agony it expresses. Narcissus dies, but not in isolation.[28]

In this superb lyric the poet's grief, his suffering when the lady proves to be unaware of the expectations aroused by her image, is explicitly connected to his relation with the members of his own class. He is really isolated, but *waz ob* . . . What if his grief should now gain him the universal compassion from which it has so far excluded him? What if he should now win solidarity with his class, such as he had hoped to achieve through service to a lady in whom grace really existed, even as he loses everything else?

Throughout the lyric the poet makes his solitude immediately felt. The third and fourth strophes reverberate with demonstrative adverbs, *dort, her, dâ. There* she stands above me at a window, a noble Venus; *here* I stand alone. Between her appearance there and his loneliness here stretches an immense distance, yet from the first he has sought to involve the audience in his very solitude, pointing there, pointing here. The leap of self-consciousness is acted out before them in the opening strophe, as he awakens from being *verdâht*.

Wolfgang Mohr cites this lyric in his study. Up to line 138, 27, he says, the lyric is composed entirely of reflections and memories, but suddenly everything is brought into the present:

The *swenne ich eine bin* and the *swenne so sie wil* seem to remove the fantasy-images from the present moment, and the phrase *so bedunket mich* even seems to signify a dream-image. But the demonstrative *dort her* draws the dream into the present, and with the line *ach so get si dort zuo andern vrouwen* the audience might almost look around to see with its own eyes what the singer is gazing upon. [P. 224.]

[28] On the strophic order, see *MU*, p. 42f.

The progress of disillusionment in the poem runs parallel to the progress of *Vergegenwärtigung*, of making the love-experience seem more and more present; so that when the poet is most in doubt, the audience is most involved. His despair seems to diminish his solitude; when the lady is most distant, and her true worth most suspect, the audience is most vividly drawn in. When she abandons him, he calls upon them. It seems as though the man no longer weeps alone, as he thought he would have to for the rest of his days. It seems as though he is attended by a society that is concerned, that has preserved a place for him. Though the lyric has begun as a formal, "objective" account of an experience, in the end it transcends its verbal limits to make the present audience essential to its meaning. The painted picture of the despairing lover steps out of its frame, out of its fictional "space," and enters the world of the beholders.

By the time the lyric ends, the poet is not alone; he is singing of his grief before an audience to whom he is well known, and in a song whose beauty awakens their envy and compassion.

But this picture of the courtly class united in its participation in the poet's grief is truly a fantasy. Grief is a disruptive state in a society for which *freude* equals *werdekeit:* it denies the efficacy of courtly love. *Sanc ist âne fröide kranc* (123, 37)—"A song without joy is worthless." The poet must learn to conceal his grief,[29] for it sets him against his society; his pain and disbelief are an indictment of the ideal.

Whoever lives in grief cannot participate in the cultural goal of a joyous life; such a person functions much more as a restrictive member of the courtly society. . . . If the courtly demeanor in Heinrich von Morungen arises entirely from the basis of joy, it

[29] This is the subject of Heinrich's lyric "Leitlîche blicke unde grôzlîche riuwe" (*MF*, 133, 13ff), in which the courtly poet tells of the conflict between the secret reality of his grief and the courtly requirement of a joyous demeanor.

extends beyond a merely egocentric level of pleasure; this joyous disposition is rather sanctioned as a social value.[30]

The Poet's Hope to Re-create the Image

The exposure of the image turns the knight into a courtly Narcissus horrified at the destruction of his hopes. He is immobilized until he can restore the image as the fitting object of his service. Such an attempt to put together again the mirror he himself has broken occupies Heinrich continually, and the alternation of shattering doubt and re-creating faith determines the pattern of most of his songs.

127, 1   Wiste ich obe ez möhte wol verswigen sîn,
       ich lieze iuch sên / mîne lieben frouwen.
       der enzwei gebrêche mir daz herze mîn,
5   der möhte si / schône drinne schouwen,   I
       si kam her / dur diu ganzen ougen
       sunder tür gegangen:
10   ôwê, solte ich von ir reinen minnen sîn
       alsô werdeclîche enpfangen!

       Der sô vil geriefe in einen touben walt,
       ez antwurt ime / dar ûz eteswenne.
15   nust der schal vil dicke vor ir manicvalt
       von mîner nôt, / wils eht die bekenne.   II
       ouch klagt ir / maneger mînen kumber
20   dicke mit gesange:
       ôwê jâ hât si geslâfen allez her
       ader geswigen alze lange.

       Wêre ein sitich ader ein star, die mohten sît
25   gelernet hân / daz si sprêchen "Minne."
       ich hân ir gedienet her vil lange zît:
       mac si sich doch / mîner flê versinne?   III

[30] August Arnold, *Studien über den Hohen Mut,* Von deutscher Poeterey, IX (Leipzig, 1930), 16.

30   nein si, niht, / got well ein sîn wunder
        verre an ir erzeigen.
        jâ möht ich baz einen boum mit mîner bete
        sunder wâpen nider geneigen.

(If I knew whether it would really be kept quiet, I would let you see my beloved lady. Whoever could break my heart in two would be able to see this beautiful person there. She passed into it through my eyes, without damaging them; she entered without doors. Ah, would that I were thus honorably received by her pure love!

A man who cried out so much in a deaf forest would get an answer from there, now and then. Now my cry of distress has reached her often and in many ways, if she wanted to know of my distress at all. And many a man also complains to her of my grief often, with song. Alas, she has indeed been completely asleep till now, or remained silent all too long.

If it were a parrot or a starling, they would have long since learned how to say "*Minne*." I have served her for a long time now: can she not become aware of my supplication? No, not she, unless God would be willing to show one of his miracles to her. Indeed, I would sooner be able to bend a tree with my prayer, without any implement.)

The lyric begins with a confiding whisper to the audience: if the poet could be sure they would not tell about it, he would let them see his beloved lady. But this hint of a great offer is immediately withdrawn, for it turns out that it is not the lady he might consent to show us, but simply her image in his heart—which, after all, no one could see even if his heart *were* "broken in two."

What are we to make of this grand promise, his urgent appeal for our discretion, his "If I knew it would remain a secret"—as if it could be otherwise, as if the audience might actually see what he has locked in his heart! Later in the strophe the poet wishes that he (or his image) might be similarly received in love. Heinrich once again explicitly distinguishes between the lady and her image, for the lady who he hopes will receive him is not the same as the figure he carries in his heart. And the effect of his seeming offer to show us a beautiful lady is to emphasize all the more that he possesses nothing more than an image, insubstantial, and invisible to every eye but his.

The defining situation of a man in love with an image immediately recalls Narcissus, whom we find in the second strophe, in the moment of his crisis: "If a man cried out so much in a deaf forest, he would get an answer out of it now and then." [31] When Narcissus cries out in distress as he realizes what the beautiful figure really is, he has gauged the full horror of his plight. But the poet's plight is even worse, for he has no Echo to repeat the words he speaks. Heinrich hears nothing in response. He has nothing but that voiceless image; the "message" is not repeated.[32]

The answer he desires must come from another being—from Echo, from the lady—and here the poet is completely bereft. The lady is silent, unaware, incapable of responding to the poet's cry of despair. It would take a miracle to make her bend from her natural indifference.

The subject of this song is therefore the image, or rather the relevance of the image to the lady. The one is impotent, the other unaware. Without going further, the meaning is already clear: the great promise of courtly love must lead in the end to this lonely despair, because it relies on a false image.

[31] See Ovid, *Met.* III, 437ff; *Narcissus*, 875ff (*ed. cit.*). Karl Helm quotes this passage from Albrecht von Halberstadt: "so man laut schreit in einen walt, ist Echo hie, gibt antwort balt" (*Wickgram*, 880f), and concludes that Albrecht was influenced by this lyric of Heinrich's ("Heinrich von Morungen und Albrecht von Halberstadt," *Beiträge zur Geschichte der deutschen Sprache und Literatur*, L[1927], 143–145).

[32] There is also the proverb, "Wie man in den Wald hineinruft, schallt es wieder aus." In other words, one deserves requital. I thank W. T. H. Jackson for calling this proverb to my attention.

But Heinrich has made this characteristic statement in such a way as to reflect his own relation to the audience and the cultural background he shares with them. It is worth looking at the lyric again to see how he does so. About the second strophe Schönbach writes:

> The basic image here refers not only to the idea that one calls in vain in the woods, for which there are examples in German literature, but even more to the classical legend of the nymph Echo, which Ovid treated in *Metam.* 3, 356–399, and which, indeed, Morungen well knew as a part of the story of Narcissus. We must bear in mind that the sound and reverberation are here, as with Narcissus and Echo, made to correspond to the conversation of two lovers. . . .[33]

To the cry of Narcissus the poet compares both the public talk about his suffering (*der schal . . . von mîner nôt*), and the performance of his songs (*ouch klagt ir / maneger mînen kumber dicke mit gesange*). Once again he gives testimony to the fame of his work and his intimacy with his audience.[34]

The immediacy of the Narcissus story and the poet's specific concern with Echo's rôle lead to the imagery with which the third strophe opens: "A parrot or a starling would have long since learned to say '*Minne.*' " In the second strophe he wishes that his words were echoed; here he wishes they were parroted, another kind of "sound and reverberation," like the "lovers' dialogue" between Narcissus and Echo. By the time she repeats his last farewell, Echo has become the aural equivalent of the image he desired: she is limited in her responses to the repetition of his words, as the image was limited to the repetition of his actions.

Love brought Echo to her fate, her own will reduced her to her final state of will-lessness. But the image has no will, it is

---

[33] Anton E. Schönbach, *Beiträge zur Erklärung altdeutscher Dichtwerke* (Wien, 1899), p. 119.
[34] See von Kraus's note in *MF*, p. 456.

unreal, it was never alive. To animate it, Heinrich wants the lady to become his Echo, for then the image will become real. He wants the image to cease to be a mere reflection and to become truly identical with the real lady, truly existing, truly another, endowed with a will that desires to be defined by *his* will. For his own salvation he must preserve the integrity of her otherness: he wants her to *desire* to be his image, while retaining a separate identity.

But in reality she is "asleep." Only a miracle can fulfill his wish, the infusion of love and concern into an essentially will-less thing like a reflection, or an indifferent thing like a tree. And this miracle is to be wrought in the manner of God, *sunder wâpen*, not with hands or implements, but with *mîner bete*, with thought and word alone.

And now we must look at the allusions in this lyric, and particularly at the pattern in which they occur.

Schönbach among many others has noted that the first strophe is "a pretty daring play with the religious representation of the Virgin Birth." [35] The root idea is that the image is received through the eyes and into the heart without any damage to the body (*dur diu ganzen ougen sunder tür*).[36]

The second allusion (Strophe II), as we have seen, is to the story of Narcissus.

The third allusion, which has also been frequently noted, is to the story first recounted in the apocryphal gospel of the Pseudo-Matthew, where the infant Jesus commands the palm

---

[35] *Beiträge*, p. 118f; see also the notes in *MF*.

[36] That is why in art, a mirror, which receives light, and a window or a transparent carafe, which allows light to pass without breaking, are frequent symbols of the Virgin. See Erwin Panofsky, *Early Netherlandish Painting* (Cambridge, Mass., 1953), pp. 142ff; Heinrich Schwarz, "The Mirror in Art," *The Art Quarterly*, XV (1952), 97–118, and the same author's "The Mirror of the Artist and the Mirror of the Devout," *Studies in the History of Art dedicated to William E. Suida* (London, 1959), pp. 90–105, which gives a full bibliography.

tree to bend down in order that his mother may taste of its fruits.

Then the child Jesus, with a joyful countenance, reposing in the bosom of His mother, said to the palm: O tree, bend thy branches, and refresh my mother with thy fruit. And immediately at these words the palm bent its top down to the very feet of the blessed Mary; and they gathered from it fruit, with which they were all refreshed. And after they had gathered all its fruit, it remained bent down, waiting the order to rise from Him who had commanded it to stoop. Then Jesus said to it: Raise thyself, O palm tree, and be strong, and be the companion of my trees, which are in the paradise of my Father; and open from thy roots a vein of water which has been hid in the earth, and let the waters flow, so that we may be satisfied from thee. And it rose up immediately, and at its root there began to come forth a spring of water exceedingly clear and cool and sparkling. And when they saw the spring of water, they rejoiced with great joy, and were satisfied, themselves and all their cattle and their beasts. Wherefor they gave thanks to God.[37]

We have no idea what version of the story Heinrich knew, since it was one of the most widespread legends in the Middle Ages. But the main elements of the story are constant.

These are the principal allusions, in the order in which the poet has arranged them.

With this order in mind, the point of the reference to Mary becomes clear: the Imago, the Verbum, is received by Mary and becomes flesh, becomes "real" in a secular sense, reappears in the Nativity as a living person who will be our guide and savior.[38] And the poet makes this allusion in order to stress the difference in his own situation. For the image in the poet's

---

[37] Pseudo-Matthew xx, 2; translation from *The Ante-Nicene Fathers*, VIII (New York, 1895), 377.

[38] Schönbach translates line 127, 10f, "Ach, wäre ich doch von ihrer reinen Minne so mit herrlicher Ehre *befruchtet worden!*" That is going too far, but it is a response to the point of the allusion.

heart is sterile. It cannot save him or care for him; the good news it bore was nothing but an echo of his own desire. It cannot become flesh; indeed, it is explicitly distinguished from the living lady who "sleeps," indifferent to his cry of distress. The allusion reinforces what the poet shows us in the beginning: he possesses nothing but an image, and the image is almost nothing.

In the second strophe, the sterility of the image evokes Narcissus. Between the figures of Narcissus and the Virgin the poet's "distress" is fully defined, the danger of his enthrallment to an unreal image, and his only hope of making the image become real. The poet pins all his hopes on the lady's willingness to comport herself as an image, on her echoing and parroting him; for this is how he, in his own way, can transform the image into a living person. He cannot work as God works: he cannot bring the image to will itself into flesh. But he can hope for the opposite, that the lady will take upon herself the qualities, the passive ideality, of her image in his heart. He wants the real lady—distant, silent, unconcerned—to turn at his bidding toward him and fulfill his need and save him.

But this cannot be, for the simple reason that the lady does not hear him. Worse than unconcerned, she is "asleep," insensate; she is incapable not only of responding but of *versinnen*, of becoming aware. With the image that glows in his heart, he suffers from the cruelty of her irrelevance.

All this leads up to the final allusion, to the inclining palm tree—and the confirmation of the poet's despair. For only God can work this miracle: the poet can neither make the image real, nor transform that which is insensate into a creature obedient to his will.

In her irrelevance and unconcern the lady truly has the nature of a mirror. She will reflect anything, even the image of his perfected identity, but she can never know what she reflects. She can have no notion of the service the courtly man has dedicated to that image. She is here, in her relation to him, degraded to the level of matter, passive and unconscious, indiscriminate as to the forms it will adopt.

All this he realizes. His consciousness stands in great contrast to her "sleep." Yet he is all the more like Narcissus in that he cannot break his ties to the mirror. Without the judicial image he sees there, his life cannot be informed by service, it will disintegrate into a succession of accidents, and the moral fiction of the beautiful Lady—the one he offered to show his audience—will be exposed as a lie.

Therefore, the poet never goes further than to reveal his doubt. He will tell all about the lady's failure to recognize his service, about his grief, his isolation, his dangerous illusions, his despair—about all that he has suffered from the shock of experience in the confrontation between public ideals and private realities. Yet it is precisely from experience that he takes up the vow again, and reinvests the image in its ideal attributes; for he will not deform his life, nor obliterate the quality of his class. Just when his doubt is most intense, when he must choose between renouncing the image as worthless and reaffirming its value, he takes his stand: *iedoch diene ich, swiez ergê.*[39]

This renewed vow to serve the lady is not taken in blind

[39] "And yet I serve, no matter how it goes." From "Ez ist site der nahtegal" (*MF* 127, 34ff), a lyric that fully treats the theme under discussion here. Similar in theme to the lyric just studied is Heinrich's "Hete ich tugende niht sô vil von ir vernomen" (*MF* 124, 32ff), except that here the regenerated image is his own. The lady's beauty causes a universal belief in her virtue, and the poet looks at her as the moon "looks at" the sun. She is the cause of his visibleness, of his public identity as a courtly man. But often she refuses him even a glance; in the forced contemplation of her image, now exposed as distinct from the lady, he wishes he had destroyed himself instead of receiving "her" into his heart; her light is not certain, it fails to appear, and then he is like the moon in another way, dark, undefined (cf. *MU*, p. 9). He will bequeath this distress to his son, who will become so handsome that to see him only rarely will break her heart. The son, like the image, is his future identity.

and untested faith, but in the aftermath of a comprehensive doubt; it is renewed in an "even so" mood. This doubt becomes, in its own way, a precious thing, a protection from the naïve faith that disarmed Narcissus. The poet cultivates doubt as a test of his faith; only after he has named all the dangers of courtly love does he reaffirm his devotion to the lady's image of perfection. To put it another way, he earns the right to praise the image just because he fulfilled the need to doubt it.

If this seems to be an empty paradox, let us think of the course of our own education. As children we are taught an idealized history of the United States: the pilgrims who came here and made friends with the Indians were impelled by their belief in religious freedom to endure the greatest hardships; the framers of our Constitution believed in the dignity of Man and sought to enfranchise every citizen; the Civil War was a noble conflict between two great cultures, the one defending its proud and cultivated way of life, the other advancing the cause of human equality; the great frontier united the whole nation in a mighty effort to achieve its manifest destiny; and so forth. A little more reading, and above all a little more experience, teaches us that these and countless other statements are the sheerest fabrications, designed, as are the schoolboy histories of all nations, to conceal the brutal and disreputable truth.

And yet these idealizing distortions of our history contain the hope of moral advancement, of the future that would come from such a past. We give our approval to the teaching of these fictions to the children, even though we know they are far from the truth, because they are indispensable: they endow the ideal with a visible form, and they define the behavior that marks our resemblance to the ideal. In other words, they are an injunctive and "crucial fiction," offering the illusion of solidarity and purpose. Were this fiction to blind us permanently to the defects of American life, it would be reprehensible; yet without that fiction the children would be blind to the moral possibilities of this life. We are all under the obligation to doubt it, to recognize it as a fiction that will become vicious if it is proclaimed as truth, and so destroy the very prospects it embodies; it will make us feel cheated of a golden age, and not spur us to create one. It is precisely our doubt that gives the myth its value.

So it is with the crucial fiction of courtly love. Heinrich towers above most of the other poets in his recognition of its deceptiveness and necessity. And in his demand upon the audience to share that recognition he performs the most refined and difficult service: he tells his society the truth about itself for all time, conscientiously identifying that part of the truth which is to come, which is now an actual lie. This service takes the form of an endlessly alternating denigration and regeneration of the image.

The Mirror

145, 1 Mirst geschên als eime kindelîne,
    daz sîn schônez bilde in eime glase ersach
    unde greif dar nâch sîn selbes schîne
    sô vil biz daz ez den spiegel gar zerbrach.   I
  5 dô wart al sîn wünne ein leitlîch ungemach.
    alsô dâhte ich iemer frô ze sîne,
    dô 'ch gesach die lieben frouwen mîne,
    von der mir bî liebe leides vil geschach.

    Minne, diu der werlde ir fröide mêret,
  10 sêt, diu brâhte in troumes wîs die frouwen mîn
    dâ mîn lîp an slâfen was gekêret
    und ersach sich an der besten wünne sîn.   II
    dô sach ich ir werden tugende, ir liehten schîn,
    schône und für alle wîp gehêret
  15 niwan daz ein lützel was versêret
    ir vil fröiden rîchez rôtez mündelîn.

    Grôz angest hân ich des gewunnen,
    daz verblîchen süle ir mündelîn sô rôt.

des hân ich nu niuwer klage begunnen.
20 sît mîn herze sich ze solcher swêre bôt,   III
daz ich durch mîn ouge schouwe solche nôt,
sam ein kint daz wîsheit unversunnen
sînen schaten ersach in einem brunnen
und den minnen muose unze an sînen tôt.

25 Hôer wîp von tugenden und von sinne,
die enkan der himel niender ummevân,
sô die guoten diech vor ungewinne
fremden muoz und immer doch an ir bestân.   IV
owê, leider, jô wând ichs ein ende hân,
30 ir vil wünneclîchen werden minne:
nû bin ich vil kûme an dem beginne.
des ist hin mîn wünne und ouch mîn gerender wân.

(To me it has happened as to a little child that saw its beautiful image in a mirror, and reached so hard for its own reflection that it broke the mirror completely. Then all its joy turned into bitter sorrow. In the same way, I thought that I would be ever more joyful when I saw my beautiful lady, from whom, along with love, much sorrow has come to me.

Minne, who increases the world's joy, behold, she brought my lady in a dream, where I was turned toward sleep and saw myself with my greatest joy. Then I saw her noble virtue, her bright image, beautiful and exalted above all women; except that her small red mouth, so rich in joy, was a little damaged.

It caused me great anguish that her small mouth, so red, should grow pale. So now I have begun a new lament, since my heart offered itself to such misery, that my eyes should make me gaze upon such distress—like a child ignorant of wisdom, that saw its reflection in a fountain and had to love it till he died.

Women more exalted in virtue and spirit the heavens can never contain, than the noble one whom I, to my misfortune, must be far from, and yet close to evermore. Alas for me, wretched man; for I had hoped to reach the goal of her joyful and noble love.

Now I am scarcely at the beginning. Thus my joy is gone, and my yearning hope.) [40]

The poet begins with a figure that sets the mood of the whole lyric. He compares himself to a child so captivated by the beauty of its own image that it reached hard for it and so broke the mirror. Why did it reach for the image? Because it did not know what an image was. The child was, as the poet says later about Narcissus, *wîsheit unversunnen:* it did not know the difference between an image and a living person. The child loved the image not because it was his own but because it was beautiful, a *schônez bilde.* In his inexperience, he thought the image was attainable.

If he does not know the difference between an image and a living person, it must mean that he does not know himself. He makes his mistake because he cannot recognize his own face in the mirror. He has never seen himself before; or at least he has never distinguished himself from the mass of other things in the world. As far as his consciousness goes, the image he loves is an unnamable thing, a *chose;* and the anonymity of the image is a reflection of the child's own lack of self-consciousness. He has not yet learned that he is a separate and distinguishable person, with qualities that belong to no one else; nor that the beauty he finds so irresistible originates in himself. Thus he is precisely in the condition of Narcissus gazing into the fountain.

It is the *idea* of a mirror that he has not grasped, the sense of a distinction between a reflected image and a projective substance. But this idea is forced upon him when he breaks the mirror and falls into grief. In this way he discovers the boundaries of his own identity through his love for the self-image, which exists in his consciousness but not in the world. The mirror reflected him, but it was separate from him.

[40] I have borrowed a number of passages from Jackson's translation (pp. 260f).

"In the same way, when I saw my lady I imagined that I would live in joy forever." The precision of *alsô* makes the comparison clear: the lady is to the poet as the mirror-image was to the child. The man's grief arises from the same *tumpheit*, the same inability to distinguish between the thing itself and the reflection that enhances it; the same unawareness that the perfection he loves has its principle in his own aspirations. He loves the ideal image of himself, yet he does not know himself. This is a paradox that need not surprise us when we have followed the experience of Narcissus.

In the next strophe, the same thing happens once again. As the poet lay dreaming of his "greatest joy," *Minne* brought him another image: his lady's beautiful lips were pale. The poet speaks of two different images: the one he was already dreaming of, and the one that was intruded into the dream.

Gazing into the dream-mirror, he "saw himself" [41] with the image that first aroused his hopes and gave him the illusion of endless joy to come, the ideal image, undistinguished from the reality it reflects. That was when "I saw my beloved lady," long ago, long before his joy had turned to bitter sorrow. In the dream he is once again like the small child, before love impelled him to reach out and so break the mirror.

In just that way he saw himself loved by the lady, entranced by her beauty and virtue, and unaware of their origin. But now comes *Minne*, "who increases the world's joy," breaking up his dream of perfection with an image that is less than perfect. The lady's beautiful small red mouth, the visible sign of her great worth,[42] is a little damaged, and now the mirror is broken once again.

---

[41] *Ersach sich* has the same ambiguity ("was lost in thought"; "saw itself") as in 144, 9f in Heinrich's *Tagelied;* cf. the *MF* note to this line, p. 476.

[42] The red mouth as a sign of perfection and unattainability occurs with extraordinary frequency. A few examples, all from *DLd:* Götfrit von Nifen, "Hî, wie wunnenclîch," II (p. 88): explicit association with *güete;* the same poet's "Ich hoer aber die vogel singen," III (p.

145, 3   unde [daz kindelîne] greif dar nâch sîn selbes
          schîne

145, 13   dô sach ich ir werden tugende, ir liehten
          schîn

Her "bright appearance" has the same status as the "appearance" which the child reached for and which does not exist apart from the mirror. Thus *schîn* means "reflection" in a very special sense here: it is the beautiful image that causes bitter sorrow when it is held to be real.[43]

And so the lady's splendor, the beautiful appearance that seems to announce her moral perfection, inevitably arouses the poet's doubt. The ambiguity of the language implies a grave and inexpressible question; do her virtue and concern have no more reality than those of an image in a mirror? Does that splendor light upon her from elsewhere, and is it as irrelevant to her true nature as another's dream?

The greatest irony is that it is in the poet's dream that *Minne* destroys his joy, shatters the image that he contemplated with such rapt expectation: he loses everything in the one moment of his life when he really can control what he sees and fulfill all his wishes. In the dream he can enjoy what he is denied in the waking day.[44] That dream of the perfect lady is

---

99): explicit association with *heil, gelucke, sælde,* and *êre;* see also Götfrit's *Nu siht man,* II (p. 107). Götfrit von Strasburg, "Diu zît ist wunneclich" (attribution doubtful), VI (p. 130): the red mouth signifies her peerless virtues and her unattainability. The same in Heinrich Hetzbolt von Wissense, "Nu wünschet alle der süezen," I and III (p. 148f); and "Wol mich der stunde" (p. 151), an entire lyric devoted to the beauty of the red mouth and the virtues it implies. Kristan von Hamle, "Wunneclîchen sol man schouwen" (p. 221f), IV. Kristan von Luppin, "Meien schïn dîn kunft mich fröit vil kleine," II (p. 228): no one can believe there is anything false in her, so red is her mouth. Von Sachsendorf, "Diese liehten tage," II (p. 397): her red mouth is the sign of her virtue and tenderness.

[43] Cf. Jackson, p. 262; Grünanger, pp. 156–60.

[44] Cf. *MF* 138, 17ff, where the lady fulfills in a dream what she refuses in real life. This, of course, is the usual pattern; see the

the star of the courtly man's life, guiding all of his experience by engaging him in the pursuit of perfection. Yet it is just there that the image is *verséret*, made less than perfect.

This is because the dream dramatizes the state of his mind—it is *his* dream, his *Minne*. For Heinrich, doubt is essential to the *Minne*-experience. The disposition to believe in *Minne*, in the ideality of a lady whom every courtier esteems, comes twinned with the disposition to distrust it. For that doubt is as crucial to the poet's salvation from the dangers of courtly love as his belief in its ethical rewards. It is only by doubting the reality of the image that he can save himself from the fate of Narcissus. His doubt is a true reflection of the conditions in which he consecrated himself to the ideal; for the very root of the *Minne*-relation is itself composed of truth and falsehood inextricably mixed: it is true that the knight ought to be in reality like the image, but it is false that the image is real.

Therefore, to believe entirely in *Minne* is to falsify its nature; in other words, it is not to believe in it at all.

Only so long as the lady has no individualizing qualities can her image be the recipient of the perfections he bestows upon it. To be a mirror, she must be distant; and so for the advantage of seeing the ideal in a familiar and favoring figure, the lover must face the danger of wasting away in sterile longing. For secular love requires an object that must be particular even if it is imperfect; but the lady of the lover's dream has qualities that are stylized and abstract. His doubt individualizes her, seeks out the imperfections that make her mortal and actual. It makes her turn away "to go to other women," to the people of here and now, the actual society of flesh and blood. His doubt preserves all that *is* real in courtly love, it gives

---

discussion of Arnaut de Mareuil, above, Chapter Two. Cf. also Friderich von Hûsen's famous "In mînem troume ich sach" (*MF* 48, 23–31), in which he also blames his eyes for depriving him of the dream he had been enjoying. See also Schwietering, p. 96; Kolb, pp. 19–37.

some substance to his hopes of winning her. If she is no longer an ideal, she is no longer an image either, and he ceases to be Narcissus. His doubt diminishes her, but it realizes her.[45]

His own love turned him away from the contemplation of an ideal image to show him a deliberate imperfection; his own eyes (*durch mîn ouge*) made him gaze upon the sad sight of her mouth grown pale; his own heart "offered itself" (*sich . . . bôt*) to "such distress." He proves that the image has no true existence. Only the mirror, the lady, is real, and the mirror has no quality of its own except as it reflects what is projected into it. The adoration of the image and the breaking of the mirror are the twin acts of his own will. He desired to believe, he desired to doubt.

It is necessary to remember that in the *Aufgesang* of the first strophe, where the poet tells of the time he first saw his beloved, he is speaking of the real lady, the "mirror"; but in the next two strophes he speaks exclusively of the image of her that he bore away. This distinction between the real lady and her image is important in this lyric. The image has become his possession; it is he who has made its mouth imperfect. The awareness of this distinction precipitates "the crisis of Narcissus," but also preserves the indispensable doubt.

[45] Compare this beautiful passage from Leo Spitzer, *L'amour lointain de Jaufré Rudel et le sens de la poésie des troubadours* (Chapel Hill, 1944), p. 16: "A la mélancolie de l'homme imparfait devant l'univers parfait s'ajoute la 'peur de la joie' d'un chrétien qui s'observe. *L'amor de lonh* ne vient-il pas chez Jaufré Rudel de cette 'mélancolie de l'imperfection,' qui sent que 'quelque chose' manque toujours au bonheur absolu, et de cette auto-limitation volontaire, qui a besoin du lointain? Le lointain est un élément nécessaire de tout amour, aussi nécessaire que le contact—ces troubadours ont en somme senti la *selige Sehnsucht* de Goethe, aspirant au milieu du plaisir du lit conjugal vers une *andere Begattung.* C'est le lointain qui donne à la tenue morale un rayonnement métaphysique et un sens à l'amour, comme la mort le donne à la vie. Les troubadours n'auraient-ils pas senti cela, qui est si grand et si simple, si triste et si réconfortant, qui nous fait pleurer *auprès* de la bien-aimée parce que nous la voyons déjà loin, et qui nous fait exulter *loin* d'elle parce que nous la sentons *proche?*"

Thus the explicit reference to Narcissus in the third strophe has been inevitable from the beginning, although in one respect he is very different from the "child ignorant of wisdom." Narcissus never quite experienced the denigration of the image that makes the poet suffer. The reflection in the fountain never grew less beautiful—that is why Narcissus had to go on loving it even after he had found out what it was. His will was fixed upon loving it, not upon "damaging" it. The difference between the poet and Narcissus is that the poet knows the story of Narcissus, and therefore a real choice is available to his will. He knows that he loves an unreal image; he knows what happens when a man believes in the reality of the unreal. For this reason he resembles Narcissus less than he does the Dreamer in the *Roman de la Rose:* his awareness of the exemplum of Narcissus enables him to choose, to turn from the image to the beloved thing itself—the rose, the mirror—and to the experience, the direct encounter with it. In turning from the ideal attributes of the image to the free, real, distant character of the lady, he offers himself to a great distress, but he saves himself from the fate of Narcissus. He cultivates doubt to preserve his life.[46]

But he cultivates faith to perfect it. *Minne* ennobles the lover. That is why the purpose of the final strophe is the re-creation of the image. "Heaven can contain no woman more virtuous, more high-minded, than the noble one, whom I, to my sorrow, must be distant from, and yet ever close to." [47] With the real lady he must maintain his distance, for at the least approach the mirror breaks. But he will be bound to her forever through the image that he has incorporated, and

[46] For an interesting comparison between line 145, 27f, and similar passages in Ovid's story of Narcissus, see Schönbach, *Beiträge*, p. 149.

[47] Theodor Frings and Elisabeth Lea show how these lines reflect the traditional praise of the Virgin Mary in their exhaustive study of this lyric, "Das Lied vom Spiegel und von Narziss. Morungen 145, 1, Kraus 7," *Beiträge zur Geschichte der deutschen Sprache und Literatur*, LXXXVII (1965), 40–200.

that he here exalts once again. He has denounced its unreal existence, but now he affirms the reality of its perfection. It is really unreal, but really perfect.

He is "scarcely at the beginning" of his struggle to win her love, for it is a perpetual beginning, endlessly alternating with the doubt that eradicates her meaning. He has lost his illusion, his *wân;* he had falsely believed (*wând*) that he could be at one with his own ideal, but in seeking to be united with it he obliterated it. He is at the beginning because he must now restore that image of perfection.

But for the moment he is in a state of suspense, midway between the faith that perfects and the doubt that preserves, between *wünne* and *wân.* These two words are twinned in the last line; *wân* is an inspiring illusion consciously perceived as such,[48] *wünne* the joy of believing in the reality and concern of the image.[49] The two are inseparable, and they are to resume their endless alternation when the image has been restored.

All that we have seen so far pertains to the personal concerns of the poet: the first word of the lyric is *mir,* and what follows is the effect of *Minne* on his inner life. But there is another presence here, explicitly recognized. For *Minne* "increases the joy of the world"; *Sêt!* says the poet to this "world"—"Behold! See how *Minne* brought my lady in a dream." The consequences of this sudden turn are considerable.

He calls upon his listeners to witness what has happened to him in *troumes wîs.* The dream is brought into the here and now with a demonstrative gesture that assumes the involvement of the whole audience. In making the dream at once

[48] Compare his use of *wând,* 145, 29; see above, p. 100, n. 28.
[49] Compare: "dô wart al sîn wünne ein leitlîch ungemach" (145, 5); und ersach sich an der besten wünne sîn" (145, 12); "ir vil wünneclîchen werden minne" (145, 30).

public and present, he shatters the "theatrical space": it becomes the dream of the man we know; we see it, he dreams it, before us. And it is the dream of the courtly class. When the poet is most alone, in the solitude of the dream of his future life, and in his greatest anguish as that future is eradicated—at that moment his consciousness engulfs the listeners, and all the manifold relations between them and him are brought into play.

For this lyric is the moral mirror of "those who strive for joy." It shows them their image, the qualities that define them, the conditions that permit them to make themselves more real—that is, to make their resemblance to the courtly ideal come closer and closer to true identity. The poet is a mirror of the audience.

It is for these listeners that he sings of the necessity of *Minne's* fiction, and the doubt that must be one of its consequences, the doubt that clarifies the difference between present reality and future hope, between actual experience and the meaning we long to see in it. It is for them that he makes public his dream, his hope, his disillusionment, his renewed consecration; for them he restores the mirror and reinvests the image. He performs this service for them, and affirms his solidarity with them. The extent of his consciousness is immeasurable, in many important ways distinguishing him from Narcissus, whose final outcry does not have the social resonance that we hear always in Heinrich's poetry.

Summary

In this great lyric we see the whole meaning of courtly love. The knight's idealized self-image—the image of the self in the perfection of the courtly ideal—is, by an overwhelming necessity, transformed into the renowned image of the lady; and the love that binds the man to her is the love that consecrates the life of the knight to the service of his own, and his class's, ideal. In the deeds by which he hopes to win her love, he becomes a more perfect knight. Loved by her, reflected by her, he would be united with the ideal, "saved"; for the lady is a mirror that perfects the image it bears by endowing it with its own ideality.

But in order that the lady may be a mirror, she must be distant; and such remoteness is the source of the greatest danger, not only because of the doom of unrequital, but also because of the final sterility it imposes upon life. The mirror can idealize experience, but as an object of desire it will ultimately destroy the sources of experience. It will order every desire and act to an object glorified far beyond its true worth, insensate and deceptive; and every faculty of the flesh and blood will wither away. The material mirror cannot participate in experience; it merely reflects an ethical ideal that dwells in the lover's consciousness alone. The remote and glorified mirror is anti-Eros, preventing not only carnal union but every direct, un-preformulated encounter with experience. It binds the knight with the promise of perfection actually to be realized, but it will leave him with an emptiness exactly like its own, making every immediate move toward experience the cause, as in this lyric, of profound revulsion. Spenser's Bower of Bliss delineates a possibility inherent in the whole system when it is no longer restrained by doubt.[50]

Heinrich's aim is to strike a balance between the indispensability of the mirror and the dangers of unquestioning faith, between the aspiration to perfect knighthood and the doom of Narcissus. No poet preserves this balance more steadfastly.

Appendix to Chapter Three

Before leaving Heinrich, a word about the method of studying his lyrics is in order.

Carl von Kraus, in his edition of Heinrich (1925), arranged

[50] See C. S. Lewis, *The Allegory of Love*, pp. 324ff.

the lyrics not as they appear in the manuscripts, but in a "cycle." [51] Since then, other critics have attempted to establish a song-cycle on various bases. [52] I want to explain why I have not treated Heinrich's lyrics as part of a cycle.

Von Kraus made his arrangement on the basis, whenever possible, of verbal or thematic relation, otherwise out of purely esthetic considerations. Julius Schwietering later wrote a study of the cycle in von Kraus's edition, in which he saw a "development," a series of "stages on the path of *Minne*," [53] from the initial illusion of reciprocal love to the painful but ennobling results of disillusionment. A brief look at Schwietering's approach will show how it works.

The first lyrics in the cycle concern mutual love; and in 143, 22 (number VI in the cycle) the very form of the *Wechsel* corresponds to the illusion of "Partnerschaft," of reciprocal exchange—an illusion that is soon to end. In the following lyric (145, 1—the "mirror lyric"), the pallor of the beloved's red mouth and the breaking of the mirror both signify the deprivation of her personal presence, just as the child's act signifies the lover's reaching for the lady, who is physically close. The mirror as a symbol presupposes her actual presence, which the poet must henceforth renounce. Coinciding with the disturbing realization of the lady's remoteness is the new emphasis upon her spiritual and moral characteristics, in contrast to the descriptions in the early lyrics which stressed the beauty of her physical presence. This renunciation of the lady's real presence signifies the first step on the path of *Minne*, in which the lover sees not the lady but only himself reflected in her.

[51] Published by the Bremer Presse, München; reprinted in 1950 by the Carl Hanser Verlag, München, with a few additions by von Kraus in the "Nachwort." The text I have used is from this 1950 reprint.
[52] See *MFU*, pp. 272ff, and Schwietering, pp. 71ff, for a discussion of the various cycles proposed.
[53] "Der Liederzyklus Heinrichs von Morungen," p. 103f.

The effect of the dream of the damaged red mouth is the *fröidelôser tage* of the following lyric (143, 4), the decline of the poet's joy because of his distance from the lady. His greatest anxiety now is that the loss of joy may cause him to stop singing. This is the opening thought of the lyric, which also reveals to the society—"the society must always be taken into account in the Minnelied"—the fact of her *fremden* (in the third strophe); while the second strophe contrasts the misery of his present condition with his joy in the past. This contrast darkens the poet's recollection of happiness in former days, when he still believed in the illusion that mutual physical love was in prospect; and now the lady appears hostile to him, deceptive and cruel: this is the theme of the next lyric (130, 9—Number IX in the cycle) and of those that follow.

From this summary of a small part of Schwietering's article, one can see how he argues his thesis. For him, the song-cycle is an account of the poet's progress on the *Minneweg*. The poet advances from the "I-bias" of the early lyrics, from the ex-clusively personal concern and desire for physical possession, to a higher level where his song becomes an impersonal, objec-tive hymn to joy, a glorification of the virtues that are vener-ated by the courtly society. This advancement is the result of his adjustment to the *Fernliebe*, to his loss of the hope of reciprocal love. The lady becomes transfigured, and before her exalted spirituality the poet is at first confused,[54] but he finally recognizes her as the ideal. All of this occurs with endless conflict—the early "I-centered" desires never end. But the general development revealed in the cycle is a shift in emphasis from the love of the *person* in the first phase to a love of the distant ideal in the second.

This development is analogous to the "mystical path from the historical Christ to the Transfigured Christ. . . . As the mystic's love for the incarnated God (*amor carnalis*) is not

[54] As in 135, 9; 141, 14; 136, 1—all concerning the poet's inability to speak in the lady's presence.

submerged in the love for the transfigured (*amor spiritualis*), but rather joins with it, so Morungen causes the love for the transfigured lady to be pervaded by the memory of his earlier love for her person" (p. 102). This union of the two kinds of love is also the cause of continual conflict, for the transfigured lady is seen by the poet, according to his mood, both as the ideal *and* as the uncompassionate one, who uses power without grace. This ambivalence of the poet toward the lady reveals his resistance to the mystic's desire for union with the ideal, and to the total annihilation of the self which such a union requires.

Now everyone will agree that Heinrich's lyrics are "related," and it is natural to suppose that they represent progressive stages of an experience that unfolds in time. But we also have to consider the alternative, namely that the lyrics do not reveal "stages" but are rather reflections upon one and the same experience, which is already complete and does not "develop."

In discussing the lyric that appears next to last in the cycle (138, 17–139, 18—the "Venus-lyric" that we have studied), Schwietering makes the following observations: The memory of mutual joy has the power of evoking the physical image of the beloved lady; in the dream the beloved grants what in real life she refuses—she comes to the lonely man, steps through the walls, soars with him; the "belief" (in strophes iv and v) is vain because it includes the belief in the compassion of the lady, who is, in fact, as empty of grace as Venus, powerful but cruel and unfeeling (pp. 96ff).

All this is undoubtedly true. But it is also true that the same themes have already occurred numerous times in the cycle—indeed, they occur in nearly every single lyric, and Schwietering points them out.

A few examples will suffice. In the twelfth lyric of the cycle (134, 14) the lady is explicitly described as a superhuman figure devoid of grace; this is also the theme of the fifteenth lyric (126, 8), which uses different images. In the twenty-fourth lyric (127, 1) the memory of former joy in the expectation of mutual love—the moment when the lady first turned her eyes upon the lover and sent her image into his heart—evokes the figure of the beloved, which, in the imagery of the echo and the parrot, is imagined as fulfilling what the real lady refuses; and this lyric, like the thirty-second, concludes with a distinction between the requiting image and the refusing lady. The twenty-ninth lyric exemplifies all the observations Schwietering makes about the Venus-lyric. The *tumben wâne* of mutual joy is followed by the image of the beautiful lady who never gave consolation or help; and her power, the graceless might of her charm, causes the man to be struck dumb before her; finally, the lyric ends by distinguishing the cruel power of the goddesslike lady from the compassionate grace of God. But we can go back to the ninth lyric to find all of these themes once again: the malevolent and irresistible power of the lady is a threat not only to Heinrich but to *vil mangem man,* and the poet was overwhelmed when she captured him with a friendly greeting—thus causing the illusion, now lost, of mutual joy. In the mirror-lyric (VII in the cycle), the lady fulfills the poet's desire in the dream, and, just as in the Venus-lyric, this fulfillment immediately exposes the dream as a worthless illusion.

These few examples (there are many others) suffice to demonstrate that Heinrich's lyrics are not "related" in a single straight line, that they show no "development." Schwietering sees in Heinrich's poetry the "germ of a development" that leads to Dante's *Vita-Nuova* cycle; but he adds that there is no real comparison between the two—and it is well that he does so, for in fact Heinrich's lyrics do not, in this sense, lead *anywhere.* Aside from an obvious difference in style and content between the first six lyrics and the remainder, there is no question of "development": the poet is, at the close of the cycle, in precisely the same condition as he was in the seventh lyric, where his characteristic style begins.

Heinrich's lyrics are like so many mirrors reflecting the same object—an extraordinarily complicated but static situation. It is true that the lyrics differ in tone and emphasis: the image is reflected from different points of view, which *collectively* define the courtly experience in its every aspect—from the initial illusion, to the exposure of the image, to its restoration in full consciousness of the society it defines. These may be "stages" of an experience, but they are not seen to unfold in time; they are present simultaneously in the singer's consciousness, for he has already passed through them all before he begins his song.

Therefore, when one studies *Heinrich's* lyrics—one may not generalize but must decide the question for each poet separately—one is not obliged to study them in any particular order, but may deal with them in the order most convenient for the accomplishment of the task. One is, however, under a different obligation: whatever he says must be said in full knowledge of Heinrich's total work. And corresponding to this is another injunction: one may not draw any conclusions from isloated lines and strophes; everything that is said must arise from the structure of the lyric as a whole.

The value of von Kraus's arrangement is not the issue here. The extraordinary perceptiveness that enabled him to group the songs according to their thematic, linguistic, and structural similarities enables us, as Schwietering points out, to see both in the individual lyrics and in the total work many things that might otherwise elude us. But the idea of a "cycle" would be fatally misleading if it made one look for a "development," for evidence of the poet's "growth," or "progress." There is no beginning, middle, or end. The figure these lyrics describe is truly that of a cycle, and it makes no difference where one begins, so long as one travels the entire circumference.

CHAPTER FOUR

Ulrich von Lichtenstein and the Mirror of the Actual World

ULRICH would have us believe that his *Frauendienst,* which he began in 1257 as he was growing old, is a true account of his life. But very quickly we realize that this is no autobiography, despite the claim of its author. The story that takes twenty-five thousand lines to tell, and fifty-eight lyrics to meditate upon, is much too simple to be the narrative of an actual life. Minus the digressions, it goes like this: As a youth Ulrich dedicates himself to a noble lady and serves her faithfully for many years, despite her indifference. He eventually withdraws from her service, and for a time he is his own man, in the service of no one. Finally he becomes the knight of another lady, who is more appreciative of his courtly qualities, and his life thereafter is one unbroken joy.

Thus, aside from glancing references to his wife and children, there is barely a word concerning what we would today call Ulrich's personal life, or the Austrian politics in which he played an active rôle, or anything irrelevant to the representation of a courtly lover and a courtly poet. What he describes, in endless detail, are the conditions under which he composed his songs and engaged in feats of arms, the twin aspects of his service to a noble lady. Ulrich's intention is, therefore, clearly not to give an account of his life but to idealize it, to transform it by literary means into a long career of service. He edits and revises certain events of his life in order to make them resemble the adventures of the hero of romance. However, *Frauendienst* is not exactly a romance, either.

Rather, it is an actualization of romance. Everything is intended to show how, in his relations with historical persons, in real places, on specific dates, Ulrich achieved the life that had formerly existed only in fiction; and how he carried on the work of the classic poets of the Minnesang, to whom he frequently alludes. And so, like Tristan, Ulrich performs the service of song; like Parzival, the service of action. The description of his childhood is deliberately reminiscent of the *enfances* of Parzival in Soltane.[1] The niece who acts as a messenger between Ulrich and his first lady is a *niftel*,[2] like Brangæne in Gottfried's *Tristan*. The lady's page greets him on the road with the first strophe of Walther's *Ir sult sprechen willekomen*.[3] Though little in the work is to be read naïvely as historical fact, the enemies Ulrich defeats and the lord he serves are historical figures whose names appear in documents. At the same time, every detail of what he represents as autobiography or history has a literary resonance. In countless allusions to the heroes of romance or to his literary forebears, Ulrich tries to make his life coincide with the ideal image of knighthood. Raw experience attains the form and purpose of idealized adventure: testing and amelioration.[4] This careful

[1] *Frauendienst*, ed. Karl Lachmann (Berlin, 1841), 3, 5–4, 4; ed. Reinhold Bechstein (Leipzig, 1888), 8–11. In this chapter both editions are cited for the narrative portions: the first citation refers to Bechstein; the second, separated from the first by a semicolon, to Lachmann. But for the text of the lyrics I use *DLd—Deutsche Liederdichter des 13. Jahrhunderts*, ed. Carl von Kraus, 2 vols. (Tübingen, Max Niemeyer Verlag, 1952–1958; quoted by permission). The word "Kommentar" designates the second volume of *DLd*.

[2] Meaning, generally, a female relative, but here specifically a niece. See, for example, *Tristan*, v, 9421.

[3] Bechstein, 776f; Lachmann, 240, 9ff.

[4] Cf. *Parzival*, III, 172 (the counsel of Gurnemanz) with *Frauendienst* 10, 5–11, 8; 3, 25–4, 4; and Ulrich's apprenticeship in the house of Markgraf Heinrich, 8–35; 3, 5–10, 4.

adaptation of a literary tradition to the form of a documentable autobiography gives *Frauendienst* its special character. And it forever shatters the mirror of courtly love as we have come to know it.

Ulrich is an accomplished second stringer, a born follower, correctly imitating a movement that he has observed, without entirely committing himself to it. All that is implied or inchoate in the classic poets he draws out with a numb meticulousness, in his desire to possess what he cannot be. He knows every gesture, every strain, every proper response of the courtly posture, and he is very careful to get it all down right. The soul of the *hoher Minnesang* is not altogether at home in the body of his work, but its skeleton has the precision of an anatomical chart.

In trying to square this literary image with the purported facts of his autobiography, Ulrich cannot avoid testing the adequacy of the courtly ideal to the demands of actual life. His great care to demonstrate the formal correctness of his behavior is a reaction to the failure of the courtly code in the actual world. Much of *Frauendienst* is deliberately comic, and the butt of the joke is always the absurdity of courtliness, its irrelevance to everyday life; the knight of La Mancha is on the way. As Ulrich reveals his contemporaries, they are equally aware of the absurdity of courtly love but far less aware of its appeal and its moral rewards. Ulrich is drawn both ways at once.

This ambivalence can be seen, for example, in Ulrich's famous vindicating acts of self-mutilation. Early in the courtship of his first lady, she angrily demands that he stop pursuing her; for, as she says, even if he were perfect in every kind of virtue, his uncouth mouth would still be offensive to a noble lady. Ulrich's reaction: since his mouth displeases her so, he is going to have it cut. That will show her.

We then get an extended description of the *Mundoperation*, the doctor with his scalpel, the lady's little page staring in wonder, and so forth. Afterwards, his mouth swells up like a ball and gives off a terrible smell. He suffers from pain, and hunger, and thirst (80, 1–105, 3; 22, 5–28, 15). Nor is this the only part of his body that Ulrich is willing to dispense with because it offends. Later on, acting with the same literal-mindedness, he has his little finger cut off in response to another of the lady's countless accusations (418–456; 131, 29–156, 20).

We read all this with wonder. What did Ulrich hope to accomplish in offering this surgical evidence of the force of *Minne?*

> Er het mich meisterlîch gesniten;
> daz het ouch ich manlîch erliten.
> [97, 1f; 26, 13f]

> mir was wol, mir was wê:
> wê dâ von, mîn lîp was wunt:
> sô was mîn herze wol gesunt.
> der minne twingen twanc mich sô,
> daz mir was wê, und was doch frô.
> [102, 4–8; 27, 24–28]

(He cut me in a masterly way; but I bore it like a man, too.

I was well, I suffered: suffered because my body was wounded; yet my heart was quite healthy. The force of *Minne* forced me so, that I suffered and yet knew joy.)

He bore it like a man; and while his body suffered, his heart rejoiced in this act of service. Thus the operation served the same purpose as any *aventiure* in the life of a true knight: it made visible to the whole world the reality of a manhood disciplined by *Minne*. But everyone must feel something in this episode not only inconceivable in the classic literature but inimical to it. "*Der minne twingen twanc mich sô*" has an eloquent ugliness, betraying a special attitude to this dubious deed of surgery. The difference between the knight's adventures in the great romances and this showy operation is the difference between the hidden scars of heroic battle and a red tattoo purchased long after the battle is over, by a youth who was born too late. What drives the young knight here is a desire for the *mark* of an experience which in itself is no longer available.

This literal execution of the doctrines of *Minne* suggests the impoverishment of actual life beside the formal and purposeful adventures of the fictional hero. Ulrich has to make arrangements with a doctor. There is no giant to test his skill; no desperate woman to test his chastity; no uncouth lord to test his discipline; no Grail to test his piety. All that is available to him is a *meister*, an astounded boy as witness, and a great deal of leisure. He tries to make do with these, but it is not possible to re-create the life of Lancelot in his own. He cannot find in actual life the formal experience of courtly love. Ulrich can only copy forms, forms without meaning in everyday life.

As a result, the ideal image of the knight has to be modified, actualized. First of all, it must be dissociated from the moral code of chivalry, for actual experience has no such purpose—it has no ethical purpose of any sort. The image is now studied for the details of its posture and dress: it becomes an "image" in the public-relations sense, a relatively easy acquisition if one can pay for the clothes and the other props; a manageable substitute for true refinement, for a moral commitment that would have cost much effort and have hampered one in dealing with friends and enemies. At one point in *Frauendienst*, Ulrich dresses up like King Arthur and leads his retinue in a kind of parade through several cities, where he is saluted and "served" by his peers, who delight in playing the other knights of the Round Table to the last flicker of an eyelash.

Something similar happens to the lady's image. Those who read Ulrich's later lyrics, in particular, will note their tastelessness. They are silly erotic fantasies, sickeningly coy, public daydreams of seduction, in which the poet, or his *hôher muot,* does what he likes with the imperious lady's image. That image is represented as will-less and mindless, a veritable doll, and Ulrich rejoices before his listeners in all the pleasures he gets from it in his mind. The most striking example is the forty-first lyric, *Guot wîp, mîner fröiden lêre.* The first three strophes are full of classic Minnesang clichés as the poet begs to enter the "paradise" of the lady's heart. But she keeps the gates shut, and there is an abrupt change of scenery. His own *hôher muot* appears to execute a detailed erotic revenge upon the lady's passive image. The poet joins the audience as a spectator of his own fantasy; he watches his *hôher muot, "alse er im eine fröide tihtet in / dem herzen mîn mit dir"*—"as he composes, makes up, a joy for himself in my heart with you." Thus the image is emancipated from the distant and refusing lady of the classic period, and from every moral injunction. That is why we never see "the crisis of Narcissus" in Ulrich's work: because the image no longer stands as an ambivalent reflection of the actual lady, it simply replaces her. The service of song is fulfilled in the recounting of an erotic fantasy.

The fantasy replaces experience; the image replaces the living woman, reduces her to the condition of an object. Narcissus, the medieval literary Narcissus, is in danger only so long as courtly love is the one form of experience available to him. But that is all changed now. The hero is an actual man, and the doctrines of *Minne* are irrelevant to his experience. It is precisely the poet's intention to deny the possibility of experience within those doctrines: only a fantasy can live in them, only images.

The one value relevant to actual experience is what Ulrich, much later in *Frauendienst,* calls *gemach.* This comes in the course of his long conclusion; he speaks of "four things" that everyone strives to attain:

> Noch weiz ich vier dinc, daz ist wâr,
> dar nâch die liute alle werbent gar.

swelch wîser man ir einez wil
erwerben, der mac des wol vil
gewinnen: wizzet, daz nie man
si elliu vieriu gar gewan.

. . . . .

Daz eine ist: swer des hulde hât,
in des gewalt es allez stât,
daz ie wart oder immer wirt.

. . . . .

Daz ander ist diu êre hie,
dâ man ê vaste mit umbe gie;
daz dritte gemach, daz vierde guot.

[1827, 1ff; 587, 19ff]

(And I know four things, in truth, that all people strive for. Any wise man who tries to attain a single one of them may win much: but know that no man ever won all four. . . . The first thing is: whoever has the grace of Him in whose power everything stands that ever was or will be. . . . The second is earthly honor, which people used to care about; the third is comfort, the fourth possessions.)

Ulrich's point of departure is the famous lyric by Walther von der Vogelweide, *Ich saz ûf eime steine*. Three of the "four things" are exactly as in Walther's lyric; but the fourth most precious thing is Ulrich's own: "comfort."

Because these things are mutually exclusive, he continues, a man's life is beset by conflict. One man renounces all the other things for the sake of God's grace—such a man has chosen the best part. Another forsakes this precious gift in order to win earthly fame; another cares only to increase his wealth. (1832f; 588, 27ff)

Die vierden, die ich iu nennen wil,
der vindet man ouch leider vil.
die sint alsô diu swîn gemuot,

> die gotes hulde, êre, und guot,
> lâzent niht wan durch gemach.
> ach owê und immer ach!
> pfy, wie swendet er di zît,
> der durch gemach als ein swîn lît!
> [1834, 1–8; 589, 11–18]

(The fourth kind of man, unfortunately, is also found in abundance. These men have the disposition of pigs; they surrender God's grace, honor, and wealth for nothing but comfort. Ach, alas, ach! Pfui, how he squanders his life who for the sake of comfort wallows like a pig!)

It would be a mistake to think that *die vierden,* about whom Ulrich writes with such vivid distaste, are a new force, one that never existed before the decline of the Minnesang—a decline for which they are at least partially responsible. Not even their explicit recognition here is new. They forsake everything for comfort; they fly from every intense commitment; they make no demands upon themselves; they distrust every vision of the future, every ideal, that would necessarily entail effort and the risk of unfulfillment. No more invincible enemy of courtly love could be conceived; not the *huoter,* but *die vierden* suffocate *Minne* in their comfortable indifference. Before all the spies and slanderers and jealous ones, who are, after all, defined by the ideal they blaspheme, courtly love could survive, even flourish; but before "the fourth type of man" it dies in its irrelevance.

Gemach is "comfort," to be understood as a condition deliberately chosen, like the life of chivalry, and no less rooted in an active principle: to enfeeble the consciousness, to make impotent every idea and every desire that would demand an intense personal commitment. The form of a life of comfort is not the ritual, but the routine; its goal is not to perfect itself, but simply to "function." Intellectual comfort, in the sense I mean, is smugness; emotional comfort is unconcern, a refusal to "get involved"; moral comfort is conformism. It is the opposite of the chivalric virtue of *mesure, mâze*. *Mâze* is the virtue of controlling powerful emotions: "that inner restraint which governs the appetites and keeps them subject to the intellect."[5] But the life of *gemach* seeks, not to restrain the emotions, but to enfeeble them, in order that they may be more easily satisfied.[6]

Thus all the tensions that drove the knight in his career of amelioration are dissipated. The courtly ideal is made to coincide with actual conditions; the lady is denigrated, service is reduced to mere display. Everything that was remote is debased and actualized; things as they ought to be merge with things as they are. The movement of aspiration ceases; all things come to rest, not in perfection, but in comfort. "That Sabaoths sight"[7] is now available on weekdays. These principal features of Ulrich's work—the attempt to reflect in the mirror of an actual life the ideal image of the knight, a sense of the inadequacy of the courtly ideal, and a valuation of comfort—will critically affect the meaning of the mirror in his lyrics. Therefore, it is worth dwelling a little longer on the quality of the whole work before we turn to the mirror-lyrics.

The Inclusion of the Actual World
(The Venus Journey)

Still in the course of his first service, Ulrich goes on a long journey (470–985; 160–292) to engage in tournaments with the best knights of Europe. But he is dressed in a special

---

[5] Maurice Valency, *In Praise of Love*, p. 176.

[6] The *Minne*-doctrine set forth by Hartmann von Aue in the *Büchlein* employs many of the same terms. The Body desires *gemach* and shuns all pain, which it regards as useless. But to the Heart, the essence of *Minne* is *arbeit*, unending constancy and moral refinement. See de Boor, pp. 68ff.

[7] Spenser, *Faerie Queene*, VII, VIII, 2 (second Mutabilitie canto).

way, in *"küneginne wîse"*; he puts on woman's clothes and a wig and calls himself "Queen Venus." His explanation for this masquerade is that he wishes to make the journey incognito. But needless to say, the masquerade fools no one: people all know who and what he is. From the lingering descriptions of his feminine clothes—his twelve white gowns, his thirty white sleeves and chemises, his three white samite mantles, his golden wig—we see the real intention: such beautiful accouterments, worn not only by himself but by everyone in his retinue, including his horses, attract the most renowned representatives of the courtly society of Italy, Austria, Switzerland, and Germany to a public symbol of their class.

The Venus Journey is the actualization of an allegory, and not comparable to anything in the earlier literature. For essential to every allegory is the explicit exclusion of the actual world: it takes place in a garden behind high walls and a locked wicket, or in a dream, or on the other side of an impassable river, or in the forge of Nature. This is so for a very good reason. The personification of ideals must become a parade the moment it is enacted on a real street. And one's reaction to the Venus Journey is the same as to a really good parade, where one sees one's own good friend dressed up as Uncle Sam, or the neighbors' daughter in the robes of Liberty. As we watch a parade, we experience the alternating pleasures of recognition and transformation. We are conscious of the true identity of the people who are acting in rôles, of the ideal past these rôles evoke, and of the actual world in which the ideal is depicted and which it dignifies, transforms.

But one difference is that there are no pure spectators in Ulrich's journey. The whole courtly society of southern Europe consciously participates in the pretense. And the mock solemnity of its behavior is ultimately an attack on the courtly ideals to which it seems to do honor. For we are never allowed to forget that the whole thing is a deliberate parody, and the actors know it.

Thus, for example, at Feldsberg, Ulrich the Queen is received by Sir Cadolt, who promises to show him many noble women.[8] After a number of jousts, in which Ulrich excels, Cadolt makes good on his promise. He takes Ulrich to Mass with him, where Ulrich gazes on Cadolt's wife and many others whose beauty and courtesy rejoice his heart. The women laugh because he wears feminine clothes and pretty *zöpfe*, plaits. They blush when Ulrich kisses them in greeting. "In truth," he says, "God was not served much that day" (935, 7f; 280, 15f). Ulrich wishes to go to the offering, and gestures to Cadolt's wife to precede him. But she refuses on the grounds that it would offend her *zühte*, her sense of decorum, if she went before a queen. So Queen Ulrich must go first, and all the ladies laugh at his mincing steps—they are scarcely a hand's breadth long—as he advances to the offering and returns (945, 1–8; 282, 25–32).

Then a gracious, noble lady offers him the *pæce*, the kiss of peace, which during the Mass passes from one to another, among members of the same sex.[9] He most willingly receives it but finds himself unable to pass it on, for none of the many ladies to whom he offers it will accept it. "You must excuse me from this kiss," one of them says, "for you are supposed to be a man." [10]

Ulrich tells us how much the Venus Journey cost him—307 spears, 271 gold rings, etc. (978–985; 291, 1–292, 32)—but it is not the price of this sustained charade that strikes us. Rather, it is the universal willingness to perform, to the letter, ritualistic acts whose meaninglessness, far from dogging the enthusiasm of the participants, actually heightens their pleasure. The public figure of *Minne* is here the masquerade of a male impostor. Every speaker who greets this startling

---

[8] The episode begins at 906, 1; 273, 1.
[9] See Bechstein's note to 536, 7.
[10] 947, 7f; 283, 15f. A similar incident has taken place earlier, in the episode of the Grafin's kiss, 537–543; 178, 25–180, 16.

figure—*Venus, vil edeliu künegîn*—is not simply pretending that the mask is the reality. If that were all, it would not be very different from what the classic poets did, with the hope that the mask was not a complete deception. But all who salute Queen Venus here, with those plaits pinned on, those mincing steps taken by the big feet, are affirming that there is no pertinent reality beyond the mask, that nothing ever existed except this mask which does not enhance but simply falsifies the face beneath it, that the integrity of courtly love is truly reflected in the figure of a male queen.

This celebration of the emptiness of old forms is the chief intention of the Venus Journey. Therefore, it is not quite accurate to say that "Die Venusfahrt scheint zunächst eine anachronistische Groteske." [11] Insofar as it is a Groteske it is not "anachronistic" but a precise reflection of the attitude of the actual world to the ideals of its forebears. [12]

The manifold relations between the singer and his audience in the earlier generations have now been reduced to a collec-

[11] Otto Höfler, "Ulrichs von Liechtenstein Venusfahrt und Artus-fahrt," in *Studien zur deutschen Philologie des Mittelalters*, Festschrift Friedrich Panzer, ed. Richard Kienast (Heidelberg, 1950), p. 133.

[12] The Venus Journey abounds in similar episodes. For example: Hademâr's anger at the accusation of sodomy (878, 2ff; 266, 2ff); the knight who is dressed as a monk (616–641; 199, 5–205, 20); an identical episode later on (685–698; 216, 13–219, 21); Ulrich's visit to his wife and children (707–710; 221, 29ff); the various requests for entry into the retinue of Queen Venus (e.g., 752ff and Bechstein's note, 813–816; 234, 9ff and 249, 25–250, 24); the repeated exclamations that "I never saw a woman throw down a man like that" (e.g., 866, 4–8; 263, 4–8). Compare the similar incidents in the Arthur Journey: the Prince of Austria's gratitude that "Arthur" has returned from Paradise, and, especially, Ulrich's reply (1455ff; 465, 25ff); Heinrîch von Habechspach's remarks about Ulrich's thirty-second lyric (1467ff; 468, 25ff); the political and economic reasons for which Frederick orders the journey to end (1599ff; 501, 27ff); the many men who mock the courtly code, e.g., Râpot von Valkenberc (1491ff; 474, 25ff). Compare the farcical wooing of the first lady in her castle—the hoisting sheet, the offending steward, etc.

tive caricature of the courtly ideal. It was not only because the doctrine that exalted the lady was recognized to be a fiction, a mere fiction that could still sometimes relieve the impoverishment of actual life. It was also because of the dread of nominating a human being to be the agent of one's salvation on earth. That gave to the lady more authority than the human fact could justify. At the same time, it robbed the man's life of its actuality, the sense of its participation in a mortal world where every moment could not be experienced as part of a moral and aesthetic system. It was a world of money problems (many a high-born man was short of funds), dishonest servants, family obligations, heartbreakingly cautious political leaders, winter visits to friends and neighbors . . . a world so complicated and so ordinary that "service" and "requital" were not adequate to define its experience, or moral refinement its purpose. When once that world is explicitly acknowledged, the lady can no longer stand as the arbiter of the courtly man's life. Either the doctrines of *Minne* are to be abandoned altogether, or they are to be retained on the condition that they do not contemn man's unheroic and unconsecrated life but accommodate it, divert it, adorn it. A man could not hope for his salvation in another human being and still be capable of sharing the experience of his contemporaries. That is why the lady had to be brought low, and her fall was great. Her humanity was never acknowledged, and she changed from angel to object.

The older poets never permitted the actual world to intrude in this way. When the living lady proved unworthy of her exalted image, they knew that only the image could hold such sway, that only in the fictional "space" could courtly love survive without debasement. In other words, they acknowledged that *Minne* demanded the exclusion of the actual world; that courtly love was not a representation of the world but an absolute system within the world. Painful though it was to admit this, they did so, because they wanted to protect the ideal image. In *Frauendienst* the distinction between the "two spaces" is obliterated.

The Inadequacy of the Courtly Ideal

Particularly in the last quarter of *Frauendienst*, frequent and detailed passages are devoted to historical events and conditions—the death of Herzog Friedrich in the battle against the Hungarians, a long account of the kidnapping of Ulrich and his family for ransom, the denunciation of the robber-barons, and so forth. Alternating with these factual accounts are other passages full of the platitudes of courtly literature; every sordid reality is followed by a string of literary phrases. As the world crumbles and lawlessness roams the land, Ulrich turns to his "lady"—who becomes more and more a simple literary construct—and sings of her beauty, her free gift of requital, the invulnerability to all care which her goodness confers in a world that is going to pieces. This juxtaposition of the reportorial and the literary exposes the meanness of the one and the debased idealism of the other.

The educative power of *Minne* was now valued far less than its sedative power. The image no longer impelled the knight into great adventures; rather, it was "used" as an antidote to anxiety. With the death of Friedrich and the decline of the courtly class, even such "adventures" as the Venus Journey were out of the question. Courtly life appears more and more sedentary, freed from the compulsion to ameliorate reality, enjoying the comfort of tolerating it.

Ulrich's reaction to the death of Friedrich illustrates all this. After describing Friedrich's funeral, the poet continues:

> Got müeze sîn pflegen: er ist nu tôt.
> sich huop nâch im vil grôziu nôt
> ze Stîre und ouch ze Oesterrîch.
> dâ wart maniger arm, der ê was rîch.
> für wâr ich iu daz sagen wil:

nâch im geschach unbildes vil:
man raubt diu lant naht unde tac;
dâ von vil dörffer wüeste lac.
Die rîchen wurden sô gemuot,
daz sî den armen nâmen ir guot.
daz was iedoch ein swachez leben:
den got het guotes vil gegeben,
daz die den armen tâten leit,
dâ mit si swanden werdicheit.
swen sô die armen erbarment niht,
daz is hie und ouch dort enwiht.
Swâ sô der edel rîche man
sich nimt sô grôze untugende an,
daz sîn lîp ze einem rouber wirt,
ich weiz wol, daz in gar verbirt
gotes hulde und vrowen gunst.

                  · · · · ·

Swelhem edelen got gibt lîp und guot,
der als übel wirt gemuot,
daz sîn lîp ze einem rouber wirt,
gar elliu tugent in verbirt.
die armen hœrt man über in klagen.
des muoz er gar wol missehagen
guoten wîben: daz ist alsô.
von im wirt selten iemen vrô.
Der edel rîche der sol geben
den armen: daz ist rehtez leben.
swer zweinzigen nimt und einem gît,
diu gâbe brüefet alle zît
schelten, sünde; daz ist alsô.
ob sîner gâbe wirt einer frô,
sô werdent ir tûsent trûric gar:
die schelten in alle sîniu jar!
Die rouber die sint selten vrô.
ir künftec leit daz toettet sô,
daz sî dort immer sint verlorn:
si wæren bezzer ungeborn.

diu helle ze lône in ist bereit:
si trûrent ir künftigez leit.
swen hie die armen erbarment niht,
daz selbe âne ende im dort geschiht.
Der edel junge sol wesen vrô
und sol mit zühten tragen hô,
und freu sich edele, guotes, jugent.
tuot er des niht, er ist âne tugent.
swer trûret âne hertzen leit,
dem muoz sîn hôhez lop verseit.
trûren daz ist niemen guot:
dâ von sol man sîn hôchgemuot.
Ez sol des edelen jungen lîp
sîn hôchgemuot durch ein guot wîp.
und ist er niht von wîben vrô,
sô muoz er immer leben sô,
daz er an freuden ist verirt.
sîn trûren im unsælde birt:
schelten, spotten alle zît
im sîn swachez trûren gît.
Swâ sô ein schoeniu vrowe guot,
diu reiniclîchen ist gemuot,
von hertzen treutet einen man
und im ir süezen lîbes gan
ze treuten wol sus unde sô,
und ist der niht von hertzen vrô,
der ist an freuden gar verzagt:
von reht er niemen wol behagt.
Mich hât ein reiniu vrowe guot
von trûren alsô her behuot,
daz ich bin vrô în aller zît.
ir güete mir hôchgemüete gît:
ich bin ir stæter dienestman,
mit triwen dienstes undertân
vil stæteclîchen sunder wanc.

[1677, 1–1688, 7; 530, 13–533, 11]

(May God protect him: he is dead now. And after his death a
great distress arose in Styria and Austria. There, many a man

became poor who was rich before. I tell you truly that after he died many iniquities occurred: men robbed the lands both day and night, and many villages lay waste. The rich were disposed to take the possessions of the poor. It was a despicable life, that those to whom God had given much did harm to the poor and thereby lost their virtue. Whoever is not moved to pity by the poor is despised both in this world and in the next. Wherever a noble and rich man takes upon himself the vice of becoming a robber, I know well that he is denied the grace of God and the favor of women.

. . . . .

If a nobleman to whom God gives life and wealth is so evilly disposed that he becomes a thief, he is completely without virtue. The poor are heard complaining about him. And thus it is true that he must ever displease good women. No one is made joyful by him.

The noble rich man should give to the poor: that is the proper life. Whoever takes from twenty and gives to one, his gift always brings insult and sin—that is true. If one is made happy by his gift, a thousand are made to grieve. They curse him all his life!

Thieves are never happy. The pain that awaits them in the future so destroys, that they shall be lost forever in the world to come. It would have been better for them had they not been born. Hell is ready for them as requital: they grieve over their future anguish. All this shall happen in the next world to the man who does not pity the poor.

The young nobleman should be joyous and bear himself high with courtliness, and rejoice in his nobility, his possessions, and his youth. If he does not do this, he is without virtue. High praise shall be denied to whoever grieves without heart's pain. Grieving is pleasant for no one: therefore one must be high-spirited. The young nobleman should be high-spirited for the sake of a good woman. If he is not made joyous by women, then he must live forever with joy denied him. His grieving brings him a life without blessings: his unmanly grieving always brings him blame and mockery.

Ulrich von Lichtenstein

Whenever a beautiful and good woman who is minded to purity embraces a man with all her heart and grants to him her own sweet body to embrace well, thus, and so—if he is not then joyful with all his heart, he is excluded from all joy: it is right that he should please no one.

A pure good woman has kept me from grieving, so that I am always joyful. Her goodness gives me high spirits: I am her loyal servant, obedient to her in true service, without wavering.)

Ulrich treats the death of Fredrich as though the moral solidarity of the courtly class were centered in him, and with his removal there could only be a vast dissolution. The victory over the Hungarians on the Leitha, and the sumptuous formal burial of the Herzog, are celebrated as the last enactments of the old ideals of knighthood and nobility. They mark an explicit, formal, ceremonial conclusion to the old courtly life: it is all buried with Friedrich. To be sure, the fear of moral dissolution after the death of a great sovereign is a venerable theme in medieval literature. But nowhere else is an expression of this theme confirmed by a report of historical fact: the nobles are really stealing cattle.

"Many a man became poor who used to be rich before." That is the end of everything, for the life of adventure was the dream of a class that had a lot of time and money. This is no news to Ulrich. At the conclusion of his narrative of the Venus Journey he gives us a precise accounting of how much he spent, and it was plenty. Against the ruthless hungers of the actual world, what can Ulrich say? The armed robber-barons who lead away the cows of unarmed peasants are supposed to suffer from the thought that they are to be excluded from the boudoir in this world and from paradise in the next. Now why is Ulrich not embarrassed to say such silly things?

What we see in Ulrich is that the world of experience has not yet formulated its ideal, except vaguely in the valuation of *gemach;* so that while it must renounce the courtly ideal as the form of experience, it retains that ideal as the only coherent moral code available. We can see this clearly in the present passage. Ulrich tells us that the nobles became poor and resorted to robbery; but whom does he condemn? Not the impoverished nobility but the *edel rîche*, the noble rich, those to whom "God has given much." He reports that the nobles steal, and he responds with the rule that a rich man ought to pity the poor. The moral judgment has nothing to do with the nobles' actual stealing, or with the reasons why they have been forced to steal in the first place.

He sees one thing, but he judges another. When he is reporting history, he can recognize that the nobility have become impoverished; but when he takes a moral stand, he must ignore what he has reported. He has no choice but to do this. The moral basis on which he could condemn the robber-barons pertains to a fictional world that had never been able to accommodate questions of expense and income. The leisure class is disappearing, and its ideal fiction no longer has any integrity. So Ulrich has to falsify the nature of the crime in order to apply the only moral doctrine he knows, a doctrine that has indeed provided for the condemnation of the selfish rich but has never foreseen the case of a desperately poor man of high birth resorting to plunder. So Ulrich's work becomes sentimental and disjointed.

Ulrich's advice offers nothing but a shallow sensuality and the emptiest forms of behavior, a meaningless posture of "joy." The grief that is inseparable from the moral efficacy of courtly love he despises; he is concerned more with the efficacy of appearance, with immediate sexual rewards from women who have already been reduced to the status of objects and are therefore naturally compliant. The distance that causes grief and increases desire no longer exists. And another result of this same valuation of "comfort" is a weakening of the Minnesänger's social commitment. In the last eight lines Ulrich points to himself as a specific example of the moral principles he has been urging upon others. Now Walther himself, as Mohr points out, and the classic Minnesänger in general, often testify to their own allegiance to the courtly ideal.[13] But something far different is implied in Ulrich's words, for that society is breaking up, and the illusion of solidarity essential to all the courtly lyrics is now untenable. There is no longer a question of demonstrating in the lyric, as in every act of *Ritterschaft*, the poet's own allegiance to the society. He now wants to show his success in escaping from it: "Whatever they did, I was happy, because of my good lady." This act of withdrawal is not caused by bitter disillusionment; rather, it is another way of preserving *gemach*.[14]

The inclusion of the actual world has permanently debased the courtly ideal. Ulrich and his contemporaries have hauled down that ideal and imprinted it with their own faces and the data of their own lives. It will never again be regarded as a pure mirror but as a touched-up photograph of self-congratulating noble personages.

The Mirror in Ulrich's Lyrics

Ulrich wrote a number of mirror-lyrics, and it seems that in every one of them he is at his best—most sensitive to the exalted tradition of the *hoher Minnesang*, most subtle in debasing it. The Ulrich we have come to know, comfort-loving but ambivalent, generous but unspiritual, appears in his most engaging light. All of his many sides, including the seamy side, are reflected there; he diverts us, he baffles us, he moves us, he

---

[13] Mohr, pp. 211ff.

[14] There are other references to the robber-barons, along with similar reactions by Ulrich, at 1738ff and 1750ff; 550, 19ff and 554, 27ff. The general drift is always, "der vrowen dienest was gelegen" (1751, 2; 555, 6). The contrast between the general moral failure and *his* loyalty to the old ideals continues throughout, along with the emphasis on comfort, the compliant lady, the fantasy image: see Lieder L through LII, and 1753ff; 556, 22ff.

repels us—never more deeply anywhere in the entire *Frauen-dienst* than in these lyrics.

The following lyric (XXXIII) is the second to be written in the service of his new lady. He presents it as the versification of an actual conversation he held with her (1397, 1–8; 442, 24–31).

Wizzet, frouwe wol getân,
daz ich ûf genâde hân
herze und lîp an iuch verlân.
    daz riet mir ein lieber wân: I
5 durch des rât hân ichz getân
und wil es niht abe gestân.
daz lât mir ze guote ergân.

"Sit ir dienstes mir bereit,
tuot ir daz ûf lônes reht,
10 sô lât mich erkennen daz,
wie der dienest sî gestalt,   II
den ich mich sol nemen an,
wie der lôn geheizen sî,
der iu von mir sol geschehen."

15 Frouwe, ich wil in mînen tagen
sô nâch iuwern hulden jagen,
daz ez iu muoz wol behagen,
den muot durch iuch hôhe tragen   III
unde an fröiden niht verzagen,
20 iuwer lop der werlde sagen,
und des lônes noch gedagen.

"Sit ir frô, dar zuo gemeit,
mir ze dienest alse ir jeht,
ez gefrumt iuch selben baz
25 danne mich wol tûsentvalt.   IV
tuot daz schamelop hin dan:
mirst der spiegel swære bî,
dar inn ich mîn leit sol sehen."

Iuwer lop die wirde hât,
30   daz ez wol ze hove gât,
baz dann aller künge wât
âne scham aldâ bestât.   v
"lieber herre, sælic man,
ir sît spotes alze frî.
35   dest unprîs, tar ichs gejehen."

(Know, beautiful lady, that for the sake of your grace I have surrendered my heart and body to you. A cherished hope impelled me to do that: through its counsel I have done it, and I do not wish to cease: then let it turn out well for me.

"If your service is at my disposal, and if you are doing this in order to oblige me to requital, tell me what sort of service I should be bound by, and what kind of requital you would receive from me."

Lady, I shall so strive after your grace in my lifetime that it will please you: to bear my spirit high for your sake and not to despair of joy, to say your praise to the world, and to remain silent with respect to requital.

"If you are happy and joyful in my service, as you affirm, it benefits you a thousand times more than me. Do away with this shame-bringing praise. The mirror is painfully near me, wherein I shall see my grief."

The praise of you has such honor that it will be fitting at court; it will stand without shame, better than every royal robe. "Dear lord, blissful man, you are too free with mockery. That is unworthy, if I may say so.")

Bechstein understands the lady's response in the fourth strophe as expressing suspicion of the sincerity of the poet's praise (II, p. 166). Von Kraus rejects this interpretation (if it were true, the poet would respond with an affirmation of his sincerity), and offers an interpretation of his own:

I think [she means] his praise will cause her shame, because by looking into the mirror of this praise she recognizes that the difference between her true worth and the illusive worth [attributed to her by the poet] is too great. He sets this aside by saying this praise could stand up even at court better than every royal robe *âne scham* (without her having to feel ashamed on account of it). [Kommentar, p. 543]

But this cannot be completely right, either. The glorifying "mirror of praise" does not reflect the harm that might come to her at court, or any diminution of her stature: it shows her as a lady in whose hands all power lies. As von Kraus correctly suggests, the lady is mostly afraid of notoriety: the "pain" that she sees in the mirror is the reaction of the society that is to hear this praise and identify her as its object. In other words, there is no question of the lady's being grieved by the difference between her true worth and the perfection the poet attributes to her; she is concerned only about the damage to her reputation. That is why the poet assures her that his praise will fit her well at court.

The context puts one point beyond dispute: the image in the mirror stands in opposition to the flattering *schamelop* and the *spot* of the fifth strophe. This mirror reflects the truth at hand, the image of reality, of everyday unenhanced reality which the *schamelop* strives to glorify—and falsify. It shows her what she really is, it is a "steel glass." It reflects a plain lady, artless though full of caution, unimperious, unremote. In the second strophe she asks how much his service will cost her; in the end she replies that she cannot afford it. This is the first time in our study that we have encountered such a plain mirror, such an anti-metaphorical and anti-idealist mirror.

The whole tradition of courtly love is beautifully encapsuled in Ulrich's strophes. Moret quotes the third strophe at the beginning of his chapter on *Minnedienst*.[15] Here, in seven little lines, is the program of the whole informed and aspiring life of the knight, its consecration to service, its present dig-

[15] André Moret, *Les débuts du lyrisme en Allemagne* (Lille, 1951), p. 173.

nity in the world, its dependence upon grace, the renunciation that prevents despair.

These winged words fall flat in the ears of the practical lady who has to decide carefully whether or not to believe them. She is as solid and actual as her mirror, and from her point of view she does well to turn that praise down. She does not want to have put upon her the attributes of the ideal lady, to be lauded as a golden image that shines like the sun for all to adore and celebrate, or as an inspiring angel who comes in the night to lead the poet toward heaven—that would all be too embarrassing at court, she says. Here, in this contrast between the idealizing praise and the plain facts reflected in the flat mirror, we are back in the atmosphere of a parade, where the attempt to dress up actuality evokes the same ambivalence, the same cynicism and nostalgia. Only now the absurdity of it is made explicit by the lady, for she wants no part of it. She is not willing to play a rôle, as were the people in the Venus Journey.

Commentators have made a great deal of the narrative strophe that precedes this lyric:

> Sich fuogt aber von ir tugenden daz,
> daz ich ir nâhen bî gesaz
> und redet mit ir sus und sô.
> ich was si an ze sehen vrô:
> von hertzen ich si gerne sach.
> swaz ich des tages gegen ir sprach,
> zehant dô ich dâ von ir schiet,
> ich sanc von ir sâ disiu liet.
>
> [1397, 1–8; 442, 24–31]

(Owing to her virtue, it came to pass that I sat with her and spoke to her, thus and so. I was happy to see her: I saw her willingly with all my heart. Immediately when I parted from her, I sang these strophes about her, consisting of what I said to her that day.)

Bechstein considers this to be evidence that an actual conversation provided the subject of the lyric.[16] Von Kraus thinks that the narrative lines are derived from the lyric, "just as elsewhere so much in his report owes its origin not to reality but to literatuure" (Kommentar, p. 543).

The important point for us is that whether or not there actually was such a conversation—for that matter, whether or not there actually was such a lady—the lyric is presented as a metrical rendition of a real conversation. Thus the lady's response is presented as explicitly non-literary—she speaks, as it were, off the record. Thus Ulrich once again intrudes the actual world into a literary form. The lady is guided by common sense; her attitude is the same as that which lies behind all the illusion-shattering incidents in the *Frauendienst*. Her voice is the voice of the actual world, addressed to a sentimental literature that seeks to invest that world in a glory it cannot sustain day in and day out.

The poet is speaking literature, but the lady is—merely speaking. The prosaic quality of her verses is one effect of the rime-scheme Ulrich has devised for her. Each of her strophes is composed of *Waisen*, "orphan" lines that rime only when they are matched with the corresponding lines of the other strophe. Von Kraus rightly declares that ". . . the impression of complete rimelessness at the first hearing . . . is hardly accidental."[17] He thinks that Ulrich is thereby seeking to show the lady as a "Dilettantin" with respect to poetic composition.[18] But the most obvious impression produced by the concealment of the rime is of ordinary, prosaic, spontaneous discourse. And it is she who speaks the last word.

It is important to note that the spirit of the pastourelle is not

[16] Note to 1397, 6. Walther Brecht agrees with this conclusion in "Ulrich von Lichtenstein als Lyriker," *Zeitschrift für deutsches Altertum und deutsche Literatur*, XLIX, n.s. XXXVII (1908), 17f.

[17] Carl von Kraus, *Walther von der Vogelweide, Untersuchungen* (Berlin and Leipzig, 1935), p. 442.

[18] See also Kommentar, p. 543.

found here. The lady is no peasant girl thrilled by a smattering of upper-class talk. She is herself a noble lady, with a good reputation, and in her remarks one can discern the real attitude of Ulrich's contemporaries toward the literary forms he acts out here in his praise, and earlier in the two Journeys. The contrast is somewhat like that between Don Quixote's romances and the world in which he sets them going, except that no one here is baffled or moved by the knight, nor is the knight out of sympathy with the world's condition. The lady is altogether satisfied to be an everyday lady. She does not want to be a mirror of the courtly ideal. She has a more practical mirror, and she sees there how little all that elaborate praise will become her, and how they will react at court. That is why her final remarks are so common-sensical and angry.

This plain mirror never appears in the *hoher Minnesang*. It belongs to a world that refuses the claim of the ideal, of a future reality implied in the present but infinitely better. What a plain piece of coated glass reflects is the first and last condition on earth, and though the image lacks splendor it is not deceptive and heartbreaking. It ends the discomfort of striving; things as they are are good enough. The courtly world shrugs off its ideal: it does not want to be better in the future, it wants to be comfortable now; it wants order, security, heart's ease.

The intent of this lyric is to deny the necessity of the ideal. It makes a mockery of the poet's effort to convert a simple, normal lady into the remote, angelic image of his salvation on earth. In the lady's eyes, such an effort is simply an unfriendly gesture. That is why the alternation of the point of view is finally the meaning of the poem, as it shifts back and forth from the raw material to the idealized and un-actual image of it; from the world of experience, unenhanced, realistic, self-satisfied, to the literary world of the image, where the knight is consecrated to remake himself in the form of perfection. When the two points of view are set side by side, the man who makes demands upon himself seems absurd when viewed by the common sense of *gemach*.[19]

In the thirty-fifth lyric, one of Ulrich's finest, the idea of the mirror is much more traditional.

> Warnet iuch gar, junge und alde,
> gein dem winder: des ist zît.
> niemen blôzer vor im halde:
> er sleht tiefe wunder wît.   I
> 5 lât die schilde stille ligen,
> sît iu selben kleider milde:
> sô mügt ir im an gesigen.
>
> Ich wil iuch des besten wîsen.
> welt ir vor im sîn behuot,
> 10 sô sult ir diu hiuser spîsen:
> gein im ist iu niht sô guot.   II
> swer mit witzen nû niht vert,
> sît er wil diu hûs besitzen,
> der ist von im unernert.
>
> 15 Für sîn stürmen, für sîn slîchen,
> für sîn ungefüege drô,
> sul wir in die stuben wîchen,
> dâ mit wîben wesen frô.   III
> wîbes güete dast ein dach,
> 20 daz man nie für ungemüete
> alsô guotes niht gesach.
>
> Aller guoten wîbe güete
> müeze immer fröiden pflegen.
> vor ir zürnen mich behüete
> 25 got: daz ist mîn morgensegen.   IV

[19] The thirtieth lyric is also represented as originating in an actual conversation, and is likewise in the form of a dialogue. The content and intention are similar, although much lighter in tone, the lady being much more coquettish. See Brecht, p. 17f.

guotes wîbes werdikeit
ist für wâr gar mînes lîbes
hôhster trôst für sendiu leit.

Mînes herzen fröiden lêre
30   ist ein süezer wîbes lîp.
diust mîn trôst für herzen sêre.
sist für wâr ein wîplîch wîp   v
unde ein frouwe manger tugent.
swanne ich in ir ougen schouwe
35   mich, sô blüet mir fröiden jugent.

(Prepare yourselves fully against winter, young and old, for it is time. Let no one be uncovered before it: it strikes deep wide wounds. Let the shields lie still, wear comfortable clothes: in this way you may defeat winter.

I want to guide you in the best way. If you want to be protected from winter, then stock up your houses: you will find nothing so good against it. Whoever does not do this prudently will lack protection against winter, which wants to take possession of the house.

Before winter's storms, before its creeping advance, before its rough threat, we shall retire to our chambers, there to be joyful in the company of women. The goodness of women is a protection, the best one ever saw against grief.

The goodness of all good women shall ever foster joy. May God protect me from their anger: that is my morning prayer. The excellence of a good woman is truly my greatest consolation against longing pain.

A sweet woman is the guide of my heart's joy. She is my consolation for the heart's pain. She is truly a womanly woman and a lady of many virtues. When I behold myself in her eyes, my youth blooms in joy.)

The poet appears as one of us, to give us good advice about protecting ourselves against winter's assault. There is no description of winter as such, yet the dread of winter is there in the very advice he offers. We are impressed as when we look out of the window of a warm room into the street: the frigid air does not touch us, yet we respond to the images of winter's fury as we see the people passing by, trying to shrink within their overcoats or to push themselves into their hats. Similarly, Ulrich's evocation of winter is the more effective because of its indirectness. We do not see the winter, but we hear the advice to let the shields lie where they are and to wear warm clothes. We do not see the barren meadows, but we hear that we had better stock up our houses. Ulrich rejects the traditional images of winter's rage, the snow on the ground where the flowers bloomed, the ice on the branches where the birds once sang, the sun that shines but does not warm—all the images of barrenness and despair. Instead, he shows us a society unified by its common dread of the winter that is coming.

The tone of the lyric is set by this advice, with its specific details and its *tanzwîse* rhythm. The accurate references to the life of a specific class in a specific place, and the very posture of a man speaking to his friends, make of this lyric a communal song. A traditional *Natureingang* would be followed by the voice of a solitary singer comparing his desolation to the winter's barrenness; but here the rough threat of winter binds together all the members of the society, and the stocking up of the houses, like the *ritterschaft* of milder seasons, becomes a communal activity.

The opening strophes of this lyric thus evoke a society collectively threatened by winter; and the threats and storms and deep wide wounds produce in the end a rejoicing consciousness of protection, solidarity, comfort; a sense of immunity to all ills, enjoyed by everyone, as winter storms outside batter each house.

The enjoyment of the company of ladies—"We shall all retire to our chambers, there to be joyful with women"—has the same communal resonance. The act of withdrawal (*wi-*

chen) is essential. Each man goes his own way, but collectively they retreat into well-stocked sanctuaries of comfort and exclusiveness, protected from the rages of the outside world.

The center of the poem is the line, *dâ mit wîben wesen frô.* The well-stocked house is the best protection against winter; the goodness of women is the best protection against *ungemüete.* Each half of the lyric is an analogy and a setting for the other: warm rooms and comfortable clothes are to the winter what the goodness of good women is to grief. For *ungemüete* is, like winter, a threat to the entire society: we have heard Ulrich pronounce grief discourteous and unmanly. The welfare of the community resides in the disposition of its women: their anger is the sign of the knights' failure.

The fourth strophe presents the reverse of this theme: the poet's morning prayer is that God may protect him from the anger of women. For women's anger produces *ungemüete,* just as their goodness prevents it. The goodness of good women makes them protective, but their anger makes them dangerous; from that danger there is no protection on earth.

In other words, the poet makes it clear that their anger is the very menace from which protection is to be sought, and then the whole classic picture comes into focus. When we enjoy the goodness of women who love us, in the comfort and plenty of the warm rooms that lock out the winter, we are immune to all grief. When they love us, their goodness loves us, they reflect their own worth upon us, and we are at one with the ideal image whose remoteness at other times and in other conditions belabors us. These sheltering rooms are thus the representation of a psychic state—as is the winter outside.

Like all the other true knights, the poet has one special *süezer wîbes lîp* to whom he is devoted. He, too, is part of the community he addresses. He can give advice because his voice is the voice of the whole society, his life is in harmony with the life of the group.

This consciousness of living in harmony with others is

heightened in the final strophe. "She is, in truth, a womanly woman, and a lady of many virtues. Whenever I see myself in her eyes, then, in joy, my youth blooms." Her eyes are a mirror that rejuvenates the image it reflects. When the poet looks into them he sees a perfect man, a man in the bloom of his youth, because her eyes reflect not only the image that he casts there but also the courtly virtues that are perfect in her and that are identical with her very womanliness. In the medium of her eyes, in that mirror, his image is united with her ideality. Now those virtues with which she endows his image are the very ones that distinguish the courtly class. From this consciousness of being united with the idealized self-image, and therefore with the whole society, arises true joy.

But the strength of this lyric is not in these ideas, which, after all, are common to all courtly lyrics, and which have here been separated from their moral context to serve as artificial compliments; and certainly it is not in the language, which is platitudinous in the extreme. The tiniest poetic triumph crowns the poem and unites all its images. Outside, the world is barren, it is bitter cold, nothing grows. But in one little circle in the dead of winter, in the world enclosed by the lovers' eyes, it is *Blütezeit*, the time of renewal, of spring: "My youth blooms."

What he experiences in that pleasant room is not *joie*, that exultation which could make a Bernart de Ventadorn insensible to the ice of winter.[20] The man who sees the snow he walks in as red and white and yellow flowers—we do not expect from such a man any practical advice about stocking up the larders and dressing sensibly. And the delicate equilibrium of a man who can experience such joy, balanced like a ship on the wave, about to pitch into bottomless grief—that is not the condition of a man looking forward to a warm fire and good company.

[20] "Tant ai mo cor ple de joya," Appel, No. 44. Cf. Lazar, *Amour courtois*, p. 59f.

This lyric is a celebration of comfort, of generous, guiltless comfort unconscious of any tradition to uphold or debase. That is why it is so successful and attractive: for once, there is no pretense that comfort is the same as joy, that *gemach* is the same as *hôher muot*. The ideal is not made to coincide with actual conditions, as it usually is in Ulrich: it is simply excluded. The sense of class is replaced by the sense of community. It is true that the mirror is still conceived of as endowing the man's image with the virtues that make him acceptable to the society. But those virtues are mere social graces, and that society is full of acceptance, for comfort is its chief aspiration.

What is locked out of the room along with the winter's rages is the demanding, consuming, unattainable ideal, the image as cold as ice. Nothing is promised for the future; the lady and the image are altogether present. The mirror neither deceives nor inspires. Nobody demands much of anyone or of himself. The happiness of this house is the acceptance of the present condition of all things. There is nothing more inimical to such a mood than the harrowing consciousness of an ideal, nothing that makes a man more dissatisfied with himself as he is. But such discontent is absent here, and with it its elusive hope. In this complete exclusion of the ideal, in this release from the desire to become worthy and this comfortable acceptance of present worth, one is aware not simply of the decline of the classic Minnesang, but of its total disappearance.[21]

In the forty-third lyric, Ulrich treats the figure of the mirror in still another way, showing his thorough familiarity with the Minnesang tradition.

---

[21] In the thirty-sixth lyric each of the lovers sees himself in the other's eyes, and to each it seems that he becomes the other. Thus the mirror has largely the same meaning as in the lyric we have just considered. The thirty-fourth lyric expresses this theme in almost the same terms as XXXV. His image in the lady's eyes confers the same sense of invulnerability before the storms of winter.

Wunneclîchen hôhe mîn gemüete
stât. des habe ich mîn frouwe danc,
diu mir mit ir manicvalten güete   I
mînen muot ie hôhe twanc.
5   diu vil reine süeze tuot mir sô
daz ich bin in aller zît von herzen frô.

Diu vil guote zweier hande lachen
lachet, diu ich nennen wil.
diu kan sî sô minneclîchen machen,   II
10   daz si sint mîn herzen spil.
so ich ir süezer lachen einez sol
sehen, sô ist mir in dem herzen wol wol wol.

Einez sî mit rôsenvarwem munde
kan: daz ist sô minneclîch,
15   daz ein man dar inne fröide funde,   III
der ê nie wart fröiden rîch.
sîst der minne gernden meien zît:
in ir lachen fröuden hort der süeze lît.

Lachen kan mîn tugentrîchiu frouwe
20   mit ir spilnden ougen sô,
swanne ich mich dar inne rehte schouwe,   IV
daz ich bin von herzen frô.
swen ir ougen güetlîch lachent an,
der muoz immer sîn ein fröiden rîcher man.

25   Mit ir spilnden ougen lachen schône
kan diu reine süeze wol.
des trag ich der hôhen fröiden krône,   V
alse ir ougen touwes vol
werdent ûz ir reines herzen grunt,
30   von ir lachen: sâ sô wirde ich minne wunt.

Ir vil kleinvelwîzer hals, ir kinne,
munt, brâ, wängel, ougen liht,
ist der minnen spiegel, dâ man inne   VI
manger hande wunne siht.
35   solde ich in den süezen spiegel sehen
alle zît, mir kunde nimmer baz geschehen.

Ulrich von Lichtenstein

Wolde got, sold ich ir hals, ir ougen,
brüstel, kinne, wängel, munt
mit ir guotem willen küssen tougen   VII
40   hundert tûsent tûsent stunt!
manger giht, des wær mir alze vil,
der mit wîben niht kan spiln der minne spil.

(My spirit is high in joy, because of my lady, who, with her many
kinds of goodness, forced my spirit upward. The pure sweet lady
has such an effect on me that my heart is always joyful.

The good one laughs with two kinds of laughter, which I shall
name. She can make these two kinds of laughter so lovely, that
they are the pleasure of my heart. If I should see but one sort of
that sweet laughter, then in my heart there is joy, joy, joy.

One she makes with her rose-colored mouth. It is so lovely that a
man would find joy in it who never had been rich in joys. That
joy is of the love-desiring May-time: in the hoard of joys in her
laughter, sweetness lies.

My lady rich in virtues can laugh with her sparkling eyes, so that
whenever I look upon myself within them, my heart rejoices. The
man upon whom her eyes smile with kindness must always be a
man rich in joys.

The pure, sweet lady knows well how to laugh beautifully with
her sparkling eyes. Therefore I bear the crown of lofty joys, as
her eyes become full of dew from the ground of her pure heart,
with her laughing. Immediately I am wounded by *Minne*.

Her slender white neck, her chin, mouth, brow, cheeks, and
bright eyes are the mirror of love, wherein one sees many kinds
of pleasure. If I could look into that sweet mirror at every moment, nothing better could ever happen to me.

Her neck, her eyes, her little breast, chin, cheeks, mouth—would
God that I could kiss them secretly with her good will a hundred
thousand thousand times! Many a man asserts that that would be all
too much for me, who cannot play the game of love with women.)

200

This lyric suffers from the slovenliness of diction that is Ulrich's chief fault as a poet. Ulrich goes too far with his endless *frô*'s and *süeze*'s and *wunne*'s. But the lyric also reveals one of his virtues, the ability to sustain a single theme, revitalizing even the oldest clichés.

Thus the two kinds of laughter that he distinguishes here are united in their association with fertility and plenitude. The joy the lady gives with the laughter of her mouth is of the "love-desiring May-time," the season of growth; in that laughter lies a "hoard" of joys. Similarly, the garden-metaphor—already old and soon to be a standard item in the *Minnesangswende* [22]—is vital here; and the laughter of her eyes is a mirror containing innumerable images of pleasure. This theme of abundance and variety is sustained in the language as well: her goodness is *manicvalten;* the man on whom she smiles becomes *fröiden rîch.* The *hundert tûsent tûsent stunt* of the last strophe, otherwise a childish hyperbole, gains credit as a reflection of the constant theme of limitless abundance.

When he looks into the eyes of the lady who is rich in every kind of virtue, he sees his image in a setting of inexhaustible fertility and variety. The lady reflects all the joys and virtues of the earth, the plenitude which is the earth's own mirror of God's grace. Thus, once again, it is the image of his own immortality that he sees in her eyes, an image that is ageless, constantly renewed, indestructible. Furthermore, it participates in that same grace by which the world is reborn in May, which creates, as an image of purity and fertility, the manifold dew that rises toward heaven. So immense is the goal he seeks; to win her would indeed be "all too much" for him.

In the distinction between the laughter of the red mouth and the laughter of the eyes, Ulrich is following what seems to have been a well established tradition in the classic period.

[22] See Hugo Kuhn, *Minnesangs Wende* (Tübingen, 1952), especially the first and second chapters.

The red mouth is the center of the lady's physical beauty; and so the laughter of the mouth is associated with the regeneration of May. The eyes reveal the lady's interior beauty, her exalted moral condition; they are mirrors of the lady's inner life.

The elaborate expression of physical desire at the end unites the two aspects of the lady into one single mirror. Sexual desire sustains courtly love. The desire to unite with the lady's body begins the *Minne*-relation, and it never grows less intense or less immediate. But in the heat and refinement of *Minne* the desire of the flesh is endowed with meaning, because the wish to unite with the body incorporates the wish to unite with virtue. That carnal desire is the great integrative force of courtly love, preventing the total fragmentation of the lady, her division into aspects, some of which it is proper and safe to desire, some shameful and dangerous. The intensity of physical desire affirms the integrity of the lady, the inseparability of her beauty and her virtue; at the same time, it preserves the integrity of the lover, bending his body and soul together toward one single fulfillment. Thus, in this lyric, there is a relocation of the self-image. When the poet is distinguishing the two kinds of laughter, he sees himself in the mirror of her eyes; but at the end, when he is putting everything back together again, the mirror consists of her whole person, of eyes and mouth and body together.

The chief disruptive element in the lyric is its tone, that *wol* thrice repeated, all the insistent and reiterated *frô*'s and *fröide*'s. Once, as a tag, the poet thinks to say, *sâ sô wirde ich minne wunt,* but these words fall flat. This is not the tone of a man "wounded" by love and desire, consumed in longing, dedicated in service. It is the utterance of a man for whom courtly love is a *spil,* as he calls it; a man, so to speak, professionally dedicated to happiness. That is why the effect of the lady's beauty and goodness is described so vaguely, in the emptiest of clichés. The man who sees her becomes "a man rich in joys," Ulrich makes this statement twice, but what does he convey?

We have heard another poet describe the effect on all those who have had a vision of the lady. In a hundred ways Heinrich and the others of his society act out the evidence of the lady's power. They are dazed as when one stares into the sun, yet they long for her as one longs for the morning star; there is probably not one who has kept his senses, but if there is such a one, let him hasten to implore mercy for one who is truly "wounded"; her virtue and her beauty are a source of danger in every land (*MF* 130, 15ff), yet a word that she speaks startles the body with joy (*MF* 125, 19–126, 7); the man who raves all the time in longing is struck dumb by the actual sight of her beauty, the singer torments himself for losing the power of speech (*MF* 135, 9–38); she is an angel, she is a murderess (*MF* 147, 4–16). These countless paradoxes of passion and doubt confirm the reality of the lady in her ambivalent effect on the lover.

Ulrich offers nothing but the vaguest of clichés. "Whomever she smiles upon must become a man rich in joys." And when he is not too general, he is too specific. That mechanical naming of her parts at the end—neck, chin, mouth, brow, cheeks, eyes, breast, chin again, cheeks again, mouth again—is a mere catalogue, a desperate substitution of compulsiveness for imagination. Equally vague and mechanical is the diction: *manger hande wunde; in ir lachen . . . der süeze lît; mir kunde nimmer baz geschehen.* These are mere résumés.

Of course, Ulrich's talent is second-rate to begin with. But aside from the question of talent, he has a vested interest in preserving his mediocrity in his lyrics.

If his generalities and clichés are anti-sensory, leaving the flesh cold, the nerves undisturbed, that is precisely his intention. Such clichés relieve the poet and his audience from the experience of beholding the lady's terrible beauty, her maddening perfection. It is not simply from want of imagination that Ulrich fails to specify the experience—the joy, the anguish—of loving her; it is from an aversion to intensity of any sort, to passion, to despair, to ecstasy. It is from a decision that his whole generation has taken, to survive in the safety and mediocrity of *gemach.*[23]

[23] The forty-fourth lyric takes up the distinction between the mouth and the eyes of the lady with the same implications. In the first two strophes the poet declares that he is *hôhes muotes* because of a beautiful highborn lady; he then proceeds to describe the genesis of this *hôher muot*. The lady spoke a word with her sweet red mouth; she smiled when she spoke that word, as the poet gazed into her bright sparkling eyes (Str. iii). Her goodness took the word out of the ground of her heart, and *vreuden hôchgemüete* bloomed (*blüet*) within him as he heard that sweet word, which he shall forever treasure as the hoard of his joys (Str. iv); the word has gone into his heart (cf. 1655, 3; 523, 16). In all this there is a clear influence from Reimar (*MF* 195, 2) and Heinrich (*MF* 137, 10–26 and esp. 125, 19–126, 7).

The basic metaphor thus far is of transplantation: she took the word-seed from the ground of her heart and planted it in his; the "flower" is *hôher muot*. But Ulrich works out this metaphor in an interesting way. She speaks the word with her beautiful red mouth; but before the word was spoken it existed soundlessly in the goodness of her heart; and even as the spoken word leaves by her red lips, the other, the soundless word rises also to show its effects in her eyes, in the light of the mirror of the heart. Thus the double aspect of the lady finds a parallel in the double aspect of her word, the vocalized word perceived by the senses, the spiritual word expressed in light. And the word is inexhaustibly fertile.

The remainder of the lyric is a meditation upon that word. With it the lady gives the poet joy and endows him with every virtue (Str. v). He has honor, joy, pleasure, knighthood (*ritters leben*) from her, as *lône* for his service (Str. vi). He has also received from her the desire to seek honor. He is her true knight, and whatever she desires, he desires; she is his powerful queen (Str. vii).

Thus the idealized image becomes the word that expresses his whole existence as a knight, both in its public appearance (as the vocalized word, as the service that is visible) and in its internal attitude (as the soundless word received from her heart, the source of all virtue). That word is his salvation; it is like the word that came from the mouth of the lady Cavalcanti loved: "la salute tua è apparita" ("Veggio negli occhi de la donna mia"—see the end of the next chapter). But once again, it is the tone of the lyric that undoes all its exalted

Frauendienst does two things that are new. It discredits the idealism of the *hoher Minnesang* by demonstrating its inadequacy to the real life of the courtly class. And it relieves that class of every moral imperative by depicting its actual condition as a literal fulfillment of the courtly ideal. Thus Ulrich von Lichtenstein may be said to have "realized" the ideals of the *hoher Minnesang* in the most material sense: he uses a literary moral doctrine not as a paragon but as a sanction for the behavior of historic personages.

His main purpose in this is to create a moral disguise for the enjoyment of *gemach*, the acceptance of actual conditions. The severe discipline, the sacramental life, the consecration to service, the commitment to the perfection of one's nature, the pursuit of an ideal image and the valuation of the future, the danger of that pursuit in the devaluation of the present—all these consequences of courtly love are replaced by a new disposition to abhor intensity, to enfeeble desire, to make its object readily available and less demanding. As a result, the image loses its ideality and is often described as though it were a real lady, or a photographic likeness of her. The lady ceases to be remote and imperious; she can neither torture the lover nor redeem him.

The world of *Frauendienst* should not be at all strange to

---

pronouncements. It does not end with the knight at the beginning of a severe discipline of service; he is rather soothed, assured, satisfied—comfortable.

The lyrics that follow, especially the forty-eighth and fifty-eighth, contain the same themes as the forty-third and forty-fourth, but they have less merit. Also, the theme of the word, the eyes, the red mouth is taken up again at 1807ff; 577, 21ff, and in the fifty-sixth lyric. In the latter there is a smug and at the same time frantic attitude toward sexual union as an escape from the anxieties of the actual world. This is the final debasement of *Minne*. Immediately afterwards (LVII), we are back to fantasies (as in XLI), with the poet manipulating the lady's image as he lies alone: "Straightaway my body thought of joys with her, thus, and so." This demonstrative erotic fantasy is "paradise." It is the last stage in the ascendancy of *gemach:* the flight into fantasy is a withdrawal from experience.

us. Change the costumes and the customs, and it is our world, today, with its own distrust of experience, its creed of comfort, its convenient and insolent morality, its surrogate images.

Who knows what kind of poet Ulrich might have been? He had a way with words and images. With an inherited idealism, a mirror that could not reflect the practices of the actual world, he was in a position that has called forth many a great poet. He could have used the mirror of the ideal to show forth the unperfectible nature of the human race and the steadfastness of its dream. But he suffered a moral failure of his own. Unlike Heinrich von Morungen, he could not face the fact that man is unable to attain the ideal that he alone can engender. Instead, Ulrich chose to debase the unattainable, dressing up his contemporaries as ideal figures. That pretense brought ease and comfort to the courtly man, as it deprived him of the hope of amelioration. It was a kind of despairing indolence, and it ended the possibility of creating great poetry.

The De Trinitate of St. Augustine and the Lyric Mirror

THE outstanding feature in the "background" of a medieval poet was the Church. This hardly need be said. Today, however, in the absence of a world-wide faith and institution, we often tend to interpret the Church's influence as not only universal but also exclusive. Although no one explicitly believes any longer in the childish notion of the medieval man racked day in and day out by terror of the torments of hell and consumed with guilt for every earthly pleasure, many share a belief that amounts to the same thing, for it assumes that a medieval man was incapable of secular life. I refer to the belief that every innocent artifact is a concealed allegory of the Church's massive doctrines, and that we can discover the true meaning of any literary work, even the simplest lyric, only when we have peeled away its secularity like a bitter and untasted rind.

Despite the Church's pervasive influence, a medieval man could sing or hear a lyric without, for the moment at least, bending his thoughts to the Crucifixion or the afterlife. The Church was there for everyone at every moment, washing away his inherited sin at birth, absolving him of his personal sin at death; but each man had a thousand secular concerns as well—the neighbors' jealousy, the body's appetites, the landlord's rent—and no one knew this better than the Church.

Epilogue

The Church's knowledge of secular experience was one of its strengths before it became one of its weaknesses. Its preachers confirmed, in intimate detail, the universal existence of a temporal inner life, and private life. "The seconde spece of Envye," says Chaucer's Parson,

> is joye of oother mannes harm; and that is proprely lyk to the devel, that evere rejoyseth hym of mannes harm. Of thise two speces comth bakbityng; and this synne of bakbityng or detraccion hath certeine speces, as thus. Som man preiseth his neighebor by a wikked entente; for he maketh alwey a wikked knotte atte laste ende. Alwey he maketh a "but" atte laste ende, that is digne of moore blame, than worth is all the preisynge.
>
> [Robinson, ed., 491–493]

Through such descriptions every private secret became a universal condition:

> Thanne comth the synne of worldly sorwe, swich is cleped *tristicia*, that sleeth man, as seith Seint Paul. For certes, swich sorwe werketh to the deeth of the soule and of the body also; for therof comth that a man is anoyed of his owene lif.
>
> [*Ibid.*, 724–726]

Though the men of the Church tried to make all these events of the heart and the street a part of the drama of redemption, they clearly did not make secular life less secular.

Nor is a work of literature less secular when it adopts many terms of ecclesiastical origin. If we find not only a God of Love but a servant of his servants and many "priests," we should not assume that the poet included the dogma when he borrowed the term. Quite the contrary, he often used these terms to suggest that courtly love had a certain formal dignity and that its rewards were worth striving for. The vocabulary of the Church was frequently used to corroborate and to glorify secular experience.

Let us recognize the influence of the Church without making every medieval man its moral puppet.

In its meticulous descriptions of secular life, the Church sought to demonstrate that a man could turn to it in his every need. We may well suppose that these descriptions hold clues to the meaning of the secular values whose presence we have inferred in the courtly lyric. There is no better place to look for them than in the works of St. Augustine, the greatest single literary and philosophical influence of all the men of the Church in the period when the lyric was at its height.

St. Augustine was at once determinedly insistent upon the invisibility of God's invisible things and intimately acquainted with the visible things of ordinary life. This knowledge and integrity are nowhere more evident, or more serviceable to the author, than in the *De Trinitate,* one of his most important and most original works—and one which was widely read in the Middle Ages, judging by the number and distribution of the manuscripts. In *De Trinitate* he attempts to infer some knowledge of God from the structure and workings of the human mind and body, for both bear the image of their Creator. Thus the work is an example *par excellence* of using the "ladder of the visible."

In the course of his long search, St. Augustine gives definitive expression to many ideas and habits of perception that were to become essential for the Middle Ages: the disposition of the individual soul to seek in another being the agent of its salvation; its inability to survive, by its own powers, the deceptiveness of human experience; the belief in the ideal, not as a mental construct but as a concerned and rewarding being; the concept of all reality, of material as well as psychological reality, as so many images of that creative ideal; the concept of resemblance, not as an accidental quality, but as the creative principle of all existence and the cause of all unity; the concept of history not as a process unrolling in time but as a constantly realized metaphor, a poem of prefiguration and fulfillment in which time has no ultimate significance; the enthralled consciousness of the inner life, and the evolution of a dramatic style to express its conflicts. All these, and more, one finds fully articulated in the *De Trinitate*, as well as in Augustine's other works; no other writer is so rich in the "spirit" of the Middle Ages.

It should be clear, of course, that neither St. Augustine nor any other man is the "source" of the courtly lyric. Augustine does not explain the lyric, nor does the lyric allegorize Augustine.

The purpose of this epilogue is to demonstrate that Augustine's vocabulary in the *De Trinitate*, the terms he establishes in his analysis of the operations of the human mind, can adequately define, without distortion, the relation between the courtly man, the lady, and the love that unites them, in the secular lyric. This is true because St. Augustine's book consists of a close study of the visible, secular things. He finds the clearest image of the Holy Trinity in the condition of the mind that fully knows itself. In the later books of the *De Trinitate*, which we shall examine, he presents a meticulous description of the origin and nature of self-consciousness, its necessity, its pre-condition, its rewards; above all, its status as an image of God. He hypostatizes the condition of self-consciousness.

As we attempt to follow Augustine's path—as no one would dare to do except with the guidance of the many authoritative studies available [1]—we shall find a new light on

[1] I have particularly relied on the following: the long and illuminating notes of P. Agaësse and J. Moingt in the edition of the *Œuvres de Saint Augustin*, Bibliothèque Augustinienne, 2me série, XVI (Paris, 1955), cited hereafter as BA; Michael Schmaus, *Die psychologische Trinitätslehre des hl. Augustinus* (Münster i. W., 1927); Etienne Gilson, *Introduction à l'étude de Saint Augustin* (Paris, 1943). I have also consulted John Burnaby's translation, which has guided me through many a difficult passage: *Augustine: Later Works*, Library of

the courtly lyric. This does not mean that the poets read St. Augustine, or that they were concerned with any of the things that concerned him. It means, rather, that medieval religion and medieval literature are reflections of a single mentality, a single mode of thought which forms the "background" to the lyrics more meaningfully than any narrow and particular literary tradition.

Narcissus, with whom our study began, is also a paradigm of the evolution of self-consciousness; and between Narcissus and St. Augustine the alternatives of the medieval world are defined, the secular and the religious, in the fullest extent of their possibilities. The experience that Narcissus suffers and the one that Augustine describes are alike in their dependence on an image; but otherwise they are irreconcilable.

Narcissus first learns to distinguish between himself and his reflection. In discovering that he is different from the image he discovers his own identity, distinguishing his outward form from the life that animates it—the will, the intelligence, the memory, the capacity for desire and thought: he discovers in himself every faculty than an image cannot possess.

We today would hold this reward of consciousness to be the one redemption in Narcissus's suffering. But for Augustine it would, because of its finality, be not the reward but the very cause of his destruction. He would approve the mind's discovery that no sensible image can reflect it, but for him that would be only the first step. For in its highest state of consciousness the mind knows itself not as a discrete form, but precisely as an image. The mind's health lies in its awareness

Christian Classics, VIII (Philadelphia, 1955). The text is that of the *Patrologiae Cursus Completus*, Series Latina, ed. J. P. Migne (Paris, 1845–1855), Vol. XLII, cols. 819–1098; hereafter cited as *PL*. Other useful studies are cited in the notes.

that it is an image of an ideal reality, that it is dependent upon the substance of the Holy Trinity, which brought it into being and conferred upon it its form and aspiration. The mind's integrity is preserved by its love for what it reflects; for that love impels it to become more and more like its origin, and as it becomes a truer image, it becomes more real.

Narcissus, and the courtly man for whom he is a paradigm, love an ideal that is purely secular and must therefore have a limited and peculiar existence. For the courtly ideal was intended to make the most of a mortality that would falter many times before it had to end. Its promises were meant to be fulfilled within time; and all of the demands of the courtly ideal expressed, not the origin of human life, but its temporal possibilities. For a secular man the incorporeality of an ideal made it not only exempt from time, but unreal in time. That is why the ideal can be accorded only a kind of theatrical reality, an "as if" reality. Otherwise it will devour secular life, mock its frailty, starve it—as it deprived Narcissus of all requital. No secular intelligence can be consoled by the voice in the whirlwind; no secular love can wait till it is free of time and matter. The courtly life was a spirituality that accommodated time and matter; it was created to enhance man's temporal intelligence, to refine his material love, to confer earthly salvation—without ever depriving him of earth, and matter, and time. It made an ethical demand upon the courtier to act "as if" the ideal were alive and concerned, as if there were no such thing as a mirror. The courtly lover was in peril when that crucial "as if" was obscured, when he failed to see that the image was confined to a mirror, a mirror that would break and that could not live. His consciousness of the "as if" was the source alike of his enhancement, his anguish, and his survival.

St. Augustine renounces the moral enterprise of secular life because of that "as if," for to him it is a fatal reservation, the annihilation of true faith.

That is why he belongs to a different world. But the two worlds are still the two hemispheres of the great medieval world, and the language of one can still translate the experience of the other. It is our task now to see how the language of St. Augustine translates the courtly experience.

Preparation

God created man in His own image. God is a Trinity, three Persons, one substance. In the mind and body of man there are numerous "analogies" to the oneness of the Father, the Son, the Holy Spirit. In the human mind are the two analogies that form the closest image: Augustine terms them (1) *mens, notitia, amor;* (2) *memoria, intelligentia, voluntas.* But before he can formulate them, he must prepare the way. This he does in Book VIII.

THE REAL AND ABSOLUTE EXISTENCE OF THE IDEAL

One loves only the good. The earth, the air, the just man, the wise word—we love all these things for the same reason: we deem them good. Here is the path by which one may seek to find God:

Bonum hoc et bonum illud: tolle hoc et illud, et vide ipsum bonum, si potes; ita Deum videbis, non alio bono bonum, sed bonum omnis boni.   [VIII, III, 4; col. 949]

(This is good, and that is good: take away the "this" and the "that" and behold, if you can, the good itself. Thus you will see God, who is good not because of something else that is good, but is the very goodness of all good things.)

Because the notion of the Good is impressed on our minds, we are able to judge among all the good things we love, to say that one thing is better than another. This real and immutable Good is God himself, whom we can never see in this life. And yet it is according to the notion of the Good that we make all our judgments. This paradox, that the human mind can judge in the light of an ideal it can never see, is at the root of the whole work.[2]

The Good is not only the light of the soul's judgment, it is the hope of its reformation. Because the Good is a Being altogether different from the soul, pre-existing and transcending it, untouched by the waves of experience that overwhelm it, the soul can be saved:

Cum vero agit hoc studio, et fit bonus animus, nisi se ad aliquid convertat quod ipse non est, non potest hoc assequi.

[VIII, III, 4; col. 950]

(But when the soul endeavors and becomes good, it cannot attain this end unless it turns itself to something that is not itself.)

This *conversio*, the turning toward the Good in an act of its will, preserves the soul's integrity; for it is held together by its love for the ideal. If it turns away from the Good and places its love in an object as changeable as itself, it is pulled apart by uncertainty and conflicting desires. It loses something of its form, becomes *deformis* and unable to know itself.[3]

The soul must try to see beyond things that are considered good here and now to the Good itself, in which they participate. In other words, it must use "the ladder of the visible"; and the thing most visible to it is its own nature. We recognize the soul as good, and it pleases us, if we understand it correctly, not in itself but in the "art" that made it.[4] And as it deems itself good, the soul must love itself.

Now the soul must attach itself to the Good in love and

---

[2] Cf. Fulbert Cayré, *Initiation à la Philosophie de Saint Augustin*, Bibliothèque Augustinienne, Etudes, Philosophie, I (Paris, 1947), 189.

[3] See P. Agaësse's note, "La 'conversio' augustinienne," BA, 576ff.

[4] *Non in se ipso nobis placet, sed in illa arte qua factus est.* VIII, III, 5; col. 950.

always strive to conform itself to its idea; and yet the Good is never to be known directly in this life. Then how is it possible to love what one does not know? We must believe in the eternity, equality, and oneness of the Trinity before we can understand it, but how can we, in our believing, love that Trinity which we do not yet understand (VIII, v, 8; col. 952f)?

This question arises in other matters, too. Why do we love the Apostle Paul? Not because he was a man, for he is no longer a man but we still love him: what we love does not die. Then it must be a just soul that we love. But this means that we know what a soul is, and what "the just" is. Now we have a basis for saying that we know what a soul is, for we have a soul. But how do we know what the "just" is, especially if we are not just ourselves? Yet we do know, and the source of our knowledge is where we shall find the truest image of God:

In nobis igitur novimus quid sit justus. Non enim alibi hoc invenio, cum quaero ut hoc eloquar, nisi apud me ipsum: et si interrogem alium quid sit justus, apud se ipsum quaerit quid respondeat; et quisquis hinc verum respondere potuit, apud se ipsum quid responderet invenit. [VIII, vi, 9; col. 954]

(It is therefore in ourselves that we see what the just is. When I seek to express it, I do not find it anywhere but in myself; and if I should ask another what the just is, it is in himself that he seeks what to answer. And whoever is able to give a true answer finds that answer in himself.)

We ought not to know what a just soul is, and yet we do know. And we marvel at this baffling fact, that the soul should see in itself what it has never seen elsewhere, for it is not itself the just soul that it sees. What it sees is a *veritas interior*, an interior truth, available to each soul capable of contemplating it (VIII, vi, 9; col. 955), no matter what its moral condition.

Epilogue

The real and absolute existence of the ideal is the cause of the soul's capacity for knowledge and judgment. There lies its hope, and the peculiarity of its nature: the soul can see what it is not yet, what it aspires to become.

VERA DILECTIO

One who is not yet the just soul he contemplates can become just by "cleaving" to that ideal, so as to be reformed according to it, not only defining a rule of justice but living justly himself, truly giving to each his due. And how may he cleave to that interior truth except by loving it?

He loves the just man according to that form and truth which he perceives in himself. But this *forma et veritas*—there is no other reason for loving it than for itself alone. And so whoever loves human beings ought to love them either because they are just or in order that they might become just; and in the same way one ought to love oneself (*ibid.*, col. 955f).

What a man truly loves is within himself, and its presence is revealed every time he makes a judgment. It is not Justice that he sees, for God is Justice, and God cannot be seen; it is rather a "just soul" and a "rule" enabling him to know whether a soul or an act is just.[5] The human soul is therefore equipped with all the critical faculties of its reformation. Impelled by love for the rule of Justice, it works to resemble the object of its love.

It is love that draws the soul toward the attainment of its true end: "True love is this, that in cleaving to the truth we should live justly."[6] Love unites the soul with the interior truth. It is Justice that illuminates the mind whenever it makes a moral judgment, and that enables it to be certain—we do not

[5] VIII, ix, 13; col. 959. Cf. Gilson, *Introduction*, pp. 88–130, esp. pp. 118–124; and Fulbert Cayré's note in BA, pp. 579ff.

[6] *Haec est autem vera dilectio, ut inhaerentes veritati juste vivamus.* VIII, vii, 10; col. 956.

merely believe, we *know* that the servants of God must live according to the words of St. Paul;[7] so it is *Caritas* that bestows upon us the love with which we love our neighbor, the love with which we love Justice, the love with which we love Love itself.[8]

Thus Augustine marks out the ground of his search for the human image.[9] At the beginning of all his thought is the human mind desiring to become wholly formed, to be fully what it ought to be. For this it requires the help of God—but God helps what already exists. Therefore Augustine turns to the natural abilities of the mind, and of these two are crucial. The mind is naturally able to see itself as it ought to be, to know itself in the ideal. It is also able to love that idealized self-image, to "cleave" to it. This is the program of its salvation. Here is where Augustine will look to find the mark of the Holy Trinity in the human soul: the mind, its knowledge of itself in the ideal, the love that unites it to this ideal image.

Mens, Notitia, Amor

THE MIND THAT KNOWS AND LOVES ITSELF

Every love-relation requires three things: a lover, a beloved, and love uniting them (VIII, x, 14; col. 960). But Augustine is concerned with the mind not as it loves another created thing but as it loves itself;[10] and then there are only the mind and its love, for lover and beloved are the same. But from the preparation we know that there must be something more, for the mind cannot love itself unless it knows itself.[11]

Therefore the mind, its self-knowledge, and its love are three things, and these three things ought to be one. For if the

[7] VIII, ix, 13; col. 959f. Augustine quotes 2 Cor. vi, 2–10.
[8] See J. Moingt's note, "Méthode du Livre VIII," BA, 572ff.
[9] Cf. Schmaus, *Trinitätslehre*, p. 225f.
[10] IX, ii, 2; col. 961f. Cf. Introduction, BA, p. 20.
[11] IX, ii, 3; col. 962f. Cf. Schmaus, pp. 230ff, esp. 235f.

mind's love of itself is less or greater than its being, it sins, and its love is perverted—for example, if it should love itself as the body should be loved, or as God should be loved. Similarly, when the mind knows itself, its knowledge is neither superior nor inferior to itself, for it is the mind which knows and the mind which is known. Thus when these three things are perfect, they are equal and one.[12]

THE SUBSTANTIALITY OF LOVE AND KNOWLEDGE

Love and knowledge exist in the mind not as qualities, but as substances. Properties such as color or shape are confined to the subject: the color of one body cannot become the color of another. But the mind is able, with the love by which it loves itself, to love something other than itself; and it does not know itself alone, but many other things as well (IX, IV, 5; col. 963f).

This idea, that the mind's love and the mind's knowledge are substances no less than itself, will be less baffling if we return to the preparations of Book VIII, which J. Moingt has summarized as follows: [13] The mind is not created in a state of perfection; it is an incomplete image, and in order to realize itself it must become more and more like that of which it is an image.[14] Now God is Love, God is Justice, God is the Good. It is love that impels the soul to turn toward its origin; and what it turns toward is the immutable law of Justice—and both the love by which it turns, and its knowledge of the law to which it turns, are bestowed upon it by God.

The essential condition of the soul is to be an image; and the integrity of an image depends upon its similarity to its origin.[15] When the soul turns toward the Good, it becomes more and more like the Good, comes closer and closer to identity with

[12] IX, IV, 4; col. 963. Cf. Schmaus, pp. 253ff.

[13] "Substantialité de l'*amor* et de la *notitia*," BA, 594ff; cf. Schmaus, pp. 272ff, who makes much the same observations.

[14] Cf. *Retractationes*, II, XXIV, 2; Gilson, 291ff; Schmaus, 291ff.

[15] Cf. Gilson, p. 294; Schmaus, pp. 195–200, 223f.

it. That identity with the Good is the true identity of the soul—it is a perfection never to be achieved in this life. But the closer it comes, the more complete its identity.[16] Now love, as Moingt writes, "which makes the soul firm in the pursuit of its end and perfects it in its nature, must in itself have firmness and stability, and the same essence as the soul." Love, therefore, is not "a simple act produced by the soul." Rather, Moingt continues,

It is *"forma et veritas"*; it is not a *habit* which the soul uses at will, but it is a "law"; "always stable and immutable," it is "substance" and "spirit." Through love the soul adheres to its form and conceives its word. For love is not of a different nature from the soul, nor alien to it; being "the interior truth present to the soul," it is the *mens*. Thus *amor* and *mens* are united to form "one single spirit," "the just soul." In contrast to covetousness which divides and deforms the soul, true love gathers it to itself in its ideal perfection in relating it to God; it is a substantial principle of a spiritual unity, "a life which joins together."

The more the soul turns away from the ideal it reflects, the more it must lose the vital resemblance which is its very form; and the more it reaches to that which is eternal, the more it is thereby formed in the image of God.[17] The soul is an image endowed with the faculty to know itself as an image, and to love what it resembles. Its condition at any moment, therefore, is an expression of its will. If it should cease to love what gives it being and form, it falls apart; for to be an image means to be a resemblance, and love preserves resemblance. Therefore, the very form of the image coincides with its love. Love is the substance of the soul, its truth, its "law."

Augustine goes further. The love for its Creator that fulfills

---

[16] Cf. *De vera religione*, XIV, 28.

[17] *Et quoniam quantumcumque se extenderit in id quod aeternum est, tanto magis inde formatur ad imaginem Dei*; XII, vii, 10; col. 1004. Cf. XII, xi, 16; Agaësse, BA, 631.

and preserves the soul's identity—that love comes from God Himself, who is Love.[18] Thus there is a "Love informing" and a "love informed";[19] and corresponding precisely to this is the relation between divine Truth and human knowledge. Whatever the mind knows, it knows through illumination from the eternal and immutable truths in the mind of God. Again, this was a cardinal point in Book VIII: we love Paul because he was a just soul; and we who are not just souls yet see, and see truly, a just soul within ourselves, and the unchanging rule which Justice itself impresses upon our minds and which gives certainty to our judgments. The human mind, not fully formed and constantly in flux, contemplating things that dissolve and re-form incessantly, and experiences that rush in a welter, with "divers false colors and forms pouring into the mind as upon a mirror . . . and varying as in a revolving mirror of thought"[20]—the mind, which sees nothing but mutability, yet knows truths that are eternal and immutable. After imagining rectangles of every sort, for example, it "turns to that according to which it judges them all to be rectangles" (*ibid.*). To Augustine it is inconceivable that the mind in such conditions can reach the unchanging truth by its own habits and powers. Therefore, as Moingt writes,

True knowledge is formed directly upon the "eternal and immutable truths," it takes its rule "above the soul," it sees the soul, not as it appears to itself, but as it "ought to be," it "judges" the soul (IX, vi, 9–11). It is thus something other and greater than a habitual disposition, or something given at the moment; it has the autonomy and stability of a "substance"; knowable and knowing by itself, it has its purpose and norm in itself, it is a substantial principle of a spiritual truth (IX, iv, 4–5). [BA, p. 597]

[18] Cf. *De doctrina Christiana*, XXIX, 30; *Enchiridion*, CVIff, CXVII. Also, Adolf von Harnack, *History of Dogma* (New York, 1958), V, 225; and J. Hessen, who cites other texts in his *Augustins Metaphysik der Erkenntnis*, 2d ed. (Leiden, 1960), p. 59f.

[19] Moingt, *loc. cit.*

[20] *Soliloquia*, II, xx, 35. Cf. Agaësse, BA, pp. 597ff.

Love and knowledge therefore are not acts or constituents of the mind, but are identical with it in substance, discrete gifts of its Creator. Love draws the soul toward its ideal condition, which knowledge reveals; and it is this *movement* and *relationship* between the mind, its ideal, and the love that unites them which constitutes the one being. *Mens, notitia, amor* are a true analogy of the Holy Trinity, distinguished one from another by their relations but all of the same substance. Of course, the human trinity is never perfect in this life: the mind is never fully formed, knowledge is obscured by carnal images, love is usurped by material objects to decay into *cupiditas.*[21] Against this impulse toward dissolution the mind must struggle and call for help. Its basis for hope is that it can never lose its capacity to become a better image of God; to make *mens, notitia, amor* approach true identity.

Illumination

When the mind seeks to know itself, how does it know that what it sees is its truth, and not a false image of itself? Augustine's answer is that it is "illuminated" by the Truth itself. He gives a number of examples of the working of divine illumination.

It is one thing, he says, to know what something is, and for that there is no need of illumination. It is another thing to know what it *ought to be,* and such knowledge is impossible without divine illumination. A man may say that he understands or desires something, and all we can do is either believe him or not. When he speaks, however, not about a momentary personal condition, but about the truth of the human soul according to species and genus, then it is no longer a matter of believing, but of knowing and approving:

Unde manifestum est, aliud unumquemque videre in se, quod sibi alius dicenti credat, non tamen videat; aliud autem in ipsa veritate,

[21] IX, v, 8; col. 965. Cf. Agaësse, BA, p. 597.

quod alius quoque possit intueri: quorum alterum mutari per tempora, alterum incommutabili aeternitate consistere. Neque enim oculis corporeis multas mentes videndo, per similitudinem colligimus generalem vel specialem mentis humanae notitiam: sed intuemur inviolabilem veritatem, ex qua perfecte, quantum possumus, definiamus, non qualis sit uniuscujusque hominis mens, sed qualis esse sempiternis rationibus debeat.   [IX, VI, 9; col. 966]

(Whence it is clear that it is one thing for a man to see in himself what another may believe on his word, but without seeing; another thing, however, for a man to see in the truth itself what another may also contemplate: for the first of these changes through time, while the second subsists in unchangeable eternity. For it is not that we gather a general or special knowledge of the human mind by observing many minds with the eyes of flesh: but we have an intuition of the inviolable truth, according to which we define, as well as we are able, not what the mind of any man is, but what, according to the eternal reasons, it ought to be.)

Again, it is one thing to make a mental representation of an arch once seen in Carthage: to do so does not require divine illumination. But quite another thing is what I see with my mind, according to which this arch pleases me and by which I would correct it if it displeased me; according to which I know whether it is perfect and beautiful, or whether it fails to be so, and why. We see things by our own powers, but we judge things by the intuition of the rational mind. With the pure intelligence we apprehend the principles of their beauty (IX, VI, II; col. 967).

Illumination is absolutely essential whenever we make a judgment of what we see and imagine, and are certain of our judgment. We know the arch is beautiful, or not beautiful, because Beauty itself enables us to know—even though we do not know what Beauty is. The action of illumination is required, moreover, not only when the mind judges but also when it conceptualizes: "For we have fixed in us as a rule the idea of human nature, according to which we know immediately, when we see anything like it, that it is a man or the form of a man." [22] The *idea* of human nature we never see directly, but we always depend upon its "rule." We cannot see the Form of Justice, Beauty, Goodness; yet we know with certainty whether any act is just, or any vision beautiful, or any being Good. That certainty is ineradicable. Even when we have doubts concerning the nature of the mind, we know with certainty what "doubt" is, and that the mind doubts, and that if it doubts it exists and thinks, and that incorporeal thought is of the mind's essence—whatever the mind is, it exists, it thinks, it is a spiritual substance (X, x, 13–14; col. 980f). That certainty is the daily gift of divine illumination; the immutable ideas in the mind of God act upon us, and we know. [23]

The Word

THE EVENT OF KNOWING

In illa igitur aeterna veritate, ex qua temporalia facta sunt omnia, formam secundum quam sumus, et secundum quam vel in nobis

[22] *Habemus enim quasi regulariter infixam humanae naturae notitiam, secundum quam quidquid tale aspicimus, statim hominem esse cognoscimus, vel hominis formam.* VIII, IV, 7; col. 952.

[23] Cf. *De vera religione*, XXIX, 53—XXXIV, 64; XLIX, 97; LII, 101. See Gilson, 122ff, and Eugène Portalié, *A Guide to the Thought of Saint Augustine*, trans. R. Bastian (Chicago, 1960), p. 113, for other texts. Also, for a full bibliography on the question of illumination, see Carl Andresen, ed., *Zum Augustin-Gespräch der Gegenwart*, Wege der Forschung, V (Darmstadt, 1962), pp. 498–505, esp. 500f; and Carl Andresen, ed., *Bibliographia Augustiniana*, (Darmstadt, 1962), pp. 42ff, esp. pp. 44f.

As the reader will no doubt have suspected, Augustine's doctrine of illumination is the subject of the most far-ranging disagreement among his interpreters. On one point, however, there is no question: the effect of illumination is to regulate and grant certainty to our judgments. For our purposes, this common ground is enough, and I have followed Gilson, who offers the clearest and most thorough account.

vel in corporibus vera et recta ratione aliquid operamur, visu mentis aspicimus: atque inde conceptam rerum veracem notitiam, tanquam verbum apud nos habemus, et dicendo intus gignimus; nec a nobis nascendo discedit. Cum autem ad alios loquimur, verbo intus manenti ministerium vocis adhibemus, aut alicujus signi corporalis, ut per quamdam commemorationem sensibilem tale aliquid fiat etiam in animo audientis, quale de loquentis animo non recedit. Nihil itaque agimus per membra corporis in factis dictisque nostris, quibus vel approbantur vel improbantur mores hominum, quod non verbo apud nos intus edito praevenimus. Nemo enim volens aliquid facit, quod non in corde suo prius dixerit. [IX, VII, 12; col. 967]

(Thus in that eternal truth by which all temporal things have been created, we behold, with the vision of the mind, the form of our own being and of everything we do with true and right reason, whether within ourselves or in the world. Because of it we have within ourselves a true knowledge of things, like a word we engender with an interior speech; and this word does not depart from us in being born. When we speak to others, this word remains within us, and we use the voice or some physical sign in order that by some sensible evocation some such word may occur within the soul of our audience as remains within our own soul as we speak. Thus we perform no bodily action either in gesture or word, by which we approve or disapprove of the conduct of men, which we have not anticipated by a word uttered within our inmost selves. For no one does anything, with a free will, which he has not first spoken in his heart.)

Augustine's concept of the *word* is crucial to the whole work, and he returns to it again and again to elaborate or modify earlier definitions. The key to the whole concept lies in the reason for its necessity.

Augustine is treating the problem of identity and self-consciousness. How does a man know himself? It cannot be by "reading" his internal condition at particular moments, for in that way he must lose himself. If he knows only that he loves at one moment and hates at another; that he is resolute now but that he faltered yesterday; that he was cruel earlier but is gentle now—if his knowledge of himself is restricted to these passing states and is therefore impermanent and constantly in need of revision, then he must cry out after himself, the *I* wherein all these experiences occur. His inner life would be a mere reflection of the world's torrential changes. He may deny that there is any order in the outside world, but he cannot deny an order within himself, a stable frame for all these moods, a single subject for all these predicates; for if he did, he would be nothing more than a sequence of conditions. He could never know what he would do until he did it, or whether he would love those tomorrow whom he loved today, or whether he would refuse to do then what he simply does not do now. He preserves the coherence of his life by a greater self-knowledge than that of his momentary states.[24]

To Augustine, as we have seen, that kind of stable knowledge is impossible without the illuminating action of the ideal. A man comes to know himself truly because the eternal truth, of which he is an image and which exists *super aciem mentis* and above the manifold changes of his inner life, leaves its mark upon him (IX, vi, 11; col. 966f). When a man knows himself truly, he knows himself as an image of a divine model.

When the mind knows itself as it is, essentially, it sees itself in the light of the reasons that illuminate it from above. Then all that it sees, all that it knows, all that it is, are contained in its "word," its self-image. This is true of its knowledge of other things as well. When we desire to say aloud all those things that we know and that remain known to us even when we do not think of them, we cannot do so unless we think of them first. Even if no words are spoken aloud, whoever thinks "speaks in his heart."[25] Therefore, certain thoughts are "locu-

---

[24] Cf. Agaësse, BA, 598.
[25] XV, x, 17; col. 1069f. Cf. Schmaus, p. 337; Gilson, p. 100; Agaësse, BA, 591ff.

tions of the heart." When these thoughts are spoken, the speech is one thing, the vision of the knowledge that we speak is another.[26] That vision of knowledge is the word.

The word spoken aloud is a visible sign of the word that remains glowing within us: what issues from the mouth is the voice of the word. Just as our word assumes a corporeal voice in order to reveal itself to the senses of men, just so the Word of God assumed flesh that He might be revealed. And just as our word assumes a voice without changing into a voice, so the Word of God assumed flesh but was far from being changed into flesh. It is by assuming a sensible form, not by being absorbed in it, that our word becomes vocal, and the divine Word once became visible.[27]

Augustine offers many examples of the genesis of the word, but perhaps it is best to consider the idea in terms of our own experience. A teacher asks a question and in a flash one pupil knows that he can give the answer; and, in fact, once called upon, he does give it. Now the moment in which the word is born is not when the boy recites the answer aloud, nor that earlier moment when he "rolls around in thought" the words he is about to speak; for in both these moments the word has already "assumed the flesh" of an audible language. The critical moment is the one that precedes these, when the boy knows that he knows, before he speaks that knowledge in common words, either aloud or to himself. If the teacher asks for the parts of speech, the boy's hand shoots up long before he has said to himself, "Noun, pronoun, verb . . ." Before he

[26] XV, x, 18; col. 1070f. Just as we engender this word which abides in the thoughts of our heart and the mirror of our understanding, so God brought forth the Word: Schmaus, p. 342f, citing *Tract. 14 in Joann.*, n. 7.

[27] XV, xi, 20; col. 1071f. Cf. Schmaus, pp. 359–361, who cites other texts of St. Augustine; and *ibid.*, p. 347: As a man seeks to become identical with the image in his word, so does he thereby work to become similar to the Word of God.

speaks these words, he has had a vision of his own knowledge. He has seen two things, the fact that that knowledge exists, and the fact of which that knowledge consists. He is certain that he knows and certain of what he knows. This is clearly seen if we imagine that he forgets the names of one or two of the parts, a frequent embarrassment to those who say correctly that they know the answer and offer to speak it aloud. The boy forgets the words "preposition" and "interjection," and yet it is still true to say that he knows the answer. Not only does he know that those words exist, but he knows what they mean, the classes they denote, the principles by which each class is established. And he knows that he knows these things. Thus there is a difference between a vision of knowledge and the audible words by which we convey that vision to others. Another child may be able to recite all the terms with great facility but without the least notion of what they mean. He, too, speaks words, first to himself and then aloud, but his speaking is not preceded by the *verbum;* it does not translate, into images of sound, an inner knowledge and an inner certainty.

Or consider what happens when we have another kind of thought; when, for example, we contemplate whatever is signified by the word "France." We do not think discursively of its geographical form, its monumental history, its vineyards, its middle class, its cities, its language, its churches, its politics. We do not think of these things one by one, but we have a single "vision" of all of them, and more. Our "word" for "France" is not a parade of facts and falsehoods, but an inner event. It is an experience of certainty and recognition, and it precedes language.

Now to consider the case of a man who knows himself: The knowledge that he has of himself is infinitely greater than the things he can say of himself. The total knowledge is wordless; it coincides with the man's consciousness of its presence. That consciousness and that knowledge, causing a pervasive experience of certainty, together make up the man's word.

When the word is true, it reveals to a man his essential condition as an image of God. The mind then knows itself as a trinity of memory, understanding, and will (the second "analogy"). It knows this because the Trinity lights it up in such a way that it sees, not the Trinity, but itself according to the Trinity. Knowing itself as an image of God, the mind knows its task: to make its word resemble as much as possible the Word of God. Therein lies the "future perfection of the image":

Verum haec hujus imaginis est quandoque futura perfectio. Ad hanc consequendam nos erudit magister bonus fide christiana pietatisque doctrina, ut *revelata facie*, a Legis velamine quod est umbra futurorum, *gloriam Domini speculantes,* per speculum scilicet intuentes, *in eamdem imaginem* transformemur *de gloria in gloriam, tanquam a Domini Spiritu* (2 *Cor.* III, 18), secundum superiorem de his verbis disputationem.

Cum ergo hac transformatione ad perfectum fuerit haec imago renovata, similes Deo erimus, quoniam videbimus eum, non per speculum, sed sicuti est (1 Joan. III, 2): quod dicit apostolus Paulus, *facie ad faciem* (I Cor. XIII, 12). Nunc vero in hoc speculo, in hoc aenigmate, in hac qualicumque similitudine, quanta sit etiam dissimilitudo, quis potest explicare?

[XV, XI, 20–21; col. 1073]

(To lead us to this perfection, the good master instructs us in the Christian faith and the doctrines of religion, in order that *with face unveiled*, freed from the veil of the Law which is the shadow of things to come, *beholding as in a mirror the glory of God*, that is, contemplating it by means of a mirror, we might be transformed *into the same image, from glory into glory, as by the Spirit of the Lord*, according to our earlier explanation of these words.

When, therefore, the image shall have been renewed by that

transformation to the point of perfection, we shall be like God, for we shall see him, not by means of a mirror, but as he is: as the Apostle Paul says, *face to face.* Now, however, who can explain how great is the dissimilarity in this mirror, in this enigma, in this vague similitude?)

NOSSE, COGITARE

What remains to be explained is the genesis of the word. How is the word "born"? Augustine's fullest answer lies in his distinction between two ways of knowing, *nosse* and *cogitare*. This distinction, moreover, solves another problem: how can the mind misunderstand itself—for example, how can it believe itself to be a corporeal substance? [28]

It is because what we think is not the same as what we know that the mind can err regarding its own nature and think of itself as a body:

Ita cum aliud sit non se nosse, aliud non se cogitare [29] (neque enim multarum doctrinarum peritum, ignorare grammaticum dicimus, cum eam non cogitat, quia de medicinae arte tunc cogitat): cum ergo aliud sit non se nosse, aliud non se cogitare, tanta vis est amoris, ut ea quae cum amore diu cogitaverit, eisque curae glutino inhaeserit, attrahat secum etiam cum ad se cogitandam quodam modo redit. [X, v, 7; col. 977]

(Thus it is one thing not to know oneself, and quite another not to think of oneself—for we do not say of one who is learned in many disciplines that he does not know grammar while he is not thinking of it, because he is thinking now of the art of medicine—since, as I say, it is one thing not to know oneself and another not to think of oneself, such is the power of love that those things which the mind has thought upon lovingly for a long time it cleaves to as though with the glue of care, and draws them with it even when, in some way, it returns to itself in order to contemplate itself.)

[28] BA, n. 24, esp. p. 605.
[29] Cf. XIV, vi, 8; col. 1041f.

Since it cannot take these physical bodies into the region of the spirit, it "rolls together" the images of them, images which the mind produces in itself. For in order to form them, it gives them something of its own spiritual nature. The mind's error is to unite itself to these images with a love so great that it judges itself to be like them—when, in fact, it has made *them* like itself. It conforms itself to them in a certain way, not in the way it really is—not in the way it *knows* it is, but in the way it *thinks* it is. It never makes the error of thinking itself to be an image (for it never loses the power to know an image from a real body), but rather the thing whose image it bears within itself.[30] The mind attributes its own nature to other things and then thinks it is like them.

Augustine will develop this distinction later, but it is already clear. *Nosse* is the mind's permanent condition of knowing, which continues even when the mind does not think of the thing it knows. Since this knowledge continues apart from the mind's successive states of consciousness, it is implicit knowledge, unconscious knowledge: it remains knowledge whether or not it is contemplated or expressed.

The permanence of this knowledge makes it possible for the mind to pronounce its word: the word is the conscious experience of this ever-present, unconscious knowledge. "When the mind expresses itself in its word," writes Agaësse, "it recognizes itself only because it knows itself already."[31] There never was a time in the life of the mind when it did not have such knowledge: *nosse* is the mind's essential act, for the mind *is* its act of knowing, it knows itself *as knowing* (X, xii, 5; col. 976). *Cogitare* is the act that makes this unconscious knowledge conscious; through *cogitare* the word is born.

On this basis Augustine refutes the materialist theories of the nature of the soul. Some have thought the soul was the blood, others the brain, others the heart, and so forth. Now

---

[30] X, vi, 8; col. 978. Cf. *De vera religione*, XX, 40ff; XXXVII, 68ff; XLIX, 95f.
[31] BA, n. 25, p. 606.

the soul *knows* that it exists, that it lives, that it understands. But when, for example, the soul supposes that it is air, it only *thinks* the air understands. Let it reject what it only *thinks*, therefore, and let it look to what it *knows;* let there remain only what was never doubted even by those who thought the soul to be some kind of body. Whatever else it doubts, let it not doubt these essential acts—it remembers, it wishes to be certain, it knows—for if these acts did not exist, the mind would not be able to doubt anything (X, x, 13–14; col. 980f).

What all of these materialist theories miss is the fact that the mind knows itself even as it seeks itself. It would not think the air understood if it did not already know that it understood. The whole point of its being commanded to know itself is to make it certain that it is not any of those things of which it is uncertain; that it may be certain of being whatever it is certain it is.[32] This certainty of recognition results from the continuity of *nosse.*

It is by the second way of knowing, *cogitare,* that the mind pronounces its word. *Cogitare,* according to an old etymology, was derived from *cogo,* and "through usage came to designate the act by which the soul gathers together the scattered and latent bits of knowledge in its memory, in order to place them in some way beneath its own gaze and thus to lead them to clear consciousness. Applied to the soul, *cogitare* is thus not properly knowledge but the integrating activity by which the soul pronounces its word through the mediation of love."[33]

The mind recognizes itself in its own act of consciousness, in the word, when thought formulates the implicit knowledge that always remains. Agaësse continues:

For the mind, to know itself is to know itself as knowing. It is thus not a question of introspection, but rather of reflection; in other words, the mind is not given to itself for the purpose of psycho-

[32] X, x, 16; col. 981. Cf. Schmaus, pp. 240ff, esp. p. 244.
[33] P. Agaësse, BA, n. 25, p. 606. N.b. *Confessiones* X, xi, 18.

logical observation, but it attains itself in coinciding with the act it produces in positing its word.

The mind does not come to know itself by examining itself bit by bit to see what it is made of. Rather, it is guided by certainty: self-knowledge consists in recognition, in a reflection of the knowledge that already exists. That "reflection" is the word. The act that is reflected, *nosse*, and the act of reflection, *cogitare*, are the essential acts of the mind.[34]

KNOWLEDGE JOINED TO LOVE

There is, then, a "knowledge which is posited," the word; and this reflects the "knowledge which posits,"[35] the *nosse* dwelling in the memory. For we not only have knowledge, we are aware of having it; and this awareness is the pronouncement of the word.[36] But there is a third element uniting the first two. The word is conceived through love, whether of the creature or of the Creator.

Nascitur autem verbum, cum excogitatum placet, aut ad peccandum, aut ad recte faciendum. Verbum ergo nostrum et mentem de qua gignitur, quasi medius amor conjungit, seque cum eis tertium complexu incorporeo, sine ulla confusione constringit.
[IX, VIII, 13; col. 968]

(The word is born when a thought pleases us either to sin or to do right. Love, like a mediator between them, joins together this word of ours and the mind from which it is engendered, and binds itself to them as a third element, without any confusion, in an incorporeal embrace.)

Only that knowledge which is loved can be a word; the word occurs only *cum placet quod mente concipitur*, "when

---

[34] Our analysis of *Narcisus* bears out the distinction between these two ways of knowing; see above, pp. 43ff.

[35] Agaësse, BA, 599.

[36] Cf. Gilson, pp. 294ff.

the mind is pleased by what it conceives." We also know things that we hate; and when we disapprove of them, we approve of that disapproval, we are pleased by it, and it is a word. "Therefore, the word, which we now desire to see and suggest, is knowledge joined to love." [37] The mind and its word are united by love. It is love that impels the mind to know itself in the beginning; it is love of Justice that enables it to know itself as it is and as it ought to be; it is love that makes it cleave to the ideal self-image reflected in the word, and thus to become more and more just: "All knowledge according to the ideal is similar to the ideal it knows." [38]

True love, as it was defined in Book VIII, is love of the ideal, and of other things in the ideal. This is especially true when the mind loves itself: for it loves itself as a resemblance of the ideal that created it. But this knowledge of itself as an ideal resemblance is precisely what the word is. When it is truly conceived, the word is an image of the mind's "future perfection," of its essential capacity to know, and to become similar to, "the eternal reasons" in the mind of God. The mind's integrity, its oneness with its word, is first engendered and then preserved through love.

The Hypostatization of Resemblance

Augustine has gone far toward explaining the astonishing fact that the human mind, constantly fluctuating, observing constantly fluctuating objects, can yet make judgments according to truths which are immutable. We know, for example, not only that today an oar dipped into water appears crooked, but also that it must appear crooked, not only today but always; and we know why, and the reason why will be

[37] *Verbum est igitur, quod nunc discernere ac insinuare volumus, cum amore notitia.* IX, xi, 15; col. 969.
[38] *Sed omnis secundum speciem notitia, similis ei rei quam novit.* IX, xi, 16; col. 969.

true forever.[39] Our entire capacity for stable knowledge consists in the mind's relation to the eternal truths, which are God himself. And this relation to the ideal is not only the cause of our knowledge, it is the reality of everything that exists. "It is not one of the lesser difficulties of Augustine's thought that it proposes to us as the pattern of truth, not the empirical object seized at a particular moment in its course of becoming, but the relation of that object to the creative ideal which gave it birth." [40]

For the reality of any object is its resemblance to the ideal in which it participates. It holds together and endures because it bears a likeness to the *forma*, which is eternal. Resemblance is thus not an inconsequential attribute shared by a number of things, but a formative energy, a creative force, life itself. Life is resemblance, and all created things are images.

Resemblance is the name of "the relation of [each] object to the creative ideal which gave it birth." Resemblance is substantial, really and absolutely existing. Etienne Gilson has given the clearest account of this aspect of Augustine's thought:

All things are what they are by participation in the ideas of God, but to reach the root of this relation one must surpass it and apply this very relation of participation to participation itself. In other words, because of the way in which they imitate the ideas, all things are similar to God; thus there is a Chastity in itself, and all chaste souls are chaste by participation in it; and a Wisdom, by participation in which wise souls are wise; and a Beauty, by participation in which all beautiful things are beautiful. But if all things are what they are because they resemble something else, there must necessarily be a Resemblance, by participation in which all similar things are similar. This principal Resemblance is

[39] *De vera religione*, XXIX, 53. Cf. *De Trin.*, XIV, xv, 21; col. 1052. Also, *De doctrina Christiana*, XXXVIII, 56f.

[40] Agaësse, BA, 598. Cf. *De doct. Christ.*, VIII, 9ff; XLIII, 233ff. *Soliloq.* I, vi, 12; viii, 15. Gilson, pp. 103ff; Portalié, pp. 100, 110: Schmaus, p. 347.

none other than the Word. The perfect imitation of the Father, the Son represents identically the one who engendered him; for just as there is nothing more chaste than Chastity, nothing more wise than Wisdom, and nothing more beautiful than Beauty, so nothing is more similar than Resemblance; that is why the Resemblance of the Father is so similar to him that it reproduces his nature with absolute fullness and realization.[41]

The result of all this is that this universe of images in which we dwell is not only composed of images which are such or such because of the Ideas they represent, but also that it is, speaking universally, composed of images because there exists an Image in itself, a Participation in itself and thereby perfect, by virtue of which each thing that exists can participate in God and imitate him.[42]

Any object—a rock, a tree, a city—owes its form and its very existence to the unity of its innumerable parts, a unity created by the resemblance of those parts to each other; and its identity depends equally upon its resemblance to other exemplars of the same species. But this constitutive resemblance, by which all things are able to exist, itself exists because there is a divine Resemblance, a Resemblance so perfectly realized that it attains the supreme degree of resemblance, identity. This hypostatized Resemblance is the Word of God. Man is able to become a better image of his Creator in the course of his life because he participates in the Resem-

---

[41] To Gilson's references for this point (*De Gen ad litt. lib. imperf.*, XVI, 58; *De vera relig.*, XXXI, 58), an even more explicit passage may be added, *De vera relig.*, XXXVI, 66: the Word so resembles the sole unity that it coincides with it and is identical with it. Cf. *ibid.*, XLIII, 81ff; Gilson, p. 281, n. 2.

[42] Gilson, pp. 275–277. Gilson cites the following passage from *De Gen. ad litt. lib. imperf.*, XVI, 57, which I give in translation:

For the Similitude of God, by which all things have been created, is rightly called a similitude because it is similar to God, not through participation in some other similitude, but because it is itself the First Similitude, and all things, which God created through that similitude, are similar by participation in it.

blance of the Son; because, being already an image, he is able to resemble Resemblance.

The "Translation"

THE HUMAN IMAGE AND COURTLY LOVE

That resemblance is less close when the mind contemplates external objects, closest when it contemplates itself. When it is fully conscious of itself, the mind sees itself as a trinity, because the Trinity enables the mind to know itself according to the eternal and immutable form of God. In that moment the mind "expresses" itself, articulates its self-knowledge so that the expression is its true image. That knowledge in the light of the eternal *forma* is the mind's truest "word"; and the love that first impelled the mind to seek its word now unites them both.

Hence we may say that the mind loves its own image. And now it is crucially important to distinguish this psychic state from that of Narcissus, who dies at the fountain.

The word is an image of the mind, but it is also of the same substance and identical with it: the word is the mind's defining self-consciousness. The existence of the word is implied in the very existence of the mind, and the love that unites them proceeds from them both. The mind loves its image; consciousness loves its object. Image and object are not two different things, as they were for Narcissus; the image is not borne in the medium of another.

And for St. Augustine the mind's life goes on beyond this moment. Just as our love for Paul is love for the ideal of Justice exemplified in Paul, so the mind's love for itself is love for the Creator it represents, the Trinity, from which it draws its own life as an image.[43] The mind loves itself not as a final

---

[43] Here, it will be recognized, we are at the root of Augustine's distinction between *uti* and *frui*.

term, but as an image of the true object of its love; not for what it is in itself, but for what it reflects. Thus, in the well-ordered mind, that act of self-love is a kind of internal and invisible sacrament, the use of a present object—the mind itself—to act out a devotion to a Being who cannot be known, but whose existence is, by the very fact of the mind's ability to know, pervasive and certain.[44] But Narcissus's love rests in the image as its term. He does not know that ideal Beauty, which is the true object of his love, may never itself be seen; nor that the salvation it bestows upon those who worship it may never be granted by one of its innumerable reflections.

But we have already begun the "translation." The relations in the courtly lyric are secular counterparts of the relations within the human trinity and the divine. The experience implied in the lyric may be described in Augustinian terms, without any distortion or inadequacy.

The knight achieves true self-knowledge when he knows himself in the light of the courtly ideal, when he knows that his identity consists in his resemblance to that ideal and to the others of the class it defines. In his own experience, the ideal is real and pre-existent, not an image engendered to define the possibilities of actual life. For he was born into a society already seeking to conform to it and to be justified by it. It is universally corroborated. It pre-existed him and created him.

The knight's love of the courtly ideal is the expression of his status as its image. Through love, and illuminated by that ideal, he conceives his word, his self-image perfected, in which he sees himself and judges himself. He struggles to complete an "identity" between his actual condition and the ideal that defines him. Without that love and that ideal self-image, he has no present and no future; he is merely the

[44] Cf. XIV, xiv, 18; col. 1049f. Also, *De doct. Christ.*, XXII, 21ff; Harnack, V, 230.

unformed possibility of being a knight. Like Erec's, [45] his self-consciousness is obliterated.

This is, so to speak, the implied pre-history of the knight, his condition long before the lyric begins; and thus far he does not differ from any other man of any other time. Something else has to happen, something that makes the lyric happen; for so long as the word remains purely an inner event there is no need for the mirror of the audience or of the lady. The knight for whom a private moral certainty suffices does not look to another to save him or recognize him. It is from the knight's desire to embody the word in a mirror that the courtly lyric derives its characteristic quality.

The courtly man requires a visible and immediate sanction by the ideal, and to this high office he exalts the lady. For an ideal is not merely an image of what ought to be: it also enjoins us to make the image real. Now before this formidable task of becoming perfect, every man must seek his peace. It was the knight's way to invest the lady in the moral authority of the ideal. To achieve the perfection of the courtly ideal was impossible; but one could hope to win its approval if that perfection appeared in the figure of another human being.

Thus the knight externalizes the human trinity to form a new one that is more social, more secular. He embodies the word in the lady, and she becomes crucial to his identity. He can never more be sufficient to himself; he requires another to contemplate him. He takes on the rôle of the *nosse*, of an actual condition that needs to be formulated and perfected. The aspiring knight, the lady who is the custodian of his ideal,

[45] The hero of a romance by Chrétien de Troyes, later adapted by Hartmann von Aue. Emerging victorious from a dangerous adventure, Erec achieves all that a knight can strive for: renown in Arthur's court, and the love of a beautiful lady, Enide. He then retires with her and lives in perfect contentment, until Enide becomes aware of a widespread murmuring against Erec's indolence and neglect of his duties. By revealing this criticism she rouses him to act to regain his reputation.

and the love that binds them together, are now one single being. As he is a courtly man, he must make the word visible in the lady; he must be bound to a mirror of himself, reflecting his perfected image and judging his present condition, informing all his experience and revealing the stages of his progress. The lady is the agent of his consciousness. He has externalized and re-animated a portion of his own *mens;* and that living mirror is one term of a life that has been projected into the world of visible things and secularized. Both he and his society must look to a separate figure to see how good he is, and how good he can become. Her look realizes him, her smile justifies him.

Regarded in this way, the courtly man is the psychic heir of Narcissus. It is a critical moment when he discovers that the lady is a mirror whose beauty comes from what she reflects. He cannot leave her image behind, as the stilnovist did, to elevate his love to Beauty, to God, to a Being more real and with greater rewards to offer; for the courtly man, no such reference is available. The lady reflects a word engendered not in the light of the "eternal truths," but of a purely secular ideal.

The essential act of the knight is service, and that service must have as its object not the private and pre-socialized word, but a figure well known in the world where it is to be recognized. The knight is bound to the lady, and from the moment he leaves her he ceases to be a knight. That is why it is a crisis when he discovers that the lady is an insensate mirror and thus not capable of knowing the marvelous deeds of battle and song that he has done for her: for then the meaning of his service is discredited—the acts that define him, that realize his identity as a knight.

At this point the knight is in an acute predicament, from which he can free himself in any of a number of ways. On the lowest level, with a mindless complaint, he leaves the discredited lady and finds himself another in whom he can believe for a time. This way leads to a denigration of the lady's rôle and thus of the whole ethical system, and brings no other reward than a painless and hopeless inappetence. On the highest level available to the secular knight, he cultivates his doubt as an enlargement of his consciousness, and restores the image with a new dignity as his guide and salvation.

THE KNIGHT'S QUEST FOR CERTAINTY

The soul's task, which it can accomplish only through the proper orientation of its love to the eternal truths of God, is to make *cogitare* coincide with *nosse*, to make its word precisely adequate to the unconscious knowledge it always possesses. This coincidence of its word and its actual state is its "identity." In the genesis of its word the mind is liable to error, but Augustine shows the way through this danger in his tantalizing and characteristic statement that the mind may be certain of being whatever it is certain it is.

This test of certainty explains Augustine's assertion that the mind knows itself already when it seeks itself.[46] But how far from certainty is the man we see in the courtly lyric! He is perpetually uncertain about the efficacy of his service, his estimation in the eyes of his peers, the reality of his worth. Uncertainty is the air he breathes, the impetus of his song; and the quest for certainty moves him in everything.

His uncertainty is a precise reflection of his secularity. The engendering of the word is a universal act, performed as well by those who have never heard of God; for Augustine that act is complete only when the mind sees itself as an image of a Being more real and worthy of love, and more capable of requiting it. But for the knight, that act is complete only when the word is incarnated in the figure of a universally admired person. In the first instance, the engendering of the word leads

[46] X, ix, 12; col. 980. If the soul knows what *cognosce* is, and what *te ipsam* is, it already knows itself. Cf. Schmaus, p. 239; Agaësse, BA, p. 607f, n. 27.

the mind still further in upon itself, withdrawing from the "visible things" around it in order to find greater certainty in the light of God. But for the knight, the mind must seek its certainty outside itself, regarding its self-consciousness as worthless without its formal affirmation by others: for the knight can have no enduring sense of personal reality unless he is known by others. He delegates to others the mind's proper act of *cogitare*. The struggle of his life is the struggle to be known; his "identity" lies in the coincidence of his self-knowledge with the knowledge that others have of him. It is for others to ratify his existence, to formulate him. He must look into the mirror for all the certainty he can have in his life.

This is to oversimplify things somewhat, for the knight does not lack a word that remains with him, a conscious self-knowledge, apart from the lady and the others of his society. The point, however, is that he is utterly without that certainty which, according to Augustine, defines true knowledge. This vital certainty the courtly man can never have, for self-knowledge alone is of no value to him. Thus in the lyrics we have studied, lyrics which are purely secular (always excepting those in which the conflict between *Minne* and devotion to God is explicit, and which really make up a class by themselves), the society is shown to be essential to the identity of the knight: without his favorable reflection in their eyes, he cannot be a knight, and he cannot know himself. He splits the act of *cogitare* in two, and he can never recognize himself with certainty in his word unless that word coincides with a public image. The loss of the sense of identity—the madness of Yvain, the indolence of Erec, the aimlessness of Parzival [47]—always coincides with the loss of fame and reputation. The knight dies to himself when he ceases to be known.

The scope of these generalizations ought to be made clear.

[47] Heroes of romances by Chrétien de Troyes, Hartmann von Aue, and Wolfram von Eschenbach.

Epilogue

Needless to say, they pertain only to the secular courtly lyric, and in a special way to the courtly romance. Furthermore, although these statements are adequate to the work of a lesser poet like Ulrich, there is a body of lyrics and romances—among them the greatest of the Middle Ages—for which they will not suffice, for the simple reason that the poet takes as his theme just this problem of the knight. Such a poet we have found in Heinrich von Morungen, and he is not alone. One of Gottfried's [48] themes is the inability of the society at large to understand the inner life of the truly refined and educated man. For it is no accident that in desiring to present "not the knight's physical prowess, his ability to win victories or his success as a 'courtly lover,' but rather the knight as a man, as a sensitive being, a thinker and artist," [49] Gottfried must at the same time exclude all but the smallest part of the normal courtly audience. If the knight needs to be known by the society as he knows himself, then he must conform to an ideal that necessarily becomes inadequate and even dangerous, threatening to annihilate his character and the sources of his greatest pride. For if it is essential to be known fully by others, then he must never be more than what the others can know: this condition threatens the very identity it was intended to preserve. It is just this predicament that the most interesting poets examine. What, they ask, happens to the man who refuses to empty out the inner life in order to be nothing more than what he appears to be?

When the influence of courtly literature begins to be felt in England, Chaucer takes up the theme. To say that the knight assigns to others the mind's proper act of *cogitare* is to repeat what we saw earlier concerning the knight's vulnerable position of seeking his salvation in another: when the lady knows him and approves of him, the two ways of knowing coincide, the "identity" is complete, he is "saved." Now the story of

[48] Gottfried von Strassburg, author of *Tristan und Isold*.
[49] W. T. H. Jackson, "Tristan the Artist in Gottfried's Poem," *PMLA*, LXXVII (1962), 365.

Troilus and Criseyde reveals just this danger of seeking salvation in another human being, who, because she is human, can never realize the ideal perfection she is to discern in the knight, and must ultimately be inadequate to the word.[50]

After this brief "translation," we are in a position to follow the rest of Augustine's thought in the *De Trinitate*, for the meaning of the mirror is even more clearly defined in the later books.

Memoria, Intelligentia, Voluntas

THE SUPREMACY OF THE RATIONAL SOUL

In the fourteenth book, Augustine enriches many of the ideas he has introduced, and posits an even better analogy than *mens, notitia, amor*. He has to do this because, with the development of the idea of the *verbum*, he has added a fourth term to the original trinity. In the new analogy the *mens* will cease to be a relative term and will designate the one substance with which the three elements of the human trinity are identified.[51]

Once again, Augustine's concern is where to look for the least inadequate image of God. And once again the answer is in the rational soul, but now there is a slightly different emphasis:

Quanquam enim magna natura sit, tamen vitiari potuit, quia summa non est: et quanquam vitiari potuerit, quia summa non est, tamen quia summae naturae capax est, et esse particeps potest, magna natura est.   [XIV, iv, 6; col. 1040]

(However great a nature the soul may be, it can yet become corrupt, for it is not the highest. And however much it can

[50] Cf. Charles Muscatine, *Chaucer and the French Tradition* (Berkeley and Los Angeles, 1960), pp. 124–165.

[51] Cf. Agaësse, BA, n. 20, pp. 597ff. With the development of the new trinity, the term *notitia* changes in meaning to designate the primary unconscious knowledge. See Schmaus, pp. 250–253; Agaësse, BA, p. 591; Moingt, BA, p. 633.

become corrupt because it is not the highest, yet precisely because it is capable of the highest nature and able to participate in it, it is a great nature.)

Words like *posse* and *capax* are frequently repeated throughout Book XIV. The image in the human soul, its essence and its immortality, consist in its *capacity* to attain some understanding of God. That image is indestructible. Even in the soul of the sinner, memory, knowledge, and love remain always present, always capable of turning to the Creator: that is the sinner's enduring hope of salvation. The soul can restore the image it bears only by the help of God; but unless that image had remained, however distorted, during the soul's "corruption," there would be nothing left to be redeemed.[52] But now we are back to an earlier idea, which is considerably developed in the fourteenth book.

CONSCIOUS AND UNCONSCIOUS KNOWLEDGE

Augustine takes up again the distinction between *nosse* and *cogitare*. Only those things which a man thinks of are in the view of his mind; other things are hidden in a kind of mysterious knowledge which is called the memory (XIV, vi, 8; col. 1041f). He recalls the example of the man who is skilled in many disciplines, who knows and loves them all even when he is thinking only of one. Thus it is revealed to us that in the secret part of our mind we possess certain stores of knowledge which become visible to the mind's view when they are the object of thought. The mind then discovers that it remembered, understood, and loved these things even when it was not thinking of them (XIV, vii, 9; col. 1042f).

Thus there is a trinity which places in the memory that by which the gaze of thought is formed, that very formation of thought being like an image which is imprinted by the memory; and that by which both are joined together, namely, love

[52] Cf. Agaësse, "L'image inamissible," BA, pp. 630ff.

or will. Therefore, when the mind sees itself in the act of thought, it recognizes itself. For it is not the implicit self-knowledge, the *nosse*, that the mind engenders, as though it had been unknown to itself before. On the contrary, *nosse* is an enduring act, and the mind is always known to itself in the same way that other things are known which are contained in the memory, even when they are not contemplated. And these two ways of knowing are joined together by a third term, *dilectio*, which is the will seeking to possess something for the purpose of enjoying it. Thus we acquire some idea of the trinity of the mind by these three terms: *memoria, intelligentia, voluntas.*[53]

Augustine has, in effect, doubled the trinity.[54] The first trinity is unconscious, permanently existing *in abdito mentis* and consisting of the knowledge, understanding, and will that we do not think of all the time, and that we often do not know we possess. For even before the act of thinking, the mind already knows, and understands, and loves itself, though in such a way that the knowledge is unformulated, the understanding unexpressed, the love impure, the entire image of God obscured. But as soon as there is a *cogitatio*, then the mind's unconscious self-knowledge becomes objectified in a word (XV, xxi, 41f; col. 1089f). The second trinity is formed from the first through the agency of thought, objectifying in the word all that is contained in the memory.

A glance at our own experience may make clearer the difference between these two trinities. Suppose a man declines to commit some act—to steal, to betray a friend—when he has the opportunity to do so. Guided by the first, unconscious trinity alone, he refuses to do this thing because he knows it

[53] XIV, vi, 8; col. 1042. Cf. Book X, at the end. Memory is the faculty by which we maintain everything that we know, even when we are not thinking of it: XV, xxi, 40. Cf. Schmaus, p. 266; *Confessiones,* X, 8ff.
[54] Cf. Schmaus, pp. 269ff and 351ff; J. Moingt, BA, n. 46, 632ff.

would cause him inner suffering; his refusal already implies self-knowledge, self-understanding, self-love, for he would not know to avoid this suffering unless he knew and loved himself. But if he had engendered a word, he would refuse also because, in Augustine's terms, such an act is inimical to the nature of his soul, because it offends the ideal of Justice, because he knows his task is to cultivate the resemblance of his soul to the ideal in which it participates.

Now this *cogitatio* is an absolute necessity (and not, as our example may imply, a gratuitous event); it is the soul's own act of salvation. For it is only through conscious thought that the mind knows what it is and the human trinity is perfected, that the memory is purged of falsehood, understanding is informed, and love is purified.[55] Only by the utterance of the word can the soul rely on the continuity of its moral effort.

Here again the courtly romance shows the stages by which the mind becomes "present to itself so that through its act of thought it may understand itself, and through its love join together its understanding and memory."[56] The moral "deaths" of Erec, and Yvain, and Cligès; the doubt, despair, and defiance of Parzival; the ethical as well as physical leprosy of the *arme Heinrich*[57]—all of these "perversions" end when the hero gains the power to express the moral ideal that he has violated, and that defines him and his station in the world. He does not merely learn a lesson or submit to a commandment: he engenders a word, his victory is self-consciousness.

Augustine sums up what he has said about the new trinity as follows: That which is contained in the memory informs the

[55] See Moingt, BA, n. 46, pp. 632ff.

[56] XIV, xi, 14; col. 1047f. In this passage Augustine himself almost suggests the comparisons that follow. He takes Ulysses (*Aeneid*, III, 628f) as a demonstration that the memory is the faculty by which "the mind is present to itself," so that, without absurdity, it can be said that there is a "memory of the present."

[57] Cligès is the hero of a romance by Chrétien de Troyes; *Der Arme Heinrich* is a work of Hartmann von Aue.

"interior regard" of the mind as it searches the memory; and that which is engendered in the act of thought is a replica of what abides in the memory.[58]

Nam si nos referamus ad interiorem mentis memoriam qua sui meminit, et interiorem intelligentiam qua se intelligit, et interiorem voluntatem qua se diligit, ubi haec tria simul semper sunt, et semper simul fuerunt ex quo esse coeperunt, sive cogitarentur, sive non cogitarentur; videbitur quidem imago illius trinitatis et ad solam memoriam pertinere: sed quia ibi verbum esse sine cogitatione non potest (cogitamus enim omne quod dicimus, etiam illo interiore verbo quod ad nullius gentis pertinet linguam), in tribus potius illis imago ista cognoscitur, memoria scilicet, intelligentia, voluntate. Hanc autem nunc dico intelligentiam, qua intelligimus cogitantes, id est, quando eis repertis quae memoriae praesto fuerant, sed non cogitabantur, cogitatio nostra formatur; et eam voluntatem, sive amorem, vel dilectionem, quae istam prolem parentemque conjungit, et quodam modo utrisque communis est.   [XIV, vii, 10; col. 1043f]

(If we consider the interior memory by which the mind remembers itself, the interior intelligence by which it understands itself, and the interior will by which it loves itself, where they are always together and have always been together from the moment they began to exist, whether or not they were the objects of thought—then it will indeed appear as though the image of the trinity belongs to the memory alone. But because there can never be a word without the act of thought [for we think everything that we say, by that interior word which belongs to no national language], we know that image rather in the three faculties of memory, intelligence, and will. But that which I now call "intelligence" is understanding inseparable from thought, that is, when our thought is formed by the discovery of those things which were present to the memory but not yet thought of; and what I call will, or love, or delectation, is that which joins offspring and parent together, and is in some way common to both.)

[58] Cf. Schmaus, p. 271.

Epilogue

THE IMAGE IS A CAPACITY FOR KNOWING GOD

No matter how mistaken the mind may be as to its own nature, no matter how false its word or perverted its love, no matter how deformed the image, the mind never ceases to be a trinity of memory, understanding, and love; and it remains an image because it is a capacity for God.[59] And when the mind does properly remember its Lord, it becomes fully conscious of the truth, for it learns by an interior teaching that it can rise only by God's gracious act of concern (*gratuito affectu*), just as it was able to fall only by a failure of his own will (XIV, xiv, 20–xv, 21; col. 1051f).

By the truth that illuminates the mind, no one ever loses the ability, when presented with a theory regarding the nature of his mind, to say with Matthew, "This is, this is; this is not, this is not." [60]

The Mirror

THE OBSCURITY OF THE MIRROR REFLECTS THE INEFFABILITY OF GOD

As the soul's resemblance to God increases, so does its capacity for knowledge of God; for all knowledge is a resemblance, in the mind of the knower, to the object known. In that image the resemblance to God will be perfect when its vision of God is perfect. Concerning this vision, Paul says, "*Videmus nunc per speculum in aenigmate, tunc autem facie ad faciem.*" He says again, "*Nos autem, revelata facie gloriam domini speculantes, in eamdem imaginem transformamur, de gloria in gloriam, tanquam a Domini spiritu.*" [61] Similarly, John says that we shall be similar to him, for we shall see him as he is.

But the attempt to understand God through the analogy of

---

[59] XIV, VIII, 11; col. 1044. xiii, 17—xiv, 19; col. 1049–1051. Cf. Schmaus, pp. 291ff.

[60] XV, XI, 20; col. 1072. Matthew v, 37. Cf. Schmaus, 348ff.

[61] XIV, XVII,23—XIX,25; col. 1055f. Cf. Schmaus, p. 297.

the human mind must fail. For the apostle says that we see now through a mirror, and he adds, *in aenigmate*, in an obscure allegory, whose meaning we cannot fully understand. We are surrounded by images of God, yet we cannot understand God. Nevertheless, the attempt is worth while, for to experience the ineffability of God is in itself valuable. It purifies the mirror that reflects His image (XV, IX, 15; col. 1068f).

For let no one be astonished that in the mode of seeing granted us in this life—that is, through a mirror is an enigma —we must have great difficulty in order to see at all. The greatest of all enigmas is the most familiar; we encounter it every day of our lives: we do not see what we are unable *not* to see. For who does not see his own thought, and yet who does see it (XV, IX, 16; col. 1069)?

This enigma, as Moingt shows,[62] is implied in the human trinity. It is a remarkable thing that the mind is not always in its own sight, and that its knowledge is hidden in its memory without being the object of its thought. How, then, can the mind understand the divine Knowledge by which it was created when it cannot understand itself? Being obscure even to itself, the mind becomes an enigma. But the truly astonishing thing is that the mind's very perplexity about itself enables it to know better the God whom it reflects. "To participate in the incomprehensibility of God," writes Moingt, "by the existence we have received from him is what makes us most similar to him, while all that is too distinct in our trinity is what is most dissimilar to the divine unity." It is the same with the invisibility of our thought, to which everything else is visible. Our word is hidden in the memory before it emerges as a "vision of vision." Thus in our own trinity there is something seen and something unseen; and we are thereby helped to understand in the Holy Trinity what we ought to believe without being able to see. "Let no one think," says St. Augustine, "that he has discovered nothing if he has been able

[62] "L'énigme de l'image," and "Enigme et allégorie," BA, 646ff.

to discover how incomprehensible is the object of his search." [63]

THE HUMAN IMAGE REFLECTS THE HOLY TRINITY

Just as the relation of the intelligence to the memory is an image of the relation of the Son to the Father, so our will is an image of the Holy Spirit. Our will, when it is right, knows what it would seek and avoid. Then it must possess certain knowledge, which would not be possible without memory and intelligence: we cannot believe those who say that love does not know what it does. Therefore, love as well as understanding inheres in the memory, which is the principle, and in which we find, ready and concealed, that which we attain through the act of thought. We find intelligence and will in the memory when we discover, through thinking, that we understand and love something; and they were both there even when we did not think of them. And there is love as well as memory in the intelligence, which receives its form through the act of thought, to become the word we speak inwardly when we say what we know; for, without remembering, our thought would not turn upon anything, and without love it would not care to turn its vision upon anything. Thus love unites memory with thought, unties them as parent and offspring. And if love did not know what it ought to seek, a knowledge impossible without memory and understanding, it would not know what it ought to love.[64]

Now the Holy Trinity is incorporeal, indivisible, and immutable. When the vision "face to face" that is promised us shall come, we shall see that Trinity with greater clarity and

---

[63] See Moingt, pp. 647f: "This is the nature of the enigma of our soul, the image of God *although* it is obscure and *because* it is obscure. Although obscure, with respect to the reality of which it is the image. Because obscure, with respect to itself, in the mystery that binds it to God." Cf. Portalié, p. 108f.

[64] XV, xxi, 41; col. 1089. Cf. Schmaus, pp. 275ff, who compares this passage with *Sermo 52*, c. 7, n. 18. Cf. also BA, n. 62, pp. 654–656.

certitude than we now see its image, which we are. However, those who see through that mirror and in that enigma, as it is now granted us to see, are not the ones who see in their own mind the things we have analyzed and set forth; no, it is the ones who see their mind *as* an image, in order that they may be able to refer what they see to the one whose image it is; and, through the image they contemplate, that they might see by intuition what they are not yet able to see face to face. For the apostle does not say, We see now a mirror, but "We see now through a mirror" (XV, xxiii, 43, col. 1091).

Therefore, those who see the trinity in their mind but do not believe or understand it to be an image of God—those people indeed see a mirror, but they so fail to see through the mirror the God who must be seen there, that they do not even know the mirror they see *is* a mirror. If they did, they would seek through that mirror for the One whom it reflects, in order that, their hearts cleansed by a faith unfeigned, they might see Him face to face. For if they despise the faith that purifies the heart, what is the result of all their subtle understanding of the nature of the human mind except to prepare their condemnation, on the testimony of that intelligence itself?

They would not so labor to understand without reaching some certainty if they were not wrapped in shadows and did not bear the burden of a corruptible body; the shadows are their punishment, the body weighs down their soul. What has caused them this affliction but sin? Aware of the magnitude of such evil, they ought to follow the Lamb who bears away the sin of the world. At the end of this life those who belong to the Lamb shall be free of all the malicious powers that slew the Lamb and were vanquished by his blood. *Then*, cleansed of corruption and endowed with incorruptible bodies, we shall see the truth in perfect clarity, without any struggle, without any mirror.[65]

[65] XV, xxiii, 44—xxv, 45; col. 1091f. Cf. *Enchiridion*, LXIII, and Schmaus, 297–310: "Die Trinitätsmystik Augustins."

The Courtly Life Described
in Augustinian Terms

The most encompassing resemblance between Augustine's thought and the "world" of the lyric is the principle that a man knows himself by means of the ideal he resembles. That knowledge, the word truly conceived, enables him to become better than he is as he becomes more himself. It tells him not only what demands he must make upon himself, but also that he must make demands, that his present condition is inadequate and needs to be fulfilled. "No one will become what he desires to be," says Augustine, "unless he despises himself as he is." [66]

No book, no doctrine, nothing composed of language can ever hold all that is in the word; for the word is our consciousness, a reflection of all that we know and an image of what we ought to become. Andreas [67] may show us the proper way for an amorous knight to speak, and he can draw up a blueprint of courtly demeanor; but what makes the knight coincide with his knighthood, what preserves his identity, is the love that unites him with that "locution of the heart," from which can be drawn more doctrine than a hundred like Andreas can ever set down.

No writing, no lore can ever take the place of the word. The word is an image of infinite attributes. It is when we seek to incarnate the word that the whole "vision of knowledge" disintegrates into fragments; for the most expressive language, and the most beautiful figure, will be inadequate. The word is soundless, an image that is invisible and therefore capable of reflecting our whole reality all at once, transcending space and time, and the discursiveness of language and sight.

But the knight, as we have seen, cannot know himself in the

---

[66] *De vera religione*, XLVIII, 93.

[67] Andreas Capellanus, a contemporary of Chrétien, author of a work titled variously *De Amore*, or *De arte honeste amandi* ("On the Art of Loving like a Gentleman").

word alone. He must materialize it, and in so doing he diminishes it. He translates the word into another kind of image, a mirror. To the lady he attributes the word's ideality and love. He exalts her image, suppresses every accidental quality—her name, her thoughts, her humanity. For these only falsify her real origin: she was born as the word was born, from a vision of knowledge, informed by the ideal, bound in love. She is his intelligence—his *intelligentia*—and his future self, the dream of his reality. Without her he is unknowable, even to himself. But she, too, is a mortal creature after all, and must, like the language of nations, fall short of the word.

Why does the knight embody the word in her? Because he must preserve his life before the ideal, that "self-born mocker of man's enterprise," with its devouring demands; because he must complete the economy of the trinity. For Augustine, love is a substance bestowed by God to integrate the soul and lead it back to Him. But for the secular man love is a condition here on earth, without further reference; and self-love is the first necessity, the most difficult and dangerous of all. The mind of the knight loves the word it begets, but he has no certainty that the word loves him; and unless it does, he remains unfulfilled, the trinity is flawed; in the absence of an approving consciousness, he falls apart. So to save himself he animates this word, incorporates it in a being of whom a will can be predicated.

The translation of the word into the image of the lady enables the knight to labor and hope. The word is substantiated, it has a human will to love the self it reflects, to become one with it, forming an "identity" preserved by the love common to both. The fact that it is another's will puts the knight in great peril, for his own will is immobilized, and he can become as passive and desperate as Narcissus. But now he has a new hope for a secular kind of salvation: when he and the mirrored word are united in love, he has a sense of the fulfillment of his nature. In loving service to an ideal that approves, he seems to attain all the virtues of which he is capable. For love seeks to unite the lover with his beloved by the force of resemblance. It moves him to labor to resemble the ideal—to excel at arms, to compose his song, to perform every meritorious act—for these make him more and more similar to the perfection he serves.

The knight's vulnerability in this relationship we have already noted. Yet the moment of his greatest danger is the first step to salvation for another man. What threatens the courtier redeems the stilnovist: [68]

Qui ergo vident suam mentem, quomodo videri potest, et in ea trinitatem istam de qua multis modis ut potui disputavi, nec tamen eam credunt vel intelligunt esse imaginem Dei; speculum quidem vident, sed usque adeo non vident per speculum qui est per speculum nunc videndus, et nec ipsum speculum quod vident sciant esse speculum, id est, imaginem. Quod si scirent, fortassis et eum cujus est hoc speculum, per hoc quaerendum et per hoc utcumque interim videndum esse sentirent, fide non ficta corda mundante (1 Tim. 1, 5), ut facie ad faciem possit videri, qui per speculum nunc videtur.   [XV, xxiv, 44; col. 1091]

(Therefore those who see their mind, insofar as it can be seen, and within it that trinity which I have discussed in many different ways as I was able, but who do not believe or understand it to be an image of God—these people indeed see a mirror, but they do not see through the mirror Him who is now to be seen through a mirror; nor do they know that that very mirror which they see *is* a mirror, that is, an image. If they knew that, they might perhaps feel that the one whose mirror it is should be sought through that mirror and be seen through it, tentatively; in order that, their hearts cleansed by a faith unfeigned, they might be able to see face to face Him who is seen now through a mirror.)

For the courtly poet there is nothing left once he realizes that the "mirror *is* a mirror," with few qualities beyond what

[68] See above, Introduction, p. 2.

he projects there. There is no vision *per speculum* for him; he cannot be inspired to look "beyond" the mirror to see what it reflects. He is a secular man; the mirror is the secularization of his word. It reflects his absolute commitment to the values of his society. It is a mirror for *all* to see, and in it they recognize *him* as one of their own. This recognition by the others of his class is essential to him; he cannot exist without it. Thus the ideal and the mirror must be one; and when the mirror breaks, the ideal is obliterated, no longer able to grant the moral certainty he desires above all things.

It is altogether different for the stilnovist, who does not require the image to preserve his social identity.

> Veggio negli occhi de la donna mia
> un lume pien di spiriti d'amore
> che porta uno piacer novo nel core
> sì che vi desta d'allegrezza vita.
>
> Cosa m'avèn quand'i' le son presente,
> ch'i' no la posso a lo 'ntelletto dire:
> veder mi par de la sua labbia uscire
> una sì bella donna che la mente
> comprender no la può, ché 'nmantenente
> ne nasce un'altra di bellezza nòva,
> de la qual par ch'una stella si mòva
> e dica: la salute tua è apparita.
>
> Là dove questa bella donna appare,
> s'ode una voce che le vèn davanti;
> e par che d'umiltà il su' nome canti
> sì dolcemente, che s'i' 'l vo' contare,
> sento che 'l su' valor mi fa tremare;
> e movonsi nell'anima sospiri
> che dicon: "Guarda, se tu costei miri,
> vedra' la sua vertù nel ciel salita." [69]

[69] Cavalcanti, XXV. Text: *I Rimatori del Dolce Stil Novo*, ed. G. R. Ceriello, Biblioteca Universale Rizzoli, 207–209 (Milano, 1950), p. 63f.

Epilogue

(In my lady's eyes I see a light full of spirits of love which brings wonderful delight into my heart, so that it is filled with joyous life;

Such a thing befalls me when I am in her presence that I cannot describe it to the intellect: It seems to me that as I gaze at her there issues from her semblance a lady of such beauty that the mind cannot grasp it, and from this at once another is born of wondrous beauty out of which it seems that there issues a star which says: "Behold, your blessedness is before you."

When this beautiful lady appears, a voice goes forth before her which celebrates her meekness so sweetly that if I try to repeat it, I feel that her greatness is such that it makes me tremble, and in my soul stir sighs which say: "Lo, if you gaze at this one you will see her virtue ascended into heaven.") [70]

Here, as the lady becomes more and more an image, her concern becomes more and more apparent, and the lover's salvation more assured. This is a very different condition from what we have found in the Troubadour lyric and the Minnesang, and in this light it is clear why there have been no Italian lyrics in this study.

The fact is that the stilnovisti do not use the figure of the mirror in their poetry. In the entire corpus (excluding Dante), there are but two lyrics of doubtful attribution in which the poet speaks of a mirror, and in both the figure is dully conventional. This is what we must try to understand.

Actually, we have already seen the reason. For the secular poet the recognition that the real lady is different from her perfect image causes the greatest distress: the knight is paralyzed until he can regain his faith in their identity. But for the stilnovist this recognition is the source of his greatest joy. He is not immobilized but emancipated when he discovers that it is the lady's image he really loves. For that image is not some inane and deceitful shadow: it is more real than the lady

[70] Translated by Maurice Valency, *In Praise of Love*, p. 229.

256

herself, who must die, who must suffer all the fantastic dangers of the flesh. The lady passes away, but her *image* is immortal. It is a substance; it is not the image her lover has of her, but it is independently and absolutely *her* image, immutable, the same to all, because it is defined by an essence. The beauty of her image is the expression of Beauty dwelling within; its concern, the expression of Grace; its understanding, the expression of Wisdom.

All this the intellect perceives when her image is borne to it and there emancipated from all the accidental shadows that conceal her true essence. The *intellectus agens* once having removed all sensible accretions, a divine abstraction is revealed. The image is not a mere secular mirror of God; it is itself something divine, discernible to each faculty in its own manner: to the eyes as the image of a beautiful lady; to the heart, a source of joy and consolation; but to the intellect, an essence, the only object proper to it. From this thrice-refined image comes the good news to the intellectual soul: *La salute tua è apparita.*

Now when the image is more real than the lady, the mirror is simply irrelevant. Whether it is figurative or literal, the mirror always means one thing: an insubstantial image, whose only worth lies in reflecting something real. That is why it always provokes such ambivalence. It reveals something marvelous that cannot otherwise be seen, in comparison to which it is itself of small worth, or of none whatever—it can be worse than worthless, for it can replace the reality that justifies it. But the moment the image is conceived of not as a passive reflection but as a pure presence of the ideal, the mirror passes away and in its place there stands an angel.

Both in the courtly lyrics we have examined and in the *dolce stil novo*, the poet never leaves off distinguishing between the lady and her image. In making this distinction, the courtly poet exposes the bearer of the image as a blind mirror, insensate, promiscuous in its passivity. But the stilnovist discovers in the image the ideal that yearns for his salvation, the Being for which he strives. That is why the stilnovist declined to make use of a poetic figure that was certainly available to him in the lyric tradition he inherited. To dissolve the mirror and affirm the enduring reality of the image was his solution to the peril of Narcissus.

The stilnovisti were also free of an obligation which was, after all, the chief professional concern of the courtly poets: they were not called upon to preserve the unity of a social class. It was this concern that kept the courtly poet fixed before the mirror and that prevented him from looking beyond it. He was in the service of a secular ideal; and to abstract that ideal from the secular figure in which it was embodied would have disintegrated the whole ethical system, depriving the class of its *raison d'être*, and the knight of his moral certainty. Thus the knight was trapped in his idealization of another. Intelligences and angels would never betray the hopes of a man aspiring to their purity. But these beings can have no place in a secular system that claimed for itself the power to perfect man's nature on earth, and that gave to the knight the purpose that defined him. The courtly man was wedded to the mirror.

List of Works Cited

Texts

Aimeric de Peguilhan. *The Poems of Aimeric de Peguilhan*, ed. William P. Shepard and Frank M. Chambers. Evanston, 1950.

Andreas Capellanus. *De Amore Libri Tres*, ed. E. Trojel. Havniae, 1892.

——. *The Art of Courtly Love*, trans. J. J. Parry. New York, 1941.

Arnaut de Mareuil. *Les poésies lyriques du troubadour Arnaut de Mareuil*, ed. Ronald C. Johnston. Paris, 1935.

St. Augustine. *Confessiones*, ed. M. Skutella. Bibliothèque Augustinienne, 2d series, Vols. XIII–XIV. Paris and Bruges, 1962 (*PL*, XXXII).

——. *Enarratio in Psalmum CIII. PL*, XXXII.

——. *Enchiridion ad Laurentium. PL*, XL.

——. *Retractationes. PL*, XXXII.

——. *Soliloquia. PL*, XXXII.

——. *De Trinitate. PL*, XLII.

——. *De vera religione. PL*, XXXIV.

——. *De doctrina Christiana. PL*, XXXIV.

Bartsch, Karl, ed. *Chrestomathie provençale*. 6th ed. Marburg, 1904.

St. Basil of Caesarea. *Epistola CCX. PG*, XXXII.

Bernart de Ventadorn. *Bernart von Ventadorn, seine Lieder*, ed. Carl Appel. Halle a.S., 1915.

Chaucer, Geoffrey. *The Works of Geoffrey Chaucer*, ed. F. N. Robinson. 2d ed. Boston, 1957.

List of Works Cited

Chrétien de Troyes. *Werke*, ed. W. Foerster. Halle, 1884–1899.

Des Minnesangs Frühling, ed. Carl von Kraus *et al.* 30th ed. Zürich, 1950.

Deutsche Liederdichter des 13. Jahrhunderts, ed. Carl von Kraus. 2 vols. Tübingen, 1952–1958.

Dionysius the Pseudo-Areopagite. *De coelesti Hierarchia*. PG, III, 119–370.

Gottfried von Strassburg. *Tristan und Isolt*, ed. F. Ranke. Berlin, 1930.

Gregory of Nyssa. *De Beatitudinis*. PG, XLIV.

Guillaume IX. *Les Chansons de Guillaume IX*, ed. Alfred Jeanroy. Les Classiques Français du Moyen Age. Paris, 1927.

Guiraut de Bornelh. *Sämtliche Lieder des Trobadors Guiraut de Bornelh*, ed. Adolf Kolsen. 2 vols. Halle a.S., 1910.

Guiraut de Calanso. *Die Lieder des provenzalischen Trobadors Guiraut von Calanso*, ed. Willy Ernst. Romanische Forschungen, XLIV. Erlangen, 1930.

Hartmann von Aue. *Der Arme Heinrich*, ed. H. Paul. 3d ed., rev. A. Leitzmann. Halle, 1949.

Heinrich von Morungen. *Heinrich von Morungen*, ed. Carl von Kraus. 2d ed. München, 1950.

Macrobius. *Commentarius in Somnium Scipionis*. Bibliothèque Latine-Française, 2d series, Vol. XXXIII. Paris, 1847.

Narcisus. "Der altfranzösische Narcicuslai, eine antikisierende Dichtung des 12. Jahrhunderts," ed. Alfons Hilka. *Zeitschrift für romanische Philologie*, XLIX (1929), 635–675.

Narcisus (poème du XIIe siècle), ed. M. M. Pelan and N. C. W. Spence. Publications de la Faculté des Lettres de l'Université de Strasbourg, Fasc. 147. Paris, 1964.

Ovide Moralisé, ed. C. de Boer. 5 vols. Verhandelingen der koninklijke Akademie van Wetenschappen te Amsterdam, Afdeeling Letterkunde, Nieuwe Reeks, XV, XXI, XXX, XLIII. Amsterdam, 1915–1936.

Peire d'Auvergne. *Die Lieder Peires von Auvergne*, ed. Rudolf Zenker. Erlangen, 1900.

Plotinus. *The Enneads*, trans. Stephen MacKenna. New York, n. d.

——. *The Philosophy of Plotinus*, trans. Joseph Katz. New York, 1950.

List of Works Cited

Rabanus Maurus. *Allegoriae in Universam Sacram Scripturam.*
PL, CXII.
——. *Expositio in Epistolam ad Corinthios Primam.* PL, CXII.
Raynouard, M., ed. *Choix des poésies originales des trouba-dours.* 6 vols. Paris, 1816–1861.
Ricas Novas. *Les poésies du troubadour Peire Bremon Ricas Novas,* ed. Jean Boutière. Paris and Toulouse, 1930.
Richard of Saint-Victor. *Le "De Trinitate" de Richard de Saint-Victor,* ed. A.–M. Ethier. Publications de l'Institut d'Etudes Médiévales d'Ottawa, IX. Paris and Ottawa, 1939.
——. *Benjamin Major.* PL, CXCVI.
——. *Adnotatio in Psalmum CXIII.* PL, CXCVI.
Rigaut de Barbezieux. "Rigaut de Barbezieux," ed. J. Anglade.
Revue des langues romanes, LX (1918–1920), 6th series, X (January–July 1920), 201–310.
Rilke, Rainer Maria. *Briefe an einen jungen Dichter.* Leipzig, n. d.
I Rimatori del Dolce Stil Novo, ed. Gustavo Rodolfo Ceriello.
Biblioteca Universale Rizzoli, 207–209. Milano, 1950.
Le Roman de la Rose par Guillaume de Lorris et Jean de Meun,
ed. Ernest Langlois. 5 vols. Société des Anciens Textes Français,
Vol. LXXI. Paris, 1914–1924.
Spenser, Edmund. *The Faerie Queene,* in *The Works of Edmund Spenser, a Variorum Edition,* ed. E. Greenlaw *et al.*
Baltimore, 1932–1957.
Ulrich von Lichtenstein. *Ulrich's von Liechstenstein Frauendienst,* ed. Reinhold Bechstein. 2 vols. Deutsche Dichtungen des Mittelalters, Vols. VI–VII. Leipzig, 1888.
——. *Frauendienst und Frauenbuch,* ed. Karl Lachmann. Berlin, 1841.
Walther von der Vogelweide. *Die Gedichte Walthers von der Vogelweide,* ed. Carl von Kraus. 11th ed. Berlin, 1950.
——. *Leben und Dichten Walthers von der Vogelweide,* ed. W. Wilmanns. 2 vols. Halle a.S., 1916–1924.
Wolfram von Eschenbach. *Parzival,* ed. K. Lachmann. 7th ed., rev. E. Hartl. Berlin, 1952.

Secondary Works

Agaësse, P., and J. Moingt. "Notes" to St. Augustine, *De Trinitate.*
Bibliothèque Augustinienne, XVI. Paris and Bruges, 1955.

List of Works Cited

Andresen, Carl, ed. *Bibliographia Augustiniana*. Darmstadt, 1962.

——. *Zum Augustin-Gespräch der Gegenwart*. Wege der Forschung, Vol. V. Darmstadt, 1962.

Arnold, August. *Studien über den Hohen Mut*. Von Deutscher Poeterey, Vol. IX. Leipzig, 1930.

Arnou, René. *Le désir de Dieu dans la philosophie de Plotin*. Paris, 1921.

Aubin, Paul. "'L' 'Image' dans l'œuvre de Plotin," *Recherches de science religieuse*, XLI (July–September 1953), 348–379.

Bethell, S. L. *Shakespeare and the Popular Dramatic Tradition*. London, 1944.

Bradley, Ritamary. "Backgrounds of the Title *Speculum* in Mediaeval Literature," *Speculum*, XXIX (1954), 100–115.

Brecht, Walther. "Ulrich von Lichtenstein als Lyriker," *Zeitschrift für deutsches Altertum und deutsche Literatur*, XLIX, n. s. XXXVII (1908), 1–122.

Bréhier, Emile. *The Philosophy of Plotinus*, trans. Joseph Thomas. Chicago, 1958.

Burnaby, John. *Augustine: Later Works*. Library of Christian Classics, Vol. VIII. Philadelphia, 1955.

Cayré, Fulbert. *Initiation à la philosophie de Saint Augustin*. Bibliothèque Augustinienne, Etudes, Philosophie, Vol. I. Paris, 1947.

Curtius, Ernst Robert. *European Literature and the Latin Middle Ages*, trans. Willard R. Trask. Bollingen Series, XXXVI. New York, 1953.

De Boor, Helmut. *Geschichte der deutschen Literatur*. Vol. II, Die höfische Literatur. München, 1960.

Delatte, A. *La catoptromancie grecque et ses dérivés*. Bibliothèque de la Faculté de Philosophie et Lettres de l'Université de Liège, Fasc. XLVIII. Paris and Liège, 1932.

Denomy, A. J. "An Inquiry into the Origins of Courtly Love," *Medieval Studies* (Toronto), VI (1944).

——. "Courtly Love and Courtliness," *Speculum*, XXVIII (1953), 44–63.

Diez, Friedrich. *Leben und Werke der Troubadours*, ed. Karl Bartsch. 2d ed. Leipzig, 1882.

List of Works Cited

Eitrem, S. "Narkissos," *Paulys Real-Encyclopädie der classischen Altertumswissenschaft*, XVI (Stuttgart, 1935), 1723ff.

Frappier, Jean. "Variations sur le thème du miroir, de Bernard de Ventadour à Maurice Scève," *Cahiers de l'Association Internationale des Etudes Françaises*, XI (May 1959), 134–158.

Frings, Theodor, and Elisabeth Lea. "Das Lied vom Spiegel und Von Narziss. Morungen 145, 1, Kraus 7." *Beiträge zur Geschichte der deutchen Sprache und Literatur*, LXXXVII (1965), 40–200.

Gilson, Etienne. *Introduction à l'étude de Saint Augustin*. 2d ed. Paris, 1943.

Godefroy, F. *Dictionnaire de l'ancienne langue française*. 10 vols. Paris, 1881–1902.

Grünanger, Carlo. *Heinrich von Morungen e il problema del Minnesang*. Milano, 1948.

Gunn, Alan M. F. *The Mirror of Love*. Lubbock, Texas, 1952.

Harnack, Adolf von. *History of Dogma*, trans. Neil Buchanan. 7 vols. New York, 1958.

Hartlaub, G. F. *Zauber des Spiegels*. München, 1951.

Helm, Karl. "Heinrich von Morungen und Albrecht von Halberstadt," *Beiträge zur Geschichte der deutschen Sprache und Literatur*, L (1927), 143–145.

Henry, Paul. *Plotin et l'occident*. Spicilegium sacrum Lovaniense, Etudes et documents, Fasc. XV. Louvain, 1934.

Hessen, Johannes. *Augustins Metaphysik der Erkenntnis*. 2d. ed. Leiden, 1960.

Höfler, Otto. "Ulrichs von Liechtenstein Venusfahrt und Artusfahrt," *Studien zur deutschen Philologie des Mittelalters*, Festschrift Friedrich Panzer, ed. Richard Kienast. Heidelberg, 1950.

Hoepffner, Ernest. *Les troubadours dans leur vie et dans leurs œuvres*. Paris, 1955.

Hugedé, Norbert. *La métaphore du miroir dans les épîtres de saint Paul aux Corinthiens*. Thèse No. 157, Université de Genève. Neuchâtel, 1957.

Inge, William Ralph. *The Philosophy of Plotinus*. 2 vols. New York and London, 1918.

List of Works Cited

Jackson, W. T. H. *The Literature of the Middle Ages.* New York, 1960.

——. "Tristan the Artist in Gottfried's Poem," *PMLA*, LXXVII (1962), 364–372.

Jeanroy, Alfred. *La poésie lyrique des troubadours.* 2 vols. Paris and Toulouse, 1934.

Kiesewetter, Carl. *Faust in der Geschichte und Tradition.* Leipzig, 1893.

Köhler, Erich. "Narcisse, la Fontaine d'Amour, et Guillaume de Lorris," *Journal des Savants*, Avril–Juin 1963, 86–103.

Kolb, Herbert. *Der Begriff der Minne und das Entstehen der höfischen Lyrik.* Hermaea, neue Folge, Vol. IV. Tübingen, 1958.

Kraus, Carl von. *Des Minnesangs Frühling, Untersuchungen.* Leipzig, 1939.

——. *Walther von der Vogelweide, Untersuchungen.* Berlin and Leipzig, 1935.

——. *Zu den Liedern Heinrichs von Morungen.* Abhandlungen der königlichen Gesellschaft der Wissenschaften zu Göttingen, phil. hist. Klasse, neue Folge, Vol. XVI, No. 1. Berlin, 1916.

Kuhn, Hugo. *Minnesangs Wende.* Hermaea, neue Folge, Vol. I. Tübingen, 1952.

——. "Zur inneren Form des Minnesangs," *Der deutsche Minnesang*, ed. Hans Fromm. Wege der Forschung, XV. Darmstadt, 1961.

Lazar, Moshé. *Amour courtois et "Fin' Amors" dans la littérature du XIIe siècle.* Bibliothèque Française et Romane, series C, Vol. VIII. Paris, 1964.

Leisegang, Hans. "La connaisance de Dieu au miroir de l'âme et de la nature," *Revue d'histoire et de philosophie religieuses*, XVII (1937), 145–171. Translated as "Die Erkenntnis Gottes im Spiegel der Seele und der Natur," *Zeitschrift für philosophische Forschung*, IV (1949), 161–183.

Levy, E. *Provenzalisches Supplement-Wörterbuch.* 8 vols. Leipzig, 1894–1924.

Lewent, Kurt. "Zu den Liedern des Trobadors Guiraut de Calanso," *Zeitschrift für französische Sprache und Literatur*, LVII (1933), 407–446.

List of Works Cited

Lewis, C. S. *The Allegory of Love.* Oxford, 1936.

Lovejoy, Arthur O. *The Great Chain of Being.* Cambridge, Mass., 1936.

Mohr, Wolfgang. "Minnesang als Gesellschaftskunst," *Der Deutschunterricht,* VI (1954); reprinted in *Der deutsche Minnesang,* ed. Hans Fromm. Wege der Forschung, XV. Darmstadt, 1961.

Moret, André. *Les débuts du lyrisme en Allemagne.* Lille, 1951.

Muscatine, Charles. *Chaucer and the French Tradition.* Berkeley and Los Angeles, 1960.

Negelein, J. von. "Bild, Spiegel und Schatten im Volksglauben," *Archiv für Religionswissenschaft,* V (1902), 1ff.

Ninck, Martin. *Die Bedeutung des Wassers im Kult und Leben der Alten.* Leipzig, 1921.

O'Brien, Gordon Worth. *Renaissance Poetics and the Problem of Power.* Chicago, 1956.

Pätzold, Alfred. *Die individuellen Eigentümlichkeiten einiger hervorragender Trobadors im Minneliede.* Marburg, 1897.

Panofsky, Erwin. *Early Netherlandish Painting.* Cambridge, Mass., 1953.

Pillet, A., and H. Carstens. *Bibliographie der Troubadours.* Halle, 1933.

Portalié, Eugène. *A Guide to the Thought of St. Augustine,* trans. R. Bastian. Chicago, 1960.

Raynouard, F. J. M. *Lexique roman.* 6 vols. Paris, 1833–44.

Róheim, Géza. *Spiegelzauber.* Internationale Psychoanalytische Bibliothek, Nr. 6. Leipzig and Wien, 1919.

Schmaus, Michael. *Die psychologische Trinitätslehre des hl. Augustinus.* Münsterische Beiträge zur Theologie, Vol. XI. Münster i. W., 1927.

Schönbach, Anton E. *Beiträge zur Erklärung altdeutscher Dichtwerke.* Wien, 1899.

Schwarz, Heinrich. "The Mirror in Art," *The Art Quarterly,* XV (1952), 97–118.

——. "The Mirror of the Artist and the Mirror of the Devout," *Studies in the History of Art dedicated to William E. Suida,* pp. 90–105. London, 1959.

Schwietering, Julius. "Der Liederzyklus Heinrichs von Morungen," *Zeitschrift für deutsches Altertum und deutsche Literatur*, LXXXII (1948), 77–104. Reprinted in *Mystik und höfische Dichtung im Hochmittelalter*. Darmstadt, 1960.

Spitzer, Leo. *L'Amour lointain de Jaufré Rudel et le sens de la poésie des troubadours*. University of North Carolina Studies in Romance Languages and Literature, No. 5. Chapel Hill, 1944.

Stössel, Christian. *Die Bilder und Vergleiche der altprovenzalischen Lyrik, nach Form und Inhalt untersucht*. Marburg, 1886.

Thorndike, L. *A History of Magic and Experimental Science during the First Thirteen Centuries of our Era*. 2 vols. New York, 1923.

Valency, Maurice. *In Praise of Love*. New York, 1958.

Wiese, Benno von, ed. *Die deutsche Lyrik*. 2 vols. Düsseldorf, 1956.

Index

Index

Index

Index